Kimmel, Short, and Pearl Harbor

Kimmel, Short, and Pearl Harbor
The Final Report Revealed

Fred Borch
and Daniel Martinez

Naval Institute Press
Annapolis, Maryland

Naval Institute Press
291 Wood Road
Annapolis, MD 21402

© 2005 by Fred Borch and Daniel Martinez
All rights reserved. No part of this book may be reproduced or utilized in any form or by any means, electronic or mechanical, including photocopying and recording, or by any information storage and retrieval system, without permission in writing from the publisher.

ISBN: 978-159114-090-0

Library of Congress Cataloging-in-Publication Data

Borch, Frederic L., 1954–
Kimmel, Short, and Pearl Harbor : the final report revealed / Fred Borch and Daniel Martinez.
    p. cm.
    Includes entire text of: Advancement of Rear Admiral Kimmel and Major General Short. Washington, D.C. : United States Office of the Under Secretary of Defense for Personnel and Readiness, 1995.
    Includes bibliographical references and index.
    ISBN 1-59114-090-0 (alk. paper)
    1. Pearl Harbor (Hawaii), Attack on, 1941. 2. Kimmel, Husband Edward, 1882–1968. 3. Short, Walter Campbell, 1880–1949. I. Martinez, Daniel, 1949– II. Title: Advancement of Rear Admiral Kimmel and Major General Short. III. Title.
D767.92.B66 2004
940.54'26693—dc22

                              2004015516

Printed in the United States of America on acid-free paper ∞

19 18 17 16 15   8 7 6 5 4

Contents

	Foreword	vii
	Preface	xi
	Introduction	1
1	Approach and Methodology	16
2	The Report	23
3	Aftermath	99
	Conclusion	107
	Appendix A: Photocopy of Memorandum for the Deputy Secretary of Defense, Signed Edwin Dorn	113
	Appendix B: Photocopy of Letter to Strom Thurmond from John P. White	121
	Appendix C: A Critical Analysis of the Report by the Department of Defense Dated December 1, 1995, Regarding Advancement of Rear Admiral Husband E. Kimmel and Lieutenant General Walter C. Short on the Retired List	123
	Notes	175
	Annotated Bibliography	201
	Index	209

Foreword

Perhaps once or twice in a century a nation undergoes an experience so unexpected, so shocking, and so traumatic that it becomes a turning point in its history. One such event was the Japanese bombing of Pearl Harbor on 7 December 1941. In the perspective of history, the span of six decades is only a flash, but it is a long time in the life of an individual. Those today who remember Pearl Harbor as a direct experience are now senior citizens, yet the subject continues to fascinate them and their descendants. Why?

No doubt one reason is the irrational but undeniable glamour of defeat. Americans are winners, but they remember and sympathize with their losers. Another factor that keeps Pearl Harbor a living issue is the puzzle factor. The merciful years have erased much of the pain and anger, but the puzzle remains an eternal double crostic where the clues help fill in the story and the story helps provide the clues, but instead of clarifying the subject, the years have compounded the problem.

How could such an event have happened? How could the Japanese aircraft have flown three thousand miles across the Pacific without being seen? How did Japan develop a torpedo that would not sink in the mud of shallow Pearl Harbor? How did Japan develop a bomb weighing 1,720 pounds, which would penetrate the deck of a battleship? How could the Japanese pilots have avoided air detection when they came within 250 miles of their target? How could they have refueled in the cold northern Pacific three times on the way to their target and not be seen?

How could they have caught the U.S. fleet napping at Pearl Harbor, the Gibraltar of Asia? How did they manage to sink or damage 8 battleships, kill more than 2,400 men, wound 1,178, destroy almost 300 aircraft, and damage another 128, and not get caught? The Japanese losses were only 29 aircraft, 129 men, 1 major submarine, and 5 midget submarines.

Where were the U.S. carriers? What about radar? How much did President Franklin D. Roosevelt know? What about the Japanese submarines caught in the harbor? Was there a third wave? Why did the Japanese not finish off the Americans, when they could have done so? How about the breaking of the Japanese code? Could an event like Pearl Harbor ever happen again? These and other questions are still being asked and studied after more than sixty years.

These unanswered questions gave rise to a myth that still exists today: that the Japanese could not have done this by themselves; that leaders in Washington allowed the attack to happen so that the United States would have to enter the war, and that they then blamed it on the two men in charge at Pearl Harbor, Adm. Husband Kimmel for the Navy and Lt. Gen. Walter Short for the Army. In short, President Roosevelt and others deliberately withheld information, which, if Kimmel and Short had received it, would have enabled them to prevent this catastrophe, thus making both of them scapegoats.

For their alleged sins, both Kimmel and Short were relieved of their commands and were subsequently and indirectly forced to retire at the two-star rank. From 1942 through 1946 there were nine separate investigations, all of which, with one exception, concluded that the two men were guilty not of dereliction of duty but of errors in judgment; however, none of the investigations recommended that their ranks be restored.

Over the years many books have been written that support the restoration of Kimmel's rank to four stars and Short's rank to three stars. The two men's families have continued to fight for this reinstatement. Their efforts culminated in 1995 when, with the strong support and backing of Sen. Strom Thurmond, president pro tem of the U.S. Senate, Edwin Dorn, then the undersecretary of defense with responsibility for manpower and readiness matters, was ordered to investigate. The result was the Dorn Report, which found that, while Kimmel and Short were guilty of errors of judgment, they were not solely responsible for the catastrophe at Pearl Harbor, and others in Washington and on their staffs in Hawaii should share some of the blame. But the report did not recommend restoring their ranks. Since then there have been other attempts by the families of the two men, one of which came very close to being successful, but as of this date Kimmel and Short have not been exonerated.

In an effort to bring the Dorn Report's research to the public for scholars and others to study, Fred Borch, one of three writers and investigators for the Dorn Report, and Daniel Martinez, an eminent Pearl Harbor historian, have edited and annotated the report. This book is important not only because it makes available the Dorn Report, but also because it provides a synopsis of the alleged sins of omission of the two leaders and for the first time presents the ongoing story of the Kimmel and Short families and their crusade to clear their family names. This story has never been told before. This book also analyzes and summarizes the events, the failures to act, the messages sent, and the record of who knew what and when. The work is well documented. It concludes that neither Kimmel nor Short should have been surprised by the attack and that both were guilty of errors of judgment, such as the misuse of radar, failure to use reconnaissance aircraft properly, failure to coordinate, failure to pass along intelligence, and failure to read staff estimates of the situation; that both were guilty of underestimating the potential for attack and a host of other errors; and that while Washington was guilty of not informing them on several matters, such as the bomb plot message, in the final analysis, they had enough information and should have been on alert.

This book argues that Kimmel and Short may not have been able to defeat the Japanese, but they could have inflicted more damage had they been ready. The real question that the book answers is not, Could the United States have defeated or stopped the attack? but rather, Should the commanders at Pearl Harbor have been ready? The answer is probably yes.

Pearl Harbor never dies, and no living person has seen the end of this; so said Admiral Kimmel's lawyer, Charles Rudd, to my mentor, Gordon W. Prange. For forty years Prange and for thirty-three years Katherine Dillon and myself have been studying this subject. We know that this will not be the last word and that many of the same conclusions were reached by others, including Prange, Henry Clausen, and Bruce Lee, and perhaps someday these conclusions will change people's minds. But at present and until new information is forthcoming, I believe that this book is the last word on the subject of Kimmel's and Short's responsibility.

Today, with the comparison of Pearl Harbor to the terrorist attacks of September 11, 2001, it will be even tougher for anyone in the new generation of historians to reach any other conclusions, for someone has to be held accountable. As the authors so ably indicate, in the Navy the officer on the bridge (commander) is the one in charge. It may not be fair, but that is the way it is in the military, and in the final analysis both Kimmel and Short were caught sleeping.

This book is an excellent, readable addition to the literature about Pearl Harbor. It is not based upon hearsay, or would-have, should-have, could-have material, but upon actual documents and testimony concerning what happened on that fateful day, 7 December 1941. It may not change many people's minds, but unless further information comes to light, it provides the last word upon the subject.

Donald M. Goldstein, Ph.D.

Preface

On 1 December 1995 the Defense Department released a seventy-four-page report about U.S. responsibility for the Japanese attack on Pearl Harbor. But few people have seen the report and, until today, it has never been published in its entirety. Consequently, a principal aim of this book is to make the full text of the report readily available to scholars and interested members of the public. The 1995 investigative report was historically significant for several reasons. It was the first comprehensive official investigation into responsibility and culpability at Pearl Harbor to be conducted since the 1940s. Consequently it provides a fresh look at the controversy surrounding the events of 7 December 1941. Next, as the first and only inquiry to be conducted outside the Army and Navy, the report is unique as the sole Defense Department look at Pearl Harbor. Third, the report is the first official inquiry to conclude that Kimmel and Short were not alone responsible for the crushing defeat suffered by U.S. forces at Pearl Harbor; others also were culpable. Fourth, it will continue to frame the ongoing debate about responsibility for the Pearl Harbor attack. Historians, members of Congress, officials in the executive branch, and the Kimmel and Short families have all referred to the report and quoted it in support of their respective views. Fifth, the report is unique in addressing the propriety of restoring Admiral Kimmel and General Short to their wartime ranks. Those championing the Kimmel and Short cause insist that posthumous promotion is the only appropriate remedy and claim that this will constitute official exoneration for any alleged wrongdoing at Pearl Harbor. This report contains the first official statement on this remedy. Finally, the report documents the first official investigation that examined—and concluded—that the official treatment of Kimmel and Short was fair and proper.

This book contains every word of the original report of the investigation conducted under the direct supervision of Edwin Dorn, then the undersecretary of defense with responsibility for manpower and readiness matters. It also provides a context for understanding the report. The introduction sets out the story behind the Defense Department's decision to conduct an inquiry into what happened at Pearl Harbor. It shows that the decision was the culmination of efforts by Rear Admiral Kimmel, Major General Short, and their families to restore their reputations—reputations damaged after the two men were blamed for the Army and Navy's lack of defense preparedness at Pearl Harbor. After looking at these efforts between 1948 and 1995, the introduction closes with an analysis of an eventful meeting in Sen. Strom Thurmond's office—the single most important factor behind the Defense Department's decision to take a fresh look at the question of responsibility at Pearl Harbor.

Chapter 1 takes a brief look at how the inquiry was conducted, including the composition of the investigation team, how issues were framed, and the various sources considered by the team in conducting its research. Chapter 2 provides the full text of the report, with commentary and analysis. Since both of us were intimately involved in the investigation—Borch as an Army representative and a principal author of the final report, and Martinez as a professional historian and the chief outside consultant to the investigation—we are uniquely able to comment upon and illuminate parts of the report that otherwise would remain cloaked in darkness.

Chapter 3 examines what the Kimmel family, the Short family, and their advocates have done in the years since the Defense Department report was released. The conclusion provides an executive summary of the report and offers some final thoughts. Three appendices follow the main text, rounding out this work.

Pearl Harbor remains a unique event in American history. While we have definite views about what happened in the months, days, and hours preceding the Japanese attack on U.S. forces on Oahu, it is ultimately up to each reader to decide the truth. We have checked and rechecked our facts and sources, but there are sure to be errors. These are our responsibility alone.

                                                Fred L. Borch
                                                Washington, D.C.

                                                Daniel A. Martinez
                                                Honolulu, Hawaii

Kimmel, Short, and Pearl Harbor

Introduction

The impetus for Defense Department involvement in the Kimmel-Short controversy was a meeting held in Sen. Strom Thurmond's office on 17 April 1995. (1) On that spring day, sixteen people met with Thurmond to discuss the "posthumous restoration of the rank of admiral" for Husband E. Kimmel and "three-star rank" for Walter C. Short. While Thurmond described the meeting as a "full and open discussion of the issue," the attitudes expressed by some of the participants—especially Mr. Steve Honigman, then the top civilian lawyer at the Department of the Navy—convinced the senior senator from South Carolina that the Navy would never reverse its long-held view that Kimmel was responsible for the disaster at Pearl Harbor. Prior to the meeting, Thurmond had already obtained an oral pledge from Secretary of Defense William J. Perry that the Defense Department would, "without preconceptions," conduct a new investigation into Kimmel's and Short's responsibility for the defeat suffered by U.S. forces on 7 December 1941. The meeting on 27 April reinforced Thurmond's view that a Defense Department inquiry was the only appropriate course of action. Already persuaded that Kimmel and Short had been wronged by their respective services, Senator Thurmond now was also certain that institutional inertia made the Navy—and probably the Army as well—incapable of reversing this wrong. If the two uniformed services were not going to alter their views on responsibility at Pearl Harbor, he would take the issue away from them and ask for a new investigation in a more impartial and objective forum. Senator Thurmond seems to have concluded that the Defense Department, as a civilian-dominated organization with no institutional interest in Pearl Harbor, Admiral Kimmel, or General Short, was ideally suited to conduct this new inquiry. If Kimmel and Short had been wronged—and Thurmond believed that they had been—there was every reason to believe that a Defense Department unfettered by institutional prejudice would reach this same conclusion. Consequently, some three weeks after the meeting in his office, Thurmond wrote a letter to Secretary Perry in which he formally requested a Defense Department inquiry and "a decision in the Kimmel-Short matter during 1995." (2)

Perry acceded to Thurmond's request, and an investigation under the direct supervision of an undersecretary of defense, Dr. Edwin Dorn, began a few months later. Thus, the first-ever Department of Defense investigation, and the so-called "Dorn Report" that recorded its findings and made recommendations, owes its existence to Senator Thurmond and an April 1995 office meeting.

What took place in Senator Thurmond's office—who was there, what they said, and how that resulted in a new investigation—is best understood by first looking at the actions taken previously by Kimmel and Short themselves, and by their families and advocates, to restore their reputations. This is because the 27 April meeting was simply the latest battle in a long campaign waged by the Kimmels, and to a lesser degree the Shorts, to absolve their ancestors of responsibility for what happened in Hawaii on 7 December 1941. General Short and Admiral Kimmel first initiated action to clear their names in 1948, and their descendants continued to work toward this same end after the two men's deaths in 1949 and 1968, respectively. By the mid-1990s, both the Kimmel and Short families were working together toward a common goal: restoration of the four- and three-star rank they believed would constitute an official acknowledgment that Admiral Kimmel and General Short were blameless for America's losses at Pearl Harbor. On 1 March 1942, after more than forty years of active duty, Kimmel retired in his permanent grade of rear admiral. While Admiral Kimmel had worn four stars since February 1941, he left active duty as a two-star, the highest grade then authorized for retired officers. Three months later, in June 1942, Congress passed new legislation permitting an officer who had been a vice admiral or admiral for a least one year to retire in that grade. Kimmel had reverted to his permanent two-star rank after being relieved from command in December 1941. Consequently, he did not meet this time-in-grade requirement and was ineligible for his old, higher rank under this new law. In August 1947, however, Congress passed the Officer Personnel Act. (3) This new statute permitted any officer who had served as a three- or four-star admiral to retire at that higher rank, regardless of time-in-grade. While Kimmel was now eligible for advancement to four stars on the retired list, this required a nomination by the president and consent by the Senate. President Truman nominated all other officers eligible for higher rank under the Officer Personnel Act, but took no action with regard to Husband E. Kimmel.

Kimmel never formally requested advancement to his higher wartime rank. His inaction on this matter, however, did not prevent him from otherwise working tirelessly to clear his name. In 1955 he published *Admiral Kimmel's Story,* (4) a defense of his actions at Pearl Harbor. In this book, Kimmel insisted that he had done everything possible to prepare for war. Moreover, he claimed that he was being unjustly blamed for U.S. losses on 7 December. On the contrary, argued Kimmel, President Roosevelt, General Marshall, and Admiral Stark were to blame for what happened at Pearl Harbor, as these leaders had withheld critical intelligence information and thus prevented him from mounting a successful defense of Oahu.

Kimmel's public and vociferous claims that he had been wronged, however, did not result in any official action. On the contrary, in August 1957, Thomas S. Gates, Jr., then secretary of the Navy under President Eisenhower, declined to initiate action to promote Kimmel to the grade of admiral on the retired list. No further action was taken in Kimmel's case, and after his death in May 1968, his family waited almost twenty years before initiating a new campaign to restore Admiral Kimmel's reputation. Then, on 7 April 1987, Kimmel's sons, Edward and Thomas, petitioned the Board for Correction of Naval Records for posthumous advancement. The board, an administrative forum created by Congress and acting on behalf of the secretary of the Navy, is authorized to correct any error or remove an injustice in official military records. For example, a sailor or marine might request the board to correct his records to show that he was awarded a specific military decoration. But a sailor or marine may also request that the board redress an injustice, such as upgrading a bad conduct discharge based on a decades-old court-martial conviction for minor misconduct. (5)

The Kimmel family hoped to use the board as the vehicle for restoring the two lost stars but, in a 9 June 1987 letter to the family's attorney in Washington, D.C., the board's executive director explained that no action on the Kimmel request could be taken because the board lacked the authority to grant relief. (6) This was because an officer may retire at three- or four-star rank only after nomination by the president and confirmation by the Senate. It follows that neither the secretary of the Navy nor the board had the requisite power to advance Kimmel to a higher rank. With this administrative avenue closed to them, the Kimmels now began lobbying the Navy's leadership and members of Congress for relief.

In late 1987 the Kimmel family approached Adm. Carlisle A. H. Trost, then chief of naval operations, and requested that he support their efforts. Trost, however, recommended in early 1988 that the Navy decline to support Rear Admiral Kimmel's advancement to four-star rank. The Kimmels then sought and obtained a personal meeting with William L. Ball III, the secretary of the Navy. On 11 May 1988 Thomas and Edward Kimmel, accompanied by Mr. Edward Hanifly, the attorney who had represented Admiral Kimmel at the Navy Court of Inquiry held in 1944, requested Secretary Ball's support in restoring Kimmel's wartime rank. To keep up the pressure, Sen. William V. Roth of Delaware sent a letter to Ball on 6 July 1988. That letter, solicited by the Kimmels, requested that Secretary Ball support Thomas and Edward's efforts to restore their father's highest wartime rank.

On 11 January 1989 Secretary Ball replied to Senator Roth, stating that he declined to support the Kimmels. However, Ball had already forwarded a memorandum setting out Admiral Kimmel's case to the Defense Department for consideration. Eight days later, on 19 January, the deputy secretary of defense, William H. Taft IV, returned the package to Ball. Also enclosed was a memorandum with the following comments:

> I have reviewed your memorandum of December 7, 1988, and the associated material concerning the request to advance Rear Admiral Kimmel to the grade of admiral on the retired list.
>
> While the relative share of responsibility borne by Rear Admiral Kimmel and others for the tragedy that befell our Nation at Pearl Harbor may be subject to historical debate, I do not believe that it is in the best interest of the Department of Defense or the Nation to recommend his advancement on the retired list. Therefore, in lieu of forwarding this package to the President recommending disapproval, I am returning it to you.
>
> I understand the importance of this matter to Rear Admiral Kimmel's family and friends, and I regret that I cannot provide a more favorable answer. (7)

Shortly thereafter, Secretary Ball informed Edward and Thomas Kimmel of Taft's decision.

The Kimmels did not give up. On the contrary, the family now hired a public relations firm and redoubled their efforts. Secretaries Ball and Taft had departed the Pentagon after

President George H. W. Bush took office in January 1989, so the Kimmels took up the cause with the new administration. On 8 February 1990 Senator Roth wrote to Dick Cheney, the new secretary of defense. In his letter Roth requested that the Department of Defense reconsider the issue. On 13 June 1990 Cheney replied that "the possibility of promoting Rear Admiral Kimmel posthumously to the rank of Admiral has been reviewed a number of times" since World War II, "and each time the determination has been made not to proceed with such action." Secretary Cheney continued:

> I can understand the desire of the Kimmel family for the posthumous promotion of Rear Admiral Kimmel to the rank of Admiral, but I cannot on that ground alone recommend to the President that he initiate such action. The promotion process generally would not seem to be the best way to address issues about the place in history of those who are no longer with us.
>
> I regret that my response is not what you wished, but believe it is the right thing to do. (8)

In May 1991 Edward and Thomas Kimmel again wrote to Secretary Cheney, requesting that he recommend to President Bush that Admiral Kimmel's four-star rank be posthumously restored. On 21 August 1991 Cheney replied through the Navy that he would not make such recommendation. In October 1991 Sens. Joseph R. Biden (D-DE), John McCain (R-AZ), William V. Roth, Jr. (R-DE), Alan K. Simpson (R-WY), and Strom Thurmond (R-SC) wrote letters supporting the Kimmels' efforts. Thirty-six retired Navy admirals also sent a letter to President Bush requesting that he promote Kimmel. Despite this letter-writing campaign, however, the Kimmels failed to obtain their goal; on 2 December 1991 President Bush publicly announced that he would not support posthumous advancement for Admiral Kimmel.

The Kimmels now took their campaign to the U.S. Congress. On 4 August 1992 House Resolution 534 was submitted by Reps. Helen D. Bentley (D-MD), John M. Spratt, Jr. (D-SC), and Curt

Weldon (R-PA), and referred to the House Committee on Armed Services for action. Rep. Bentley's bill asserted that "it is the sense of the House of Representatives" that President Clinton should posthumously advance Kimmel to full admiral on the retired list. H.R. 534 advanced two reasons for this recommendation. First, the "naval court of inquiry found that, prior to and during the attack [on Pearl Harbor], no individual in the naval service committed any offense or incurred serious blame." Second, this same court of inquiry "specifically approved the judgements and actions of Admiral Kimmel under the circumstances prior to and during the attack." No action was taken by the House on H.R. 534. Consequently, on 5 January 1993, after a new Congress had convened, Representative Bentley submitted H.R. 13, which again urged presidential action in the case of Admiral Kimmel.

Meanwhile, Edward and Thomas Kimmel renewed their letter-writing campaign. In March 1993 they sent letters to the new secretary of defense, Les Aspin, and the new chief of naval operations, Adm. Frank B. Kelso II. The Kimmels claimed that "new" evidence supporting their request was contained in a soon-to-be-published book by a naval historian, Capt. Ned Beach (USN-Ret.). (9) Secretary Aspin took no action on the matter before his resignation as defense secretary, but his replacement, William J. Perry, responded to Edward Kimmel on 7 September 1994. "I believe that Rear Admiral Kimmel's status should not be changed," wrote Perry. He continued:

> In my view, this conclusion is compelled by society's legitimate interest in the finality of official actions, and by the weight, basis and scope of the prior judgments on this issue. While the bar of history may ultimately be more sympathetic to Rear Admiral Kimmel in the context of his times, I cannot conclude that he has been treated unjustly or advocate a revision of the Navy's records. (10)

On 19 October 1994 Senator Biden wrote to Secretary Perry, again requesting favorable action for Admiral Kimmel. Secretary Perry responded to Edward Kimmel on 22 November 1994, stating that he "adhered" to his earlier decision of 7 September. Finally, on 1 December 1994 President Clinton wrote to Mr. Manning M. Kimmel IV, Admiral Kimmel's grandson. As this was the first written statement by a U.S. president on the issue, it is worth setting out in its entirety:

> Dear Mr. Kimmel:
>
> I have reviewed the events surrounding the retirement after Pearl Harbor of your grandfather, Rear Admiral Husband E. Kimmel. While I understand your desire to see him posthumously promoted, I agree with the judgment of prior investigatory commissions, as recently validated by Secretary of Defense Perry.
>
> Your grandfather was, without question, a patriotic American who served our country with bravery and dedication. With regard to the issue of his permanent retirement grade, though, the historical record provides no compelling justification for me to reverse prior decisions that he be retired at the two-star level.
>
> I appreciate the importance of this issue to your family and respect your unwavering commitment to upholding its good name.
>
> Sincerely,
>
> S/ Bill Clinton (11)

Having failed in their efforts in the House of Representatives—and after a similar lack of success with the Navy and President Clinton in December 1994—the Kimmel family shifted their focus to the Senate. The Kimmels found a champion in Sen. Strom Thurmond, whose efforts on their behalf culminated in the 27 April 1995 meeting. That meeting, however, was about more than Admiral Kimmel, for Senator Thurmond was also interested in General Short's place in history. Paralleling the Kimmel family's efforts on behalf of their ancestor, the Short family had worked to have the general's third star posthumously restored.

While Admiral Kimmel, though he never requested the restoration of his two "lost" stars, had willingly engaged in a public battle to clear his name, General Short took the opposite approach. Short did not write a book, and rarely talked about his responsibility for Pearl Harbor. He did, however, formally request action from the Pentagon. On 2 December 1948 General Short submitted a letter to the secretary of the Army in which he asked to be advanced on the retired list to lieutenant general. In January 1949, the question of restoring this third star reached the desk of Brig. Gen. Herbert D. Hoover, the Army's assistant judge advocate general. In a memo dated 19 January, Hoover wrote that Short could be advanced "if it is administratively determined that he served satisfactorily in the grade or rank of lieutenant general." That determination, said General Hoover, was at the "discretion" of the secretary of the Army. Interestingly, Hoover included the following opinion along with his legal advice: that the historical record relating to the Pearl Harbor attack would "support" either finding, so that the secretary could properly determine that Short had served satisfactorily or that he had served unsatisfactorily. Note that the legal basis for advancing Short to a higher rank was markedly different from the law controlling Kimmel's situation: while Kimmel could only be advanced after nomination by the president and confirmation by the Senate, Short could have his third star returned to him by the secretary of the Army. (12)

Official correspondence from April 1949 reflects that Lt. Gen. Edward M. Brooks, the director of personnel and administration, relied on Hoover's legal opinion in recommending to the Army chief of staff that Short be advanced to three-star rank. Brooks concluded that Short had made errors in judgment in defending his command against attack, and wrote that "it cannot be said that General Short successfully commanded the Hawaiian Department." But, continued the Army's top personnel officer, Short's mistakes had resulted in his relief from command. General Brooks viewed this relief as "sufficient [adverse] action against him," and recommended to his superior that Short be restored to his wartime rank of lieutenant general. (13) After this memorandum was signed, and while Short's request was still under consideration, General Short died on 3 September 1949. The Army, having taken no action at the time of Short's death, simply let the matter drop. (14)

After Short's death, more than forty years passed before his son, retired Army colonel Walter D. Short, wrote a letter to the secretary of the Army asking for relief. In that two-page letter, dated 29 May 1990, Short insisted that his father had been made a scapegoat, and asked "with all his heart that my father" be posthumously advanced to lieutenant general. He offered several reasons in support of this request. First, said Colonel Short, the 1944 Army Board of Inquiry determined that his father was not derelict in the performance of his duty and that "much of the blame" lay with Gen. George C. Marshall and Brig. Gen. Leonard T. Gerow of the Army Staff War Plans branch. Second, Colonel Short relied on the 1946 Joint Congressional Committee conclusion that "the errors of the Hawaiian commands were errors of judgement and not derelictions of duty." Third, he pointed to a 1984 Pearl Harbor Survivors Association resolution calling for favorable treatment of his father. After all, if those who had survived the Japanese attack harbored no bitterness toward their old commander but rather viewed him as blameless, the Army should adopt the same attitude. Finally, Colonel Short claimed that a recently aired British Broadcasting Corporation documentary, *Sacrifice at Pearl Harbor,* gave proof that his father had been wrongly treated. That television broadcast, wrote Short, proved that intelligence critical to the defense of Oahu "was deliberately withheld" from his father. In sum, claimed Colonel Short, the "American people now realize that Lt. Gen. Short, as well as Adm. Kimmel, was a scapegoat to take the blame and protect President Roosevelt, Secretary of the Army Stimson, General Marshall, Adm. Stark the C[hief of] N[aval] O[perations], and various other officers in the Pentagon." (15)

The secretary of the Army referred Colonel Short's letter to the Army's top military lawyers for "review" and "recommendation." On 22 June 1990 the Office of the Judge Advocate General responded. In an opinion written for the chief of staff's office, the lawyers responded that the secretary of the Army had the authority to advance General Short to three-star rank "if it is administratively determined that he served satisfactorily" in that grade for at least six months. The lawyers further opined that the Army Board for Correction of Military Records was "the appropriate authority to consider whether an error or injustice" existed in Short's military records. If it found such an error or injustice, the board—acting on behalf of the secretary of the Army—could grant the requested relief. Consequently, the judge advocate general recommended that Colonel Short be advised to apply to the Army board to correct his father's military records. (16)

Colonel Short accordingly filed an application with the board, and on 13 November 1991 a three-member panel met to consider the appropriateness of correcting General Short's military records and restoring his three-star rank. They concluded "unanimously" that there was no error in the record. However, "the majority found evidence of injustice," as two of the three members were "of the opinion" that Short "was unjustly held responsible for the Pearl Harbor disaster." The board majority then made the following statement: "Considering the passage of time as well as the burden and stigma carried until his untimely death in 1949, it would be equitable and just to restore [Short] to his former rank of lieutenant general on the retired list." (17)

However, one member of the board, Mr. James T. Lucus, did not agree with the majority view. The report noted that Lucus

> [d]issents from the foregoing recommendation, contending that as the Commander of the Hawaiian Department, [Short's] sole responsibility was not only the defense of Pearl Harbor but also and most importantly, the safety and welfare of those lives he was entrusted to command. Therefore, [Short's] action or lack of action in connection with the defense of Pearl Harbor

was such a grievous error in judgement which not only warranted relief from command but also supports a determination that he did not serve satisfactorily in the grade of lieutenant general so as to grant restoration. (18)

While the majority of the board had voted for promotion, this recommendation was advisory and not binding on the secretary of the Army. Consequently, when the deputy assistant secretary of the Army, John R. Matthews, acting on behalf of the secretary, sided with the minority member and denied redress on 19 December 1991, his decision was entirely legal. (19) After Matthews denied relief, the issue lay dormant for almost four years. On 30 November 1995, however, Secretary of the Army Togo D. West, Jr., once again examined the propriety of posthumously promoting Short. Responding to a memorandum from Undersecretary of Defense Edwin Dorn, which had come to West as a direct result of politicking by the Kimmels and Shorts, West informed Dorn that he had completed "another summary review of this matter" and that, based on this review, he was "not inclined to change the Army's position." (20) By this time, however, Senator Thurmond had obtained a pledge from Secretary Perry for a new investigation.

On 25 April 1995, the following individuals met in Thurmond's office:

Strom Thurmond, senator; supporter and friend of family
John Deutch, deputy secretary of defense
John H. Dalton, secretary of the Navy
Steve S. Honigman, general counsel of the Navy; top civilian lawyer in Navy
Manning M. Kimmel IV, grandson
Edward R. Kimmel, son
Capt. Thomas K. Kimmel, USN (ret.), son
Adm. Thomas H. Moorer, USN (ret.), friend of family
Adm. James L. Holloway III, USN (ret.), friend of family
Adm. Harold E. Shear, USN (ret.), friend of family
Rear Adm. Donald M. Showers, USN (ret.), friend of family

Capt. Edward L. Beach, USN (ret.), author
John Costello, author
Michael Gannon, author
Edward B. Hanify, Esq., Kimmel's lawyer at 1944 Navy Board
Anthony DeLorenzo, district director of Pearl Harbor Survivors Association

The seventy-four-page transcript of the meeting shows that Thurmond announced that he wanted a "full and open discussion of the issue." Consequently, the senator asked "each group to state its position." But Thurmond also emphasized that he wanted "Secretaries Deutch and Dalton to... assure me that this matter will be examined without preconceptions" or, as he also put it, that judgments about the Kimmel and Short case should "be made on fact, fairness and justice." Honigman summarized the Navy position by giving four reasons why Admiral Kimmel's wartime rank should not be restored. First, "the historical record" did not show that Roosevelt, Marshall, or other Washington leaders "deliberately withheld information from Admiral Kimmel and General Short as part of a plan or conspiracy to expose Pearl Harbor to attack in order to thrust America into war." Second, continued Honigman, Kimmel and Short were responsible for failing to prepare to defend their commands. Honigman pointed to a number of items, such as Kimmel's and Short's failure to coordinate and integrate their command and control structure. Third, Honigman underscored the "principle of the accountability of the commander." As the senior naval commander, Kimmel was responsible for the disaster; it was proper to relieve him and appropriate for him to retire at two-star rank. Finally, Honigman stressed that "finality"—of official judgments previously made by Congress, presidents, and secretaries of defense and the Navy—meant that it was up to history to decide Kimmel's responsibility.

After Honigman gave his view, the Kimmels and their supporters aired their grievances.

Unfortunately for the Navy, Steve Honigman had been too strident and combative in the meeting; Thurmond was now more convinced than ever that the Navy could not be fair in examining the Kimmel-Short controversy. As Thurmond wrote in his 17 May 1995 letter to Secretary of Defense Perry:

> During our April meeting, Mr. Honigman *strongly supported not changing the Navy's position* on Admiral Kimmel. Attempting to proceed with this case, in an impartial manner, under the Navy's General Counsel would be unfair to the Navy and the families involved—all of whom have presented well-disposed and well-defined positions. While conducting an open and equitable dialogue is admirable, final judgment on this question *must be delegated to those having unquestionable impartiality and objectivity.* A fair, deliberate, and timely closure on this matter is in the best interest of the Nation and those directly involved. I suggest that we proceed and urge a decision on the Kimmel-Short matter during 1995. (21)

Some conclusions about the meeting can appropriately be made. When the Defense Department informed Senator Thurmond that it would take a fresh look at the roles played by Admiral Kimmel and General Short at Pearl Harbor, it did so because of a desire to placate Senator Thurmond, and not because the Pentagon had concluded that an investigation was necessary. Since Thurmond was at that time the head of the Senate Armed Services Committee and a man of immense power and influence, his request for an investigation simply had to be granted. The executive branch had repeatedly examined the claims made by the Kimmel and Short families and their defenders, and both Democratic and Republican presidents had denied relief. Nonetheless, Thurmond's stature in government meant there was simply no good reason to decline to conduct a new investigation. A final point: at the time of the meeting in Thurmond's office, Deputy Secretary Deutch had already been nominated to serve as director of the Central Intelligence Agency, and he was facing a confirmation hearing in the Senate.

INTRODUCTION

Denying Thurmond's request for a Defense Department investigation would have been politically unwise.

Seen from the perspective of previous efforts by Kimmel, Short, and their families to restore the two men's reputations, the meeting in Senator Thurmond's office was the cumulative result of decades of maneuvering by the Kimmels and Shorts to overturn Army and Navy refusals to promote their ancestors. Thwarted in their efforts with the executive branch, the Kimmels and Shorts looked to political action in Congress as the path to success.

While the Defense Department's investigation resulted from political pressure, in the end the decision to take a fresh look at the events of 1941 was a positive result for all parties. First, it gave both the Kimmels and Shorts a new and unbiased forum in which to air their views. Second, it resulted in the first investigation unfettered by institutional prejudice and bureaucratic inertia. Finally, it gave the executive branch a solid basis upon which to base any future decisions about U.S. responsibility for the defeat at Pearl Harbor.

1
Approach and Methodology

After the Defense Department agreed to examine whether Admiral Kimmel and General Short should be posthumously advanced on the retired list to their highest wartime grades, Deputy Secretary of Defense John P. White chose Dr. Edwin Dorn, the undersecretary of defense for personnel and readiness, to conduct the inquiry. As Dorn explained later, he took this to mean that he should investigate "whether [official] actions taken toward General Short and Admiral Kimmel some fifty years ago were excessively harsh, and if so, whether posthumous advancement to three- and four-star rank is the appropriate remedy." Although Dorn recognized that the Kimmel and Short families were convinced that the two Pearl Harbor commanders "were scapegoats for a disaster that they could neither prevent nor mitigate," he concluded that his investigation was about more than "the reputations of two officers and the feelings of their families." "The principle of equity requires that wrongs be set right," he wrote. Additionally, Dorn determined that finding the truth was critical in his inquiry, since "we owe it to posterity to ensure that our history is told correctly." (1)

Given Secretary Dorn's perspective, it should come as no surprise that from the beginning he involved himself in the details of the investigation. However, Dorn also knew that his many other duties as an undersecretary meant that he needed a small staff to conduct basic research about Kimmel, Short, and Pearl Harbor. Dorn also must have envisaged that this same team would draft a report once he had decided upon a course of action and any recommendations. In any event, Dorn selected Mr. Nicolas Timenes, the principal director for military personnel policy in the Office of the Secretary of Defense, to head the team. Timenes, a Special Executive Service employee who had worked for the U.S. government in various capacities since the mid-1960s, had already done several major studies for Secretary Dorn. Dorn had been pleased with Timenes's work product, and this factor, combined with Timenes's proven expertise in military personnel policy, made him the logical choice to head the Pearl Harbor inquiry. (2)

While Senator Thurmond did not want either the Navy or the Army to be in charge of the investigation, there was no reason to exclude uniformed personnel from participation in the process. Consequently, Dorn decided that the Army and Navy each should have one representative on his investigative team. The services in turn looked to their legal staffs for that representative, most likely because Dorn would need someone trained to ascertain the relevant facts, weigh evidence, and otherwise evaluate potentially conflicting testimony and documents about Pearl Harbor. As a result, the Army and Navy judge advocates general were both requested to nominate a military lawyer for the team. The services of Army Lt. Col. Fred L. Borch and Navy Cdr. Roger Scott were offered to Secretary Dorn, and upon his acceptance the two judge advocates joined Timenes to round out the Defense Department investigative team. (3)

On 24 October 1995 Dorn had an initial meeting with Timenes, Borch, and Scott. He told them that he intended to personally participate in the inquiry; that he wanted to immerse himself in reading about Pearl Harbor; and that he looked forward to periodic discussions of the issues at hand. From the beginning, Dorn recognized that "a judgment" about Kimmel and Short had been made long ago; President Roosevelt, General Marshall, and Admiral King decided that the two officers had failed at Pearl Harbor. "Perhaps," mused Dorn out loud, "we will feel that it isn't appropriate to change it [the Roosevelt-Marshall-King judgment]; history is full of close calls after all." But, he continued, "our mission" is to take "a fresh look at the whole picture." Consequently, if this earlier judgment about Kimmel and Short "is flawed," said Dorn, "we will look to see if the remedy [posthumous advancement] is appropriate." Dorn explained that even if he and the team determined that Kimmel and Short had been unjustly relieved of command, it did not logically follow that posthumous promotion was the proper remedy. (4)

Dorn also explained that Deputy Secretary of Defense White had rejected the idea of appointing a "blue ribbon panel, with a public forum for an exchange of views" to examine the Kimmel-Short case. According to Dorn, Secretary White rejected this investigative method as it seemed highly likely to "result in a series of arguments" with no clear-cut decision or recommended course of action. As such a result ran counter to the desired goal of taking a fresh look at the issue, including a careful consideration of the posthumous advancement remedy advocated by the Kimmel and Short families, White had decided that the best course of action was to appoint Dorn to conduct the inquiry. (5)

After these preliminary remarks to Timenes, Borch, and Scott, Secretary Dorn sketched out the methodology he wanted used in examining whether Kimmel and Short merited the restoration of their stars. According to Dorn, the team first had to define the nature of the disaster. In his view, the Japanese attack on Oahu could not have been prevented. Consequently, the nature of the disaster was not that the Army and the Navy had failed to prevent the bombardment of Pearl Harbor. Rather, the true nature of the disaster was that U.S. losses had been so heavy, while the Japanese had suffered comparatively little loss of life and materiel. It followed that the crux of any inquiry into Kimmel's and Short's performance on 7 December 1941 was not whether they could have prevented the Japanese attack on Oahu, but whether they could have mitigated its effects. Dorn insisted that this meant asking: "Did Kimmel and Short behave reasonably given their responsibility for a particular mission, and given the information and resources at their disposal?" In other words, what did the two men know, and when? And, based on what they knew, when they knew it, and the resources they had at their disposal, what could these two senior commanders have done to mitigate American losses? Answering these questions would resolve the issue of the extent of Kimmel's and Short's responsibility for the catastrophe. Only then would it be possible to decide whether their performance while in command now warranted a Defense Department recommendation that the two men be posthumously advanced in grade. (6)

After this initial meeting, the three team members set up their offices in space leased by the Defense Department in Rosslyn, Virginia. They spent the next several weeks reading as many primary and secondary sources as possible. While Timenes, Borch, and Scott read thousands and thousands of pages, they each also examined the single-volume report of the Joint Congressional Committee on the Investigation of the Pearl Harbor Attack (hereafter referred to as JCC). They also looked at selected parts of the thirty-nine-volume hearing record accompanying that report. The research team also examined the official personnel records for Admiral Kimmel and General Short, and the voluminous correspondence between their families and the Army and Navy on the issue of posthumous advancement. Each member of the team also read a large number of secondary sources. While Timenes, Borch, and Scott did not all read the same books and articles, all three did read these works: Kimmel's own book, *My Story;* Capt. Ned Beach's *Scapegoats,* a defense of Kimmel and Short; and Gordon Prange's *At Dawn We Slept,* acknowledged by professional historians as the best single-volume history of Pearl Harbor.

Within weeks of starting their research, Secretary Dorn and the three team members also decided that a trip to Oahu would be necessary. While no one was totally convinced that visiting the site of the disaster was critical to their work, the final consensus was that the Dorn Report would have less credibility if a site visit were not conducted. When the team visited Hawaii, 12–15 November 1995, they consulted with professional historians employed by the National Park Service, Army, Navy, and Air Force. The briefings from, and discussions with, experts like John R. Kuborn, deputy command historian at Headquarters, Pacific Air Forces, and Thomas M. Fairfull, chief of the Museum Division, U.S. Army Garrison Hawaii, were helpful in sharpening the issues. (7) Mr. Daniel A. Martinez, the USS *Arizona* Memorial historian, also made a key suggestion that the team should consult the archives at the University of Hawaii. Martinez believed that examining microform copies of the *Honolulu Star-Bulletin* and *Honolulu Advertiser* for the months, weeks, and days leading up to the Japanese attack would help to answer the question, "what did they know?" because these newspapers were read regularly by Kimmel, Short, and their staffs. Martinez also suggested that public statements made by Kimmel and Short might have been reported in the newspapers and might constitute new evidence. Martinez was correct: the team discovered a wealth of new information, including one newspaper account of General Short stating that an air attack was "not improbable." (8)

In addition to reading primary and secondary sources, and conducting a site visit to Oahu, Undersecretary Dorn and his team also concluded that a meeting with the Kimmel and Short families was critical to their inquiry. If this Defense Department investigation was truly to be a fresh look at the issue, then giving the Kimmels and Shorts a forum to air their views would allow the team to understand their perspective. It would also permit Dorn's team to identify those facts and circumstances relied upon by the two families to support their position—thus ensuring that no critical piece of evidence was overlooked in the investigation. Finally, meeting with the families would show outside observers that the Defense Department was serious about seeking the truth. The Kimmel and Short families met on separate occasions with Dorn and his research team on 20–21 November 1995. Among those present were Admiral Kimmel's two surviving sons, Edward and Thomas, and his grandson, Manning Kimmel, and General Short's daughter-in-law (the widow of his son, Col. Walter D. Short) and grandson. Both families were given an unlimited amount of time to present their cases; both meetings lasted several hours.

In late November 1995, with their reading mostly finished, and after the site visit and meetings with Kimmels and Shorts, Timenes, Borch, and Scott began drafting the report. Timenes as team leader chose the format for the staff report and began sketching out an outline. He decided to structure the report in five parts: "Part I: Introduction," "Part II: The Personnel Actions," "Part III: The Pearl Harbor Investigations," "Part IV: Court of Public Opinion," and "Part V: Options for Further Action." Scott worked exclusively on Part II, the legal basis for Kimmel and Short's reliefs from command, the principle of command responsibility, and the subsequent decision not to restore their higher wartime ranks. Borch focused his efforts on Part III, the detailed look at historical events prior to the Japanese attack and the nine subsequent official Pearl Harbor investigations conducted between 1941 and 1946. Timenes began drafting the remaining parts of the report. While he managed to complete much of the writing, Timenes's work was cut short when he departed unexpectedly on emergency leave. In his absence, Borch took responsibility for Timenes's work, finished it, and put the seventy-four-page staff report into final form. The final version of the report went to Secretary Dorn the first week of December.

After Dorn accepted the report and its conclusions, his office prepared a seven-page executive summary. This document, which also included Dorn's recommendation on the propriety of posthumously promoting Kimmel and Short, was written in the form of a memorandum to Deputy Secretary White, and accompanied the report when Dorn sent it to White. The full text of this memo is given in appendix A. Deputy Secretary White subsequently endorsed the findings and conclusions of the staff report, and Dorn's recommendations. White then forwarded Dorn's memo and the report to Senator Thurmond on 27 December 1995. White's cover letter to Senator Thurmond is reproduced as appendix B.

2

The Report
Advancement of Rear Admiral Kimmel and Major General Short on the Retired List, 1 December 1995

Undersecretary of Defense Dorn sent this final report to Deputy Secretary of Defense White on 15 December 1995; it was forwarded to Senator Thurmond on 27 December. The full text of the report follows; text and endnotes in normal font are the original narrative and notes; text in boldface is the authors' commentary.

INTRODUCTION

Background

On December 7, 1941, Admiral Husband E. Kimmel, USN, was Commander in Chief, United States Fleet, and Commander in Chief, United States Pacific Fleet. Lieutenant General Walter C. Short, USA, was Commander of the Army's Hawaiian Department. Later in that month, both were relieved of their commands and reverted to their permanent, two-star ranks. Major General Short retired February 28, 1942, and Rear Admiral Kimmel retired March 1, 1942. Under the laws in effect at that time, Admiral Kimmel retired as a Rear Admiral and General Short retired as a Major General, both two-star ranks. (1) General Short died in 1949 and Admiral Kimmel died in 1968.

Since the end of World War II, Admiral Kimmel, General Short, and their families have requested on several occasions that action be taken to advance those officers on the retired list to the highest grade they held while on active service. The requests were reviewed at the highest levels in the Department and the Executive Branch. Each of those requests was denied, (2) most recently by President Clinton in December 1994. (3)

Early in 1995, Senator Strom Thurmond, Chairman of the Senate Armed Services Committee, and Representative Floyd Spence, Chairman of the House National Security Committee, asked that the Secretary of Defense attend a meeting on the issue with members of the Kimmel family. (4) In response to that request, then-Deputy Secretary of Defense John Deutch, Secretary of the Navy John H. Dalton, and Navy General Counsel Steven S. Honigman met with Senator Thurmond, members of the Kimmel family, historians and others on April 27, 1995. At that hearing, Chairman Thurmond asked that the Department reexamine the matter. (5) In response, Deputy Secretary Deutch pledged that:

> this matter will be examined without preconception, that the judgments will be made fair on the basis of fact and with justice, and that we will speedily arrive at the best judgment we can on this matter. (6)

In subsequent correspondence, Senator Thurmond asked that the Department's review address the cases of both Admiral Kimmel and General Short and that the review be conducted at the Office of the Secretary of Defense level rather than at the

Navy Department level. (7) In response to that request, Deputy Secretary of Defense John White asked Edwin Dorn, Under Secretary of Defense (Personnel and Readiness), to conduct an independent review, and to report the results of his review not later than December 1, 1995. (8) This is that review.

Purpose

The purpose of this review is to ascertain and assess the facts and policies pertinent to the requests to advance Admiral Kimmel and General Short on the retired list, and to recommend appropriate action based on that assessment.

Scope and Sources

Consistent with the Deputy Secretary's commitment to "producing a final DoD decision that will be recognized as principled, fair, and based on fact," (9) this review began with a compilation and exhaustive review of the written record, and additional materials developed especially for this review. Sources examined for this review include:

1. The nine formal government investigations of the events of December 7, 1941, culminating in the report of the Joint Congressional Committee on the Investigation of the Pearl Harbor Attack (JCC). Although the JCC report is a single volume, (10) the current review is based on examination of original documents and other exhibits in the entire 39-volume hearing record, (11) which includes the complete text of the earlier investigations.
2. Personnel records for Admiral Kimmel and General Short, provided by the National Personnel Records Center (NPRC). (12) Service records of Admiral Kimmel are complete. The formal records of General Short are not in the

Adm. Husband E. Kimmel graduated from the U.S. Naval Academy in 1904. By 1939 he was wearing two stars as the Commander, Cruisers Battle Force. An extremely capable officer who believed in following rules and regulations to the letter, Kimmel was elevated over the heads of many more senior naval officers to receive four stars and become Commander-in-Chief, Pacific Fleet.
U.S. NAVAL INSTITUTE PHOTO ARCHIVE

NPRC files, and probably were destroyed during a massive fire on July 12, 1973. However, the NPRC was able to reconstruct some material regarding General Short from alternate sources at the NPRC and the Department of Veterans Affairs.
3. Unofficial assessments published since 1946, including books and articles. Among the books examined are Admiral Kimmel's own book, published in 1955 (13) and the recent volume by Captain Beach, written in support of Admiral Kimmel and General Short. (14)
4. Materials associated with the several requests for advancement, including correspondence with the families, Members of Congress, and the public; materials provided by the Kimmel and Short families; and other materials.
5. Activities conducted especially for this review, including:

Meetings with the Families of Admiral Kimmel on November 20, 1995, and of General Short on November 21, 1995.

Review of contemporaneous accounts, including newspapers such as the *Honolulu Advertiser*, the *Honolulu Star-Bulletin,* and the *New York Times* for 1941 and 1942, and references in those papers to Admiral Kimmel and General Short to the present.

Review of supplementary materials regarding accountability and responsibility provided by the Military Department Judge Advocates General and by the Service Academies.

An On-Site Survey of Pearl Harbor, including visits to Pearl Harbor, Hickam and Wheeler Air Bases, and Schofield Barracks, and discussions with Park Service, Army, and Air Force historians.

The events associated with Pearl Harbor are numerous, and the record of investigations voluminous. To assist the reader, the pertinent investigations are summarized in Figure 1.

Fig. 1. CHRONOLOGY

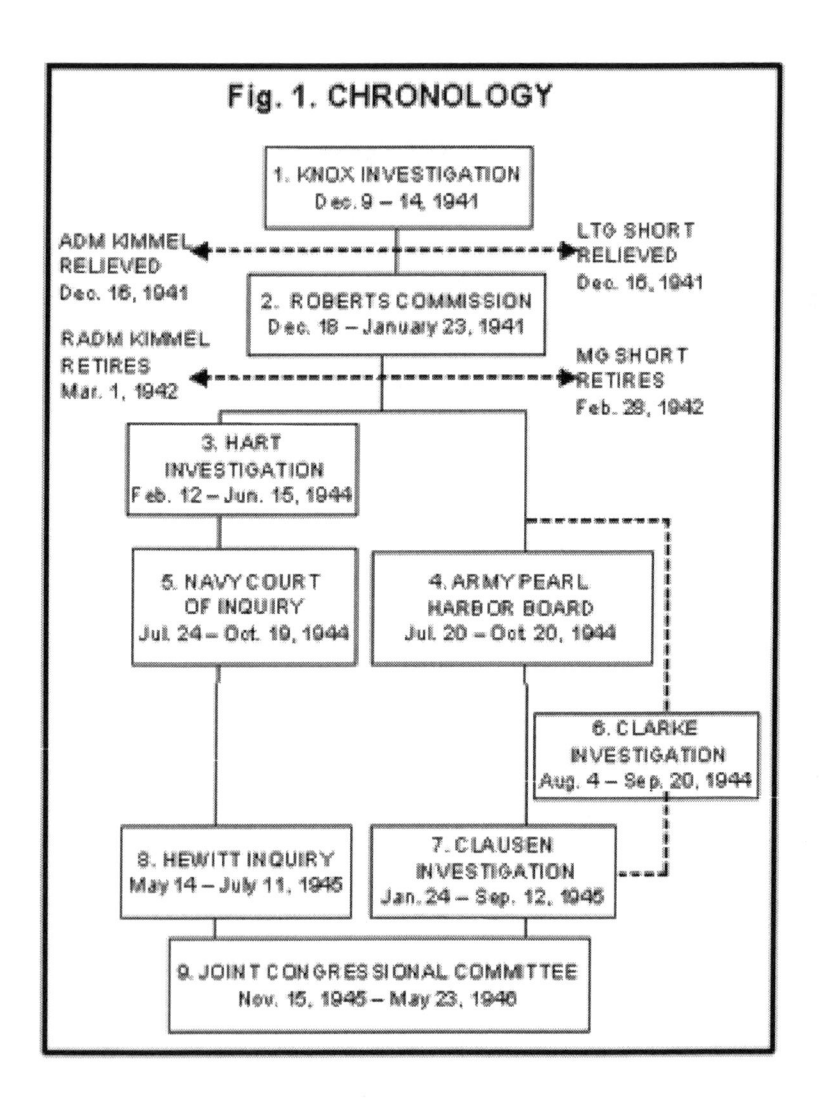

1. KNOX INVESTIGATION
Dec. 9 – 14, 1941

ADM KIMMEL RELIEVED
Dec. 16, 1941

LTG SHORT RELIEVED
Dec. 16, 1941

2. ROBERTS COMMISSION
Dec. 18 – January 23, 1941

RADM KIMMEL RETIRES
Mar. 1, 1942

MG SHORT RETIRES
Feb. 28, 1942

3. HART INVESTIGATION
Feb. 12 – Jun. 15, 1944

5. NAVY COURT OF INQUIRY
Jul. 24 – Oct. 19, 1944

4. ARMY PEARL HARBOR BOARD
Jul. 20 – Oct. 20, 1944

6. CLARKE INVESTIGATION
Aug. 4 – Sep. 20, 1944

8. HEWITT INQUIRY
May 14 – July 11, 1945

7. CLAUSEN INVESTIGATION
Jan. 24 – Sep. 12, 1945

9. JOINT CONGRESSIONAL COMMITTEE
Nov. 15, 1945 – May 23, 1946

Approach

As Deputy Secretary Deutch noted in the recent meeting hosted by Senator Thurmond, the issue turns on a balancing of accountability and fairness. (15) Accordingly, following this introduction the bulk of this report is devoted to a review of the record and an assessment of accountability, responsibility, and fairness in three distinct venues.

The retirement of Admiral Kimmel as a Rear Admiral and of General Short as a Major General was the direct result of two personnel actions in each case: relief from their Pearl Harbor commands in December, 1941, and retirements in February and March, 1942. After the war, legislation was enacted which would have made possible their advancement on the retired list; however, officials at the time declined to do so. Section II of this review addresses those personnel actions.

Much of the debate on the fairness to Admiral Kimmel and General Short has centered on the findings of the several formal investigations. (16) Section III of this review addresses those investigations.

The families are concerned with the "stigma and obloquy" flowing from early charges (17) and their persistent effect on public opinion. Thus, it is not sufficient to review only the personnel actions and investigations which constitute the Government's formal actions in these cases, so Section IV of this review addresses the "court of public opinion."

The final section of this review addresses options for further action.

II. THE PERSONNEL ACTIONS

This Section addresses three personnel actions affecting Admiral Kimmel and General Short: relief from their Pearl Harbor commands in December 1941; their retirements in February and

March 1942; and the decisions not to advance them on the retired list.

Relief from Command (18)

On February 1, 1941, Rear Admiral Husband E. Kimmel succeeded Admiral J. O. Richardson as Commander in Chief, Pacific Fleet and Commander in Chief, United States Fleet. (19) Incident to assuming these positions of command, Rear Admiral Kimmel also assumed the temporary rank of four-star Admiral. (20) At the time, the highest permanent grade that officers of the armed forces could hold was Rear Admiral or Major General (0-8). (21) Immediately after the Japanese attack on Pearl Harbor on December 7, 1941, Secretary of the Navy Frank Knox flew to Pearl Harbor on December 8 to conduct a preliminary investigation. Following Secretary Knox's report to the President on December 14, Admiral Kimmel was relieved of command and reverted to his permanent grade of Rear Admiral. (22)

Similarly, Major General Short replaced Major General Herron as Commander of the Army's Hawaiian Department, and assumed the temporary rank of Lieutenant General. General Short was also relieved of command on December 16, 1941, and reverted to his permanent grade of Major General. (23)

For reasons both legal and practical, command in the United States Armed Forces has a special character. That character is distinct from rank. The need to maintain good order and discipline at all levels of command when lives are at stake creates an environment unique to the command of military units. As the Supreme Court has noted, "no military organization can function without strict discipline and regulation that would be unacceptable in a civilian setting" (24) and that "the rights of men in the armed forces must perforce be conditioned to meet certain overriding demands of discipline and duty . . ." (25)

There is no entitlement or right to command. No one in the military has a right to any particular assignment or position, and

Lt. Gen. Walter C. Short (shown here as a major general) received a direct commission as an infantry lieutenant in 1902, when he was twenty-two years old. As he progressed through the ranks, Short's chief interest was in training. Not surprisingly, he continued to view training his soldiers as his principal mission after he assumed command of the Army's Hawaiian Department in February 1941.
U.S. NAVAL INSTITUTE PHOTO ARCHIVE

any military member may be reassigned to a position of greater or lesser responsibility by senior officials in the chain of command at their discretion. (26) This authority flows from the President's constitutional powers as Commander-in-Chief, (27) and is so well established that no court has ever recognized a right to "due process" review of military personnel assignment decisions. The authority to make such changes remains a key constitutional prerogative of the President, and the practical necessity for such authority in the unique context of the military remains central to the accomplishment of the military mission.

An officer may be relieved of command if a superior decides the officer has failed to exercise sound judgment. (28) Moreover, an officer may be relieved of command simply because of an entirely subjective loss of confidence by superiors in the chain of command. (29) The grounds for detachment of an officer in command reflect the critical importance of trust and confidence in the chain of command, and the highly discretionary nature of decisions to relieve officers in command. The guidance in 1941 was much like today's:

> The unique position of trust and responsibility an officer in command possesses; his or her role in shaping morale, good order, and discipline within the command; and his or her influence on mission requirements and command readiness make it imperative that immediate superiors have full confidence in the officer's judgment and ability to command. (30)

In sum, relief does not require a finding of misconduct or unsatisfactory performance—merely of loss of confidence with regard to the specific command in question. Given the scope of the defeat at Pearl Harbor and the need to reform the forces in the Pacific for the conduct of the war, it follows that the relief of Admiral Kimmel and General Short was consistent with military practice. Their relief also was reasonable because the Roberts Commission investigation, which began at that time, would detract their time and attention from war activities. (31)

The standard for relieving an officer in command is not whether he or she has objectively committed some misconduct that warrants such relief, but whether senior officials subjectively conclude that he or she can continue to command effectively under all circumstances. Service in positions of command is a privilege, not a right. Relief of an officer in command may cause embarrassment or injury to reputation, but that is a risk inherent in the nature of command itself, as should have been evident to Admiral Kimmel in particular when he succeeded Admiral Richardson, who had been summarily relieved by President Roosevelt. (32)

Concerns about "fairness" must yield to the needs of the country and the armed forces. Consequently, it is difficult to argue that relief of Admiral Kimmel and General Short was "unfair," given the magnitude of the disaster at Pearl Harbor and their positions in direct command of the defeated forces. Moreover, the Chief of Naval Operations was also relieved shortly thereafter, although he was reassigned to another four-star position.

Kimmel's predecessor in command, Adm. J. O. Richardson, believed that Kimmel had been wrongly blamed for what happened at Pearl Harbor. Yet Richardson also wrote that Kimmel and Short had to be relieved: "The Army and the Navy and everyone else would have understood and approved this action, because all would have recognized that, regardless of where blame lay, no armed force should remain under the command of a leader under whom it had suffered such a loss." (33) Another Kimmel defender, Edward B. Hanify, who served as Admiral Kimmel's lawyer at the 1944 Navy Court of Inquiry and attended the April 1995 meeting organized by Senator Thurmond, also agreed that relieving Kimmel and Short was necessary. In a 1987 memorandum to the director of naval history, Hanify cited with approval the comments of Adm. William H. Standley, a member of the Roberts Commission: "Under the circumstances, Admiral Kimmel and General Short had to be relieved of their commands." (34)

Retirement (35)

Following their relief from the Hawaiian commands, Admiral Kimmel and General Short reverted to their permanent ranks and were given temporary assignments. Both Admiral Kimmel and General Short sought new commands commensurate with their former ranks that would contribute to the war effort. (36)

Such assignments were not immediately forthcoming. Eventually, General Short submitted retirement papers. Although he hoped that his application for retirement would not be accepted, (37) it was, and he retired on February 28, 1942.

Admiral Kimmel learned that General Short had submitted his retirement papers, and interpreted that as a signal that he should do so as well. (38) He did, and retired on March 1, 1942. Under the laws in effect at the time, both officers retired at their permanent two-star grades. It has been asserted in several venues that Admiral Kimmel and General Short were "forced into retirement." There is no evidence to support that claim. Rather, it appears that new assignments were not immediately forthcoming, and General Short initiated a chain of events that were accepted at face value, to the disappointment of both him and Admiral Kimmel. These events give rise to two questions: (1) should Admiral Kimmel and General Short have been given new assignments, and (2) should the retirement offers have been accepted?

Three- and four-star positions are lofty and few. In the Navy in 1941, for example, there were only six. (39) It is neither surprising nor inappropriate that leaders of the time, having relieved Admiral Kimmel and General Short of their Hawaiian commands and, faced with the Roberts report findings of dereliction of duty, (40) did not immediately find other positions of comparable rank for them.

It is important to remember that the state of the Allied cause in both the Atlantic and the Pacific was extremely perilous in the dark days of early 1942. The greatest national need at the time was to prosecute the global war against both Germany and Japan.

Anything that distracted command energies from that cause could have been unwise. Under those circumstances, it would have been surprising indeed if the leaders of the time declined the opportunity to accept the retirement of the officers most visibly associated with the disaster at Pearl Harbor, and thus to put that debacle behind them.

Again, concerns about "fairness" must yield to the needs of the country and the armed forces. Nevertheless, it is difficult to conclude that accepting the offers of retirement was unfair at the time. Two-star rank is very prestigious; it is hardly ignominious.

Although post-war legislative reforms eliminated the distinction between permanent and temporary grades at two-star levels and below, today three- and four-star ranks remain in a special category. Indeed, under current law (41) positions occupied by lieutenant generals, vice admirals, generals and admirals are positions of "importance and responsibility." An officer may be assigned to such a position only if nominated by the President and confirmed by the Senate. The entire process must be repeated if a serving three- or four-star officer is transferred to another position at the same rank. Similarly, occupants of such positions may retire in those grades only if the President once again nominates them and the Senate confirms them to retire in those grades. Otherwise, an officer automatically retires at the permanent grade of two-star or below. In recent years, the Services have declined to seek nomination of several serving three-star officers for retirement at that grade, and the Senate has declined to confirm at least one other, all for what by most standards would be considered administrative oversights, personal indiscretions, or errors of judgment—none involving loss of life.

For example, Vice Adm. John M. Poindexter wore three stars as President Reagan's national security advisor. In November 1986, however, in the wake of public furor over the illegal diversion of money in the Iran-Contra operations, Vice Admiral Poindexter was forced to resign. At that time,

he reverted to his permanent two-star rank of rear admiral. Later, after President Reagan failed to nominate Poindexter for retirement at his higher three-star rank, he retired as a rear admiral. (42)

Advancement on the Retired List

The Armed Forces were governed throughout the war by laws which distinguished between permanent and temporary ranks. (43) The vast expansion of all ranks during the war created significant disparities between permanent ranks and those far higher ranks in which many officers had fought during much of the war. Recognizing that this disparity had a significant effect on retired ranks, Congress enacted the Officer Personnel Act of 1947, (44) intended among other things to permit officers to be advanced on the retired list to the highest rank held while on active service during the war. (45)

Officers at other ranks, including one- and two-star generals and admirals (some of whom had been reduced in rank when relieved), were advanced under the provisions of that Act. However, leaders at the time declined to advance Admiral Kimmel and General Short under the Act. (46) There is little in the record to indicate why those decisions were reached.

A number of general officers were relieved from command and "reduced for cause" during World War II; their relief resulted primarily from errors in judgment. They included Carlos Brewer, Lloyd D. Brown, William C. McMahon, Lindsay M. Silvester, Leroy M. Watson, Henry W. Baird, Julian F. Barnes, Joseph M. Cummins, Ernest J. Dawley, James P. Marley, James I. Muir, and Paul L. Ranson. A board of officers, consisting of lieutenant generals Gerow, McLain, and Eddy, concluded that the services of these officers in the grade of major general were satisfactory. The secretary of the Army approved this board's recommendations, and their stars were returned to them. (47)

For example, in fall 1943 Major General Dawley was relieved from command of VI Corps after the Battle of the Salerno Beachhead. His boss, U.S. Fifth Army commander Lt. Gen. Mark W. Clark, fired Dawley because "the inevitable confusion of the beachhead, the intermingling of units and the consequent lack of neat dispositions on a situation map," combined with "Dawley's failure to impress visiting officers of high rank, [and] his fatigue after several days and nights of strenuous activity and little sleep," caused Clark to lose confidence in his ability to continue in command. (48) Dawley reverted to his permanent rank of colonel and returned to the United States. (49)

By the time of those decisions, the war was over and the full record of the Joint Congressional Committee hearings on the Pearl Harbor attack (including the decoded Japanese messages which have been the basis of much subsequent debate) was publicly available. It follows that those decisions must have been informed decisions. Clearly, the decisions were within the discretion of the decisionmakers at the time. Further, those decisions have been reviewed on numerous occasions at the highest levels in several Administrations, and in each case decisionmakers have declined to propose advancement. (50)

Presumably decisions not to advance Admiral Kimmel and General Short were based on review of their performance at Pearl Harbor. Thus, determining whether these decisions were fair requires examination of that performance. The final findings by the Services and by the Joint Congressional Committee on the Pearl Harbor Attack were that Admiral Kimmel and General Short were not guilty of offenses worthy of courts-martial, but that they had committed "errors of judgment." Furthermore, the Secretary of the Navy made explicit his determination of the career implications of such errors in the case of Admiral Kimmel: that he had "failed to demonstrate the superior judgment necessary for exercising command commensurate with [his] rank and assigned duties" and therefore the

Secretary considered that "appropriate action should be taken to insure that [Admiral Kimmel not] be recalled to active duty in the future for any position in which the exercise of superior judgment is necessary." (51)

Advancement is a privilege, not a right, and must be based on performance. Admiral Trost, then the Chief of Naval Operations, wrote in connection with this issue, "there is a vast difference between a degree of fault which does not warrant a punitive action and a level of performance which would warrant bestowal of a privilege." (52) Thus, if the findings of the JCC with regard to the performance of these officers were and remain valid, advancement is not warranted. The next Section of this review addresses those findings.

III. THE PEARL HARBOR INVESTIGATIONS

The Record

There were nine separate Pearl Harbor investigations from 1941 through 1946. (53) The first began the day after the event, when Secretary of the Navy Frank Knox flew to Pearl Harbor to find out what had happened, and to try to understand why. In less than a week, Secretary Knox visited the damaged installations at Pearl Harbor and interviewed numerous individuals, including Admiral Kimmel and General Short. Secretary Knox's report (54) concludes:

> The Japanese air attack on the Island of Oahu on December 7th was a complete surprise to both the Army and the Navy. Its initial success, which included almost all the damage done, was due to a lack of a state of readiness against such an air attack, by both branches of the Service. This statement was made by me to both General Short and Admiral Kimmel, and both agreed that it was entirely true.... Neither Army or Navy Commandants in Oahu regarded such an attack as at all likely, because of the danger which such a carrier-borne attack would confront in view of the preponderance of the American naval strength in Hawaiian

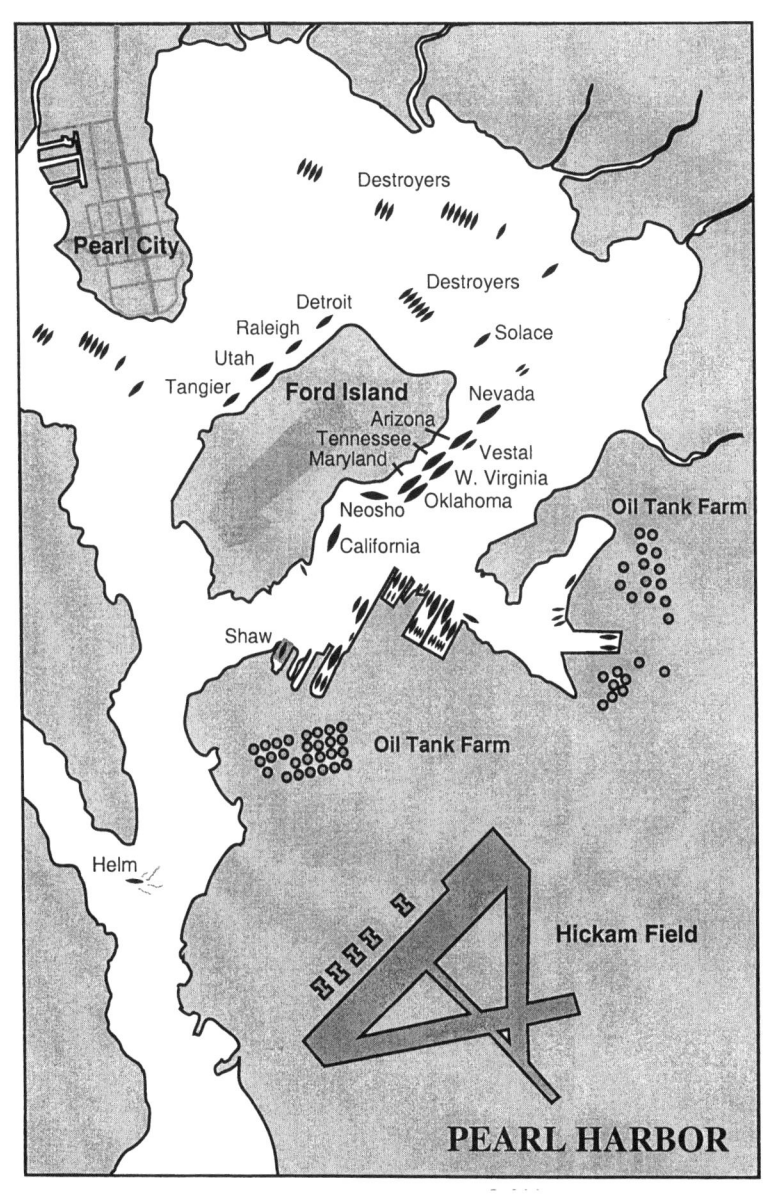

The fleet in Hawaii trained hard during the week, but its ships generally were in port on Saturdays and Sundays. This predictable ship location was the touchstone of Japanese planning, and on Sunday morning the Japanese caught the U.S. Navy completely by surprise. Only the Navy's carriers—fortuitously still at sea—escaped the attack.
© 2004 NAVPUBLISHING, LLC

waters.... Neither Short nor Kimmel, at the time of the attack, had any knowledge of the plain intimations of some surprise move, made clear in Washington, through the interception of Japanese instructions to Nomura. (55)

There was no attempt by either Admiral Kimmel or General Short to alibi the lack of a state of readiness for the air attack. Both admitted that they did not expect it, and had taken no adequate measures to meet one if it came. Both Kimmel and Short evidently regarded an air attack as extremely unlikely.... Both felt that if any surprise attack was attempted it would be made in the Far East. (56)

Secretary Knox's report was delivered to President Roosevelt on December 14, 1941. On December 16, after consultation with the President, Secretary of the Navy Knox and Secretary of War Stimson directed the relief of Admiral Kimmel and General Short, respectively. (57)

The President then established a five-member Commission headed by Owen J. Roberts, a sitting Associate Justice of the Supreme Court, to determine whether "any derelictions or errors of judgment on the part of United States Army or Navy personnel contributed to such successes as were achieved by the enemy on the occasion mentioned, and if so, what these derelictions or errors were, and who were responsible therefore." (58)

The Roberts Commission conducted meetings during the period from December 18, 1941, through January 23, 1942, interviewed 127 witnesses, and examined a large number of documents. One of the Commission's conclusions is the source of much of the controversy in the cases of Admiral Kimmel (59) and General Short and thus is worth repeating in its entirety:

17. In light of the warnings and directions to take appropriate action, transmitted to both commanders between November 27 and December 7, and the obligation under the system of coordination then in effect for joint cooperative action on their part, it was a *dereliction of duty* on the part of each of them not to con-

sult and confer with the other respecting the meaning and intent of the warnings, and the appropriate measures of defense required by the imminence of hostilities. The attitude of each, that he was not required to inform himself of, and his lack of interest in, the measures undertaken by the other to carry out the responsibility assigned to such other under the provisions of the plans then in effect, demonstrated on the part of each a lack of appreciation of the responsibilities vested in them and inherent in their positions as Commander in Chief, Pacific Fleet, and Commanding General, Hawaiian Department. (60) [emphasis added]

These are the harshest words in the report, which finds relatively little fault with actions in Washington, although it acknowledges that the "evidence touches subjects which in the national interest should remain secret." (61) The Roberts Commission report was submitted to the President on January 23, 1942, and released to the public on January 24, 1942. Admiral Kimmel and General Short retired about a month later.

"Dereliction of duty" was not then a court-martial offense as such, but it was harsh language. Although court-martial charges against Admiral Kimmel and General Short were considered during 1942, no charges were preferred, in part because of the wartime need for secrecy and in part because of doubts that such charges could be sustained. (62)

Admiral Kimmel in particular was mortified by the accusation of "dereliction of duty" and almost immediately began to press for a court-martial or other formal proceeding to clear his name. (63) In part because of continuing public debate on the Pearl Harbor issue but largely through the efforts of Admiral Kimmel's own lawyer, (64) Congress in 1944 passed a resolution that directed "[t]he Secretary of War and the Secretary of the Navy . . . severally . . . to proceed forthwith with an investigation into the facts surrounding the catastrophe." (65) To carry out those responsibilities, the Secretaries created two Boards, a Navy Court of Inquiry (66) and an Army Pearl Harbor Board. (67)

The Navy Court of Inquiry concluded "that no offenses have been committed nor serious blame incurred on the part of any person in the naval service." (68) In his endorsement, the Chief of Naval Operations, Admiral Ernest King, disagreed. He found evidence of error and concluded,

6. The derelictions (69) on the part of Admiral [Harold] Stark and Admiral Kimmel were faults of omission rather than faults of commission. In the case in question, they indicate the lack of the superior judgment necessary for exercising command commensurate with their rank and assigned duties, rather than culpable inefficiency. (70)

7. Since trial by general court martial is not warranted by the evidence adduced, appropriate administrative action would appear to be the relegation of both these officers to positions in which lack of superior judgment may not result in future errors. (71)

After further investigation and review, Secretary of the Navy James Forrestal agreed that Admirals Stark and Kimmel "failed to demonstrate the superior judgment necessary for exercising command commensurate with their rank and assigned duties" and considered that "appropriate action should be taken to insure that neither of them will be recalled to active duty in the future for any position in which the exercise of superior judgment is necessary." (72) (73)

The Army's Pearl Harbor Board generally criticized the conduct of the Secretary of State, the Chief of Staff, the then Chief of War Plans Division, and General Short, (74) but made no recommendations. The Army's Judge Advocate General, reviewing the report, suggested that General Short was guilty of errors of judgment, but that those errors did not rise to levels appropriate for court-martial. (75)

The reports of the Navy Court of Inquiry and the Army Pearl Harbor Board, together with the endorsements of the Secretaries, stand as official "corrections" by the Services of the Roberts

The USS *Oklahoma* sank within minutes of being struck by Japanese torpedoes. By the time she was raised and stabilized in mid-1943, it was no longer feasible to restore her, and she never saw active service again. Here, Secretary of the Navy Forrestal (*left*) surveys the damage to the *Oklahoma* while walking on her bottom, 6 September 1942.
NATIONAL ARCHIVES AND RECORDS ADMINISTRATION

Commission's finding of dereliction. The Court and the Board concluded that the evidence was insufficient to warrant court-martial of Admiral Kimmel or General Short. However, the evidence strongly suggested "errors of judgment."

Investigations of the events at Pearl Harbor culminated in the lengthy hearings and voluminous publications of the Joint Congressional Committee on the Pearl Harbor Attack. The JCC concluded that "[t]he disaster of Pearl Harbor was the failure, with attendant increase in personnel and material losses, of the Army and the Navy to institute measures designed to detect an approaching hostile force, to effect a state of readiness commensurate with the realization that war was at hand, and to employ every facility at their command in repelling the Japanese." (76) The JCC recognized the importance of the failure of the Army and the Navy in Washington to transmit critical information to the Hawaiian commanders. (77) Nevertheless, it found that:

> 8. . . . the Hawaiian commands failed—
>
> (a) To discharge their responsibilities in the light of the warnings received from Washington, other information possessed by them, and the principle of command by mutual cooperation.
>
> (b) To integrate and coordinate their facilities for defense and to alert properly the Army and Navy establishments in Hawaii, particularly in the light of the warnings and intelligence available to them during the period November 27 to December 7, 1941.
>
> (c) To effect liaison on a basis designed to acquaint each of them with the operations of the other, which was necessary to their joint security, and to exchange fully all significant intelligence.
>
> (d) To maintain a more effective reconnaissance within the limits of their equipment.
>
> (e) To effect a state of readiness throughout the Army and Navy establishments designed to meet all possible attacks.
>
> (f) To employ the facilities, materiel, and personnel at their command, which were adequate at least to have greatly minimized the effects of the attack, in repelling the Japanese raiders.
>
> (g) To appreciate the significance of intelligence and other information available to them.
>
> 9. The errors made by the Hawaiian commands were errors of judgment and not derelictions of duty. (78)

The *Arizona* burns in the late morning of Sunday, 7 December 1941. Of its crew of 1,777, only 46 survived. The 1,731 who died, including its skipper, Capt. Van Valkenburgh, made the loss of the USS *Arizona* the greatest single naval disaster in American history.
NATIONAL ARCHIVES AND RECORDS ADMINISTRATION

Even the minority report, which suggested greater focus on failures by the civilian and military leadership in Washington, "agree[d] that the high command in Hawaii was subject to criticism for concluding that Hawaii was not in danger." (79)

Thus, the final official pronouncements of the government on the responsibility for Pearl Harbor found that Admiral Kimmel and General Short committed errors of judgment, but that those errors did not rise to the level of court-martial offenses. Those official pronouncements make clear that Admiral Kimmel and General Short were by no means solely responsible for what happened at Pearl Harbor, and that others also deserved blame. The balance of this Section assesses whether those assessments are still valid.

A Current Assessment

In the intervening 54 years, there has been a vast outpouring of publications on the events at Pearl Harbor. Much detail has been added to enrich our understanding of those events, and many new interpretive insights have been offered.

An objective reading of the historical record suggests that the story of Pearl Harbor is far from simple. The reasons for the disastrous defeat at Pearl Harbor form a tapestry woven of many threads, including the inevitable advantage of an aggressor free to choose the time, place, and form of a surprise attack in a time of nominal peace, and the brilliant planning and flawless execution by a Japanese Navy whose capabilities were seriously underestimated by many Americans.

Two specific failures have been at the center of the historical debate: (1) the failure of officials in Washington, privy to intercepted Japanese diplomatic communications, to appreciate fully and to convey to the commanders in Hawaii the sense of focus and urgency that those communications should have engendered; and (2) the failure of the commanders in Hawaii to make adequate preparations in light of the information they did have. The balance of this review focuses on these two failures.

Given Japanese planning and determination to attack the US fleet in Hawaii and the limited American resources stretched across the Pacific, the attack on Pearl Harbor probably could not have been prevented. Consequently, the failure at Pearl Harbor is not failure to prevent that attack. Rather, the nature of the failure was the disproportionate losses in American lives and materiel when compared with Japanese losses. (80) This disproportionality resulted principally from the American failure to anticipate and prepare for the possibility of a surprise aerial attack on Pearl Harbor.

> The Japanese did not believe they would surprise the U.S. forces in Hawaii. On the contrary, Admiral Yamamoto expected his forces to be detected. In November 1941 he told about a hundred Japanese officers on the flight deck of the *Akagi* that "although we hope to achieve surprise, everyone should be prepared for terrific American resistance to this operation." In Yamamoto's view, Kimmel was "no ordinary or average man. . . . We can expect him to put up a courageous fight." He continued: "Moreover, he [Kimmel] is said to be *farsighted and cautious,* so it is quite possible that he has instituted very close measures to cope with any emergency. Therefore, you must take into careful consideration the possibility that the attack may not be a surprise after all. You *may have to fight your way in to the target.*" (81)
> Yamamoto's remarks prove that the Japanese expected their American counterparts to have prepared a defense against an aerial attack. His statements also show that there was no rational basis for Kimmel's and Short's failure to guard against such an air threat.

It is clear today, as should have been clear since 1946 to any serious reader of the JCC hearing record, that Admiral Kimmel and General Short were not solely responsible for the defeat at Pearl Harbor.

To say that Admiral Kimmel and General Short were not solely responsible does not, however, necessarily imply that they were totally blameless. To assess the degree of their responsibility, and thus their performance, it is necessary to consider their mission, the information they had, the resources they had, and what they did with that information and those resources.

General Short's mission was to protect the fleet at Pearl Harbor. On February 7, 1941, General Short's first day as Commander of the Hawaiian Department, Army Chief of Staff General George Marshall wrote to him:

> The fullest protection for the Fleet is *the* rather than *a* major consideration for us, there can be little question about that. (emphasis in original)

and in his closing paragraph reiterated:

> Please keep clearly in mind in all of your negotiations that our mission is to protect the base and the Naval concentrations. (82)

Admiral Kimmel had the "general duty" to "take all practicable steps to keep the ships of his command ready for battle." (83) This required drills and exercises ". . . done in such a manner as will most conduce to maintaining the fleet in constant readiness for War in all its phases." (84) In regards to Hawaii, Admiral Kimmel's mission was to provide long-range reconnaissance (85) and to cooperate with the Army in the defense of the fleet.

Both Admiral Kimmel and General Short asserted that information they received from Washington and their own staffs was insufficiently explicit or specific to prompt greater readiness to defend against air attack. Even the November 27, 1941, "war warning" message, testified both commanders, was ambiguous; it provided no warning of an impending surprise attack by aircraft. (86) In light of this claimed lack of information, it is important to examine what information Admiral Kimmel and General Short did have.

First, Admiral Kimmel and General Short knew that their primary mission—indeed virtually their only mission—was to prepare for war with Japan. (87)

Kimmel was very familiar with the Navy's war plan for Japan; he had studied it while a student at the Naval War College. (88)

By November 1941, Japan had occupied Manchuria and French Indo-China, and had joined in a tripartite alliance with Italy and Germany. The U.S. reaction was to stop selling Japan strategically important materials including oil and, in the summer of 1941, to freeze Japanese assets in the United States. As negotiations in the summer and fall of 1941 failed to break the impasse, Kimmel and Short—along with all other civilian and military leaders in the United States—knew that war with Japan was imminent. The only question was when and where it would occur.

© 2004 NavPublishing, LLC

Second, Admiral Kimmel and General Short knew that war with Japan was highly likely. Throughout 1941, newspapers were full of news of war in Asia and Europe. Japan had been at war in China since 1937, and reportedly had some 75,000 Japanese troops occupying French Indo-China. (89) Tensions between the United States and Japan had been increasing. President Roosevelt had taken steps to freeze Japanese assets in the United States, and US oil shipments, accounting for most of Japan's supply, had ceased. (90) Members of both the House and the Senate periodically called upon Roosevelt to declare war on Japan. (91) Japanese aggression in Asia and US determination to stop it made war almost inevitable. Germany, Japan's Axis partner, had occupied Denmark, Norway, Poland, and the Low Countries and much of France. Germany had also attacked the Soviet Union that summer, and the Wehrmacht's "blitzkrieg" had inflicted massive Soviet losses. The United States became increasingly involved in measures short of war. Honolulu newspapers reported the sinking of an American destroyer and an American tanker in the Atlantic in November 1941. (92)

Third, Admiral Kimmel and General Short knew that, if war came, Japan would strike the first blow, if only because the United States would not. (93)

Fourth, Admiral Kimmel and General Short knew that a surprise attack probably would precede a declaration of war. Japan had begun its war with Russia in 1905 with a successful surprise attack on the Russian fleet at Port Arthur. Japan's attack on North China in 1937 had not been preceded by a declaration of war either. The March 31, 1941, Martin-Bellinger Report (94) likewise noted that "[i]n the past Orange [Japan] has never preceded hostile actions by a declaration of war." (95) Additionally, on April 1, 1941, Naval Intelligence in Washington alerted all naval districts—including Hawaii—that "past experience shows the Axis Powers often begin . . . [attacks] on Saturdays and Sundays or on national holidays." (96) Admiral Kimmel's standing order to the fleet assumed "[t]hat a declaration of war may be preceded by: (1) a surprise attack on ships in Pearl Harbor, (2) a surprise submarine attack on ships in operating area, and (3) a combination of these two." (97) On February 18, 1941, for example, Admiral Kimmel wrote: "I feel that a surprise attack (submarine, air, or combined) on Pearl Harbor is a possibility." (98) General Short similarly knew that a surprise attack was likely, given that he had read the Martin-Bellinger Report. (99)

Fifth, Admiral Kimmel and General Short knew that the initial Japanese attack could fall on Pearl Harbor. Although they shared in the conventional wisdom of the era, buttressed by confirmed intelligence reports of Japanese ship movements in the Far East, that the attack most probably would occur in the Far East, (100) the fact that they took vigorous measures to defend against submarine attack and sabotage and conducted drills in repelling invasion testifies to their understanding that the war *could* come to Pearl Harbor.

Sixth, Admiral Kimmel and General Short knew that an attack on Pearl Harbor could come in the form of an attack from carriers. Shortly after taking command, both Admiral Kimmel and General Short received copies of an assessment by the Secretary of the Navy, in which the Secretary of the Army concurred, that:

> If war eventuates with Japan, it is believed easily possible that hostilities would be initiated by a surprise attack upon the Fleet or the Naval Base at Pearl Harbor.
>   . . . [T]he inherent possibilities of a major disaster to the Fleet or naval base warrant taking every step, as rapidly as can be done, that will increase the joint readiness of the Army and Navy to withstand a raid of the character mentioned above.
>   The dangers envisaged in their order of importance and probability are considered to be:
>
> (1) Air bombing attack.
> (2) Air torpedo attack.
> (3) Sabotage.
> (4) Submarine attack.
> (5) Mining.
> (6) Bombardment by gun fire. (101)

December 7, 1941

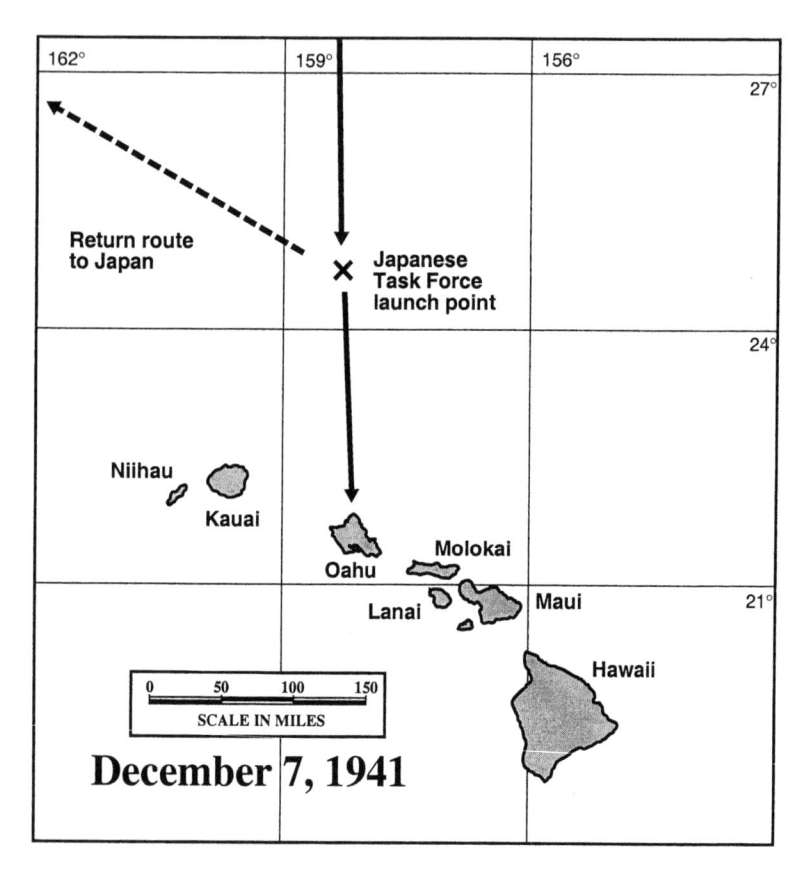

Wary of being detected as they approached Hawaii, the Japanese carriers launched their fighters and torpedo bombers while the ships were still more than two hundred miles north of Oahu.
© 2004 NAVPUBLISHING, LLC

Admiral Kimmel immediately complained to Admiral Stark of the inadequacy of the Army's air defenses at Pearl Harbor, especially interceptor aircraft and antiaircraft guns. Admiral Stark passed these concerns to General Marshall, and General Marshall emphasized to General Short his own concern about air attack:

My impression of the Hawaiian problem has been that if no serious harm is done us during the first six hours of known hostilities, thereafter the existing defenses would discourage an enemy against the hazard of an attack. The risk of sabotage and the risk involved in a surprise raid by air and by submarine, constitute the real perils of the situation. Frankly, I do not see any landing threat in the Hawaiian Islands so long as we have air superiority. (102)

General Marshall wrote these comments on General Short's first day as Commander of the Army's Hawaiian Department.

Seventh, Admiral Kimmel and General Short knew from their own staffs of the danger of surprise air attack. On March 31, 1941, Admiral Bellinger and General Martin reported to both Admiral Kimmel and General Short that "[a] successful, sudden raid against our ships and Naval installations on Oahu might prevent effective offensive action by our forces in the Western Pacific for a long period . . ." and "[i]t appears possible that Orange [Japanese] submarines and/or an Orange fast raiding force might arrive in Hawaiian waters with no prior warning from our intelligence service." (103)

Eighth, Admiral Kimmel and General Short knew from recent events that the idea of a carrier air attack on Pearl Harbor was not new. General Billy Mitchell forecast an assault by carrier launched aircraft on Pearl Harbor after his 1924 Asian tour. (104) The U.S. Navy had fleet exercises and war games involving air strikes on Pearl Harbor in the 1930s. (105) Admiral Kimmel and General Short must have been aware of the enormously successful attack by British carrier-based torpedo bombers on the harbor at Taranto in November 1940, which sank or damaged the Italian Navy's most modern battleships. (106)

The Dorn Report did not state with certainty that Kimmel and Short knew about Taranto. There is, however, no doubt that they did know, as did the Japanese. Lt. Cdr. Takeshi Naito, the assistant naval attaché in Berlin, flew to Taranto

to investigate the attack firsthand, and Naito subsequently had a lengthy conversation with Cdr. Mitsuo Fuchida about his observations. Fichida led the Japanese aerial attack on 7 December 1941. (107)

Ninth, both Admiral Kimmel and General Short made statements prior to December 7, 1941, that acknowledged the possibility of an air attack on their forces. Admiral Kimmel, for example, in a letter to Admiral Stark on February 18, 1941, stated, "I feel that a surprise attack (submarine, air, or combined) on Pearl Harbor is a possibility." (108) Similarly, the August 14, 1941, *Honolulu Advertiser*, in an article titled: "General Short Sees Danger of Oahu Air Raid," quoted General Short as saying that "an attack upon these [Hawaiian] islands is not impossible and in certain situations it might not be improbable." (109)

Tenth, Admiral Kimmel was briefed on December 2, 1941, that American intelligence had lost track of the Japanese carriers. (110)

On 2 December Lt. Cdr. Edwin T. Layton, Kimmel's intelligence officer, informed his boss that, as there had been no radio traffic from four Japanese carriers "for fully 15 and possibly 25 days," their location was unknown. Kimmel responded: "Do you mean that they could be rounding Diamond Head and you wouldn't know it?" (111) While this quip haunted Kimmel for many years, it reflects more than just ill-timed humor or bad luck. On the contrary, that Kimmel made this statement reflects that he simply did not believe that the Japanese were capable of attacking his command.

Despite this mass of evidence, the practical difficulties (112) of conducting an aerial attack may have caused Admiral Kimmel and General Short to minimize its likelihood. (113)

Finally, Admiral Kimmel and General Short knew that the initial attack could occur within weeks or days. Tension had been building between the United States and Japan, and on November 27, 1941, Admiral Kimmel received from the Chief of Naval Operations the following message:

> This dispatch is to be considered a war warning. Negotiations with Japan looking forward toward stabilization of conditions in the Pacific have ceased and an aggressive move by Japan is expected within the next few days. The number and equipment of Jap[anese] troops and the organization of naval task forces indicates an amphibious expedition against either the Philippines or Kra Peninsula or possibly Borneo. Execute an appropriate defensive deployment preparatory to carrying out the tasks assigned in WPL 46. Inform District and Army authorities. A similar warning is being sent by War Department. SPENAVO (114) inform British. Continental District Guam Samoa directed take appropriate measures against sabotage. (115)

Admiral Turner, the drafter of this "war warning" message, expected Admiral Kimmel to deploy his forces, that is, to depart the harbor with his fleet. (116) Admiral Kimmel, however, did not interpret the phrase "[e]xecute an appropriate defensive deployment" in this way, and Admiral Kimmel's interpretation was not unreasonable.

General Short received a similar message on November 27, 1941:

> Negotiations with Japan appear to be terminated to all practical purposes with only the barest possibilities that the Japanese Government might come back to offer to continue. Japanese further action unpredictable but hostile action possible at any moment. If hostilities cannot, repeat cannot, be avoided the United States desires that Japan commit the first overt act. This policy should not, repeat not, be construed as restricting you to a course of action that might jeopardize your defense. Prior to hostile Japanese action you are directed to undertake such reconnaissance and other measures as you deem necessary but these measures should be carried out so as not, repeat not, to alarm civil population or disclose intent. Report measures

taken. Should hostilities occur you will carry out the tasks assigned in Rainbow Five so far as they pertain to Japan. Limit dissemination of this highly secret information to minimum essential officers. (117)

Once General Short received the war warning message of November 27th, he was expected to have effected the best possible defense, to include defending against a possible aerial attack. (118)

It has been argued that this "war warning" language is ambiguous. (119) Yet the actions of all the parties in Pearl Harbor indicate that they took the warning seriously and responded with vigor. Admiral Kimmel issued orders to the fleet to "exercise extreme vigilance against submarines in operating areas and to depth bomb all contacts expected to be hostile in the fleet operating areas." (120) Indeed, the first shots on December 7 were fired not at dawn by Japanese aircraft but well before dawn by Admiral Kimmel's aggressive antisubmarine patrols. (121)

Ships in port in Pearl Harbor were required to keep antiaircraft guns at the ready. After meeting with Admiral Kimmel, Vice Admiral William F. "Bull" Halsey, then Commander, Aircraft Battle Force, placed his carrier task force on a war footing, instituted aircraft patrols with orders to "shoot down any plane seen in the air that was not known to be one of our own." (122) On receiving the Army war warning message, which was ambiguously worded, General Short ordered Alert Number I—an alert against sabotage. (123) Thus, the Hawaiian commands on December 7 were ready to meet almost any attack—except one arriving quickly from the air.

Additionally, Admiral Kimmel knew three things that General Short did not know. First, he learned on December 1, 1941, that the Japanese Navy had unexpectedly changed call signs. (124) This information was not shared with General Short. Second, Admiral Kimmel learned on December 2, 1941, that the location of four Japanese carriers was unknown. (125) This was because the carriers had not engaged in radio traffic for between 15–25 days. (126)

This apparent radio silence, however, also was not passed to General Short, because Admiral Kimmel assumed that the carriers remained in home waters. (127) Third, Admiral Kimmel learned on December 3, 1941, of the existence of "purple" machines (128), and that Japan had ordered certain consulates and embassies to destroy their codes. (129) Admiral Kimmel, however, did not view the code destruction as "of any vital importance" (130) and did not tell General Short about it. (131) Yet code destruction suggested that hostilities were imminent since communication between Japan and her overseas officials were at an end.

There were two things that Admiral Kimmel and General Short did *not* know.

Admiral Kimmel and General Short did not know that the initial Japanese attack would take the form of a carrier air attack on Pearl Harbor. Admittedly, there were many indications of Japanese intent to attack in the Far East, and some key members of Admiral Kimmel's and General Short's staffs shared their skepticism about the likelihood of an attack on Pearl Harbor. (132) Nonetheless, it was an error for Admiral Kimmel and General Short to draw inferences only from presumptions about the enemy's intentions, and to ignore his capabilities.

Admiral Kimmel and General Short did not know *exactly* when hostilities would start. Nonetheless, what they did know should have been sufficient to cause them to make ready defenses against air attack, as they did against other forms of attack.

The Dorn Report correctly concluded that Kimmel and Short had focused so much on divining Japanese intent that they overlooked their enemy's capabilities. The report, however, should have expanded on this point, as it was but one reflection of Kimmel's and Short's mental unreadiness. This intellectual unpreparedness—a lack of imagination about the form that a future attack on Hawaii might take—is critical to understanding what happened at Pearl Harbor and why these two senior and experienced officers were so lacking

in defensive preparations. Kimmel and Short simply did not believe in their hearts that a successful air attack was possible. Since a leader sets the tone in his command, it follows that because the two most senior commanders did not believe that an aerial attack was likely, no one else in Hawaii was mentally prepared either. Kimmel, Short, and their subordinates' mental unreadiness was manifested in a variety of areas:

1. In mid-1941 Short decided that Air Force enlisted personnel in Hawaii needed six to eight weeks of training as infantrymen; training them in Air Corps skills was not nearly as important as sharpening the ground combat skills needed to repel the waves of Japanese soldiers that might land on Oahu's beaches in the near future. (133) While this meant both lower morale and less well trained airmen, those senior officers running the Hawaiian operations of the Air Force either agreed with Short or acquiesced in his decision; certainly, no one in authority prevailed upon General Short to cease training airmen for ground combat. The ultimate example of this mental inability to envisage the threat posed by enemy air assets, of course, culminated in Short's decision—which his subordinate airmen either agreed with or acquiesced in—to line up his aircraft wingtip to wingtip on Hawaii's airfields. When the Japanese attacked on 7 December, they could not have asked for more perfect targets.
2. Although his men trained hard during the week, Kimmel kept a significantly lower state of readiness on weekends, because of his certainty that Hawaii was immune from attack. On 6 December naval officers and sailors were ashore on routine liberty. Many were enjoying the latest dance hits played at the "Battle of the Bands" at the Naval Receiving Station; more than a few awoke on

Had General Short anticipated an aerial attack, his aircraft would have been dispersed. As he believed, however, that sabotage was the greatest danger to his soldiers and materiel, the Army's P-40 fighters were parked in single file, wingtip to wingtip. While concentrating his fighters made them easier to guard, it also made them an easy target for attacking Japanese Zeros.
NATIONAL ARCHIVES AND RECORDS ADMINISTRATION

their ships with "Sunday morning hangovers" at 7:55 a.m. (134). Archie Pierce, a sailor on the USS *Oklahoma,* remembered his ship as being "never less on alert" than on the morning of 7 December. Since the battleship was scheduled for an inspection by Admiral Kimmel on Monday, its anti-aircraft guns had no firing pins and the ammunition ready boxes had no shells in them. According to Pierce, "this was so the guns and ready boxes would be clean for inspection." Similarly certain that they were safe from harm, and likewise in preparation for a Monday-morning inspection, sailors on the USS *California* had removed the covers from six of the manholes opening into the battleship's double bottom, and had loosened twelve more; this meant that water flooded through them when the *California* was first hit by a torpedo at 8:05 a.m. Finally, virtually all ships were unable to get under way because their boilers were cold—but why keep an extra boiler lit if no harm could come to the ships moored on "Battleship Row"? (135)

3. Short's obsession with guarding against a theoretical danger of sabotage inside Hawaii rendered a quick defense against an external attack impossible. For example, with their ammunition under lock and key, no Army anti-aircraft guns were in action to defend against the first wave of Japanese aircraft commanded by Cdr. Mitsuo Fuchida; the four Japanese planes brought down by American gunfire between 7:55 and about 8:30 a.m. were hit by either machine-gun or automatic rifle fire. (136)

4. Kimmel made statements that not only reflected his own certainty that Hawaii was safe from attack, but surely convinced his naval subordinates and others who heard him that there was no danger. On 6 December 1941, for example, Joseph C. Harsch, the well-known correspondent for the *Christian Science Monitor,* met with Admiral Kimmel and his staff at Fleet headquarters. Harsch asked Kimmel if there was going to be a war in the Pacific. Kimmel's reply was but one word: "No." Apparently surprised by this answer, Harsch asked Admiral Kimmel if he would "please explain why you seem so confident that there won't be a war." Kimmel answered:

> Yes. You probably do not know that the Germans have announced that they are going into winter quarters in

> front of Moscow. That means that Moscow is not going to fall this winter. That means that the Russians will still be in the war in the spring. That means that *the Japanese cannot attack us in the Pacific without running the risk of a two-front war. The Japanese are too smart for that.* (137)

Many years later, Joe Harsch wrote that while his interview with Kimmel and his staff must have continued, he did not remember any further conversation. But he did remember Kimmel's positive assertion that there would be no war for the United States in the Pacific and Kimmel's rationale for this claim. While Harsch apparently did wonder if Kimmel truly believed his statements ("I have often wondered since then how confident he actually was—whether he really believed what he said or whether it was his stance for public consumption"), there is no reason to take Kimmel's assertions at anything other than face value. Harsch's question more accurately reflects Harsch's belief that Kimmel's statement was foolish rather than any lack of belief by Kimmel in what he said. After all, in that same meeting between Kimmel, his staff, and Harsch, the public relations officer for the Pacific Fleet vividly recalled the following exchange:

> HARSCH: "Admiral, now that the Japanese have moved into Indochina .. what do you think they will do next?"
> KIMMEL: "I don't know. What do you think?"
> HARSCH: "Well, do you think they will attack us?"
> KIMMEL: "No, young man, I don't think they'd be such damned fools." (138)

This exchange between Kimmel and Harsch, of course, occurred less than twenty-four hours before thousands of Americans were killed and Pearl Harbor lay smoldering and in ruins.

5. Convinced that he could continue with "business as usual," Kimmel continued to schedule Sunday golf games with General Short. The two commanders had a game scheduled for 8 a.m. on the morning of 7 December, and had the Japanese attacked a few hours later, Kimmel and Short would have been out on the golf course with their clubs. (139)

6. Since Short believed in his heart that an attack on Hawaii was impossible, radar was discounted as a early-warning tool. Consequently, at 7:02 a.m. on 7 December, when two soldiers manning one of five mobile radar stations at Opana Point detected a large flight of aircraft some 130 miles to the north, this was only because the two men had kept their radar operating longer than their training required; the other four stations had shut down at 7 a.m. Pvts. George Elliott and James Lockard, however, had left their radar running while they waited for their breakfast to arrive by truck. After Elliott spotted "something completely out of the ordinary" on his cathode ray tube, he and Lockard decided that they should report the "blips." Lockard telephoned Fort Shafter, but the operator could find no one on duty. A few minutes later, however, Army Lt. Kermit A. Tyler, a fighter pilot and on-duty watch officer, called the radar operators. Lockard told Tyler that the blips indicated "an unusually large flight—in fact, the largest I have ever seen on the equipment." Lt. Tyler, however, reflecting the mental paralysis prevalent in the Army and Navy, assumed that Elliott and Lockard must have detected a flight of B-17s that Tyler knew was traveling from California to Hawaii that day. Convinced that all was well, Lt. Tyler took no action; he also told Pvts. Elliott and Lockard not to "worry about it." Fascinated by the electronic blips on their screen, however, the two soldiers watched for another thirty minutes. They turned off their radar at 7:39 a.m., when the breakfast truck arrived at last. (140)

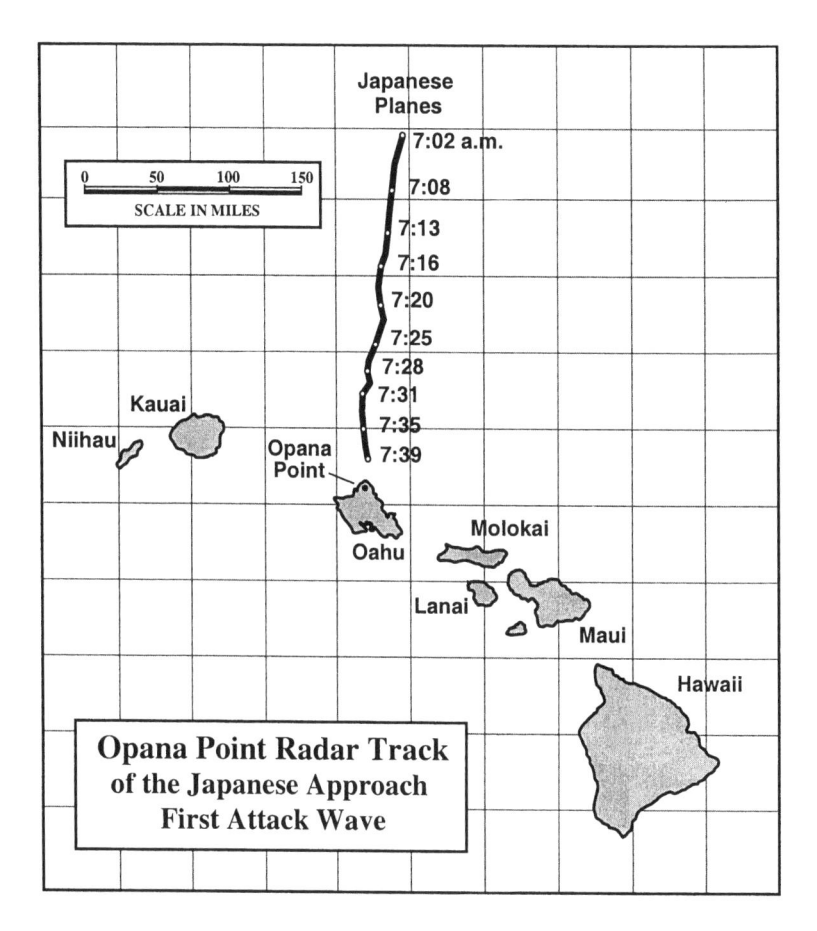

Opana Point Radar Track of the Japanese Approach First Attack Wave

Although the British had demonstrated the value of radar during the Battle of Britain in 1940, General Short used his six mobile radar stations for training only. On 7 December, soldiers at Opana Point were scheduled to cease training on their radar sets at 7:00 AM. Two men, however, had left their radar running while waiting for their breakfast to arrive by truck. As a result, at 7:02 AM they detected "blips" reflecting that a large formation of aircraft was heading toward Oahu. The radar operators notified the on-duty watch officer at Fort Shafter, who told them "not to worry about it" as these were a flight of B-17s arriving from California. In fact, the Opana Point radar operators had detected the incoming Japanese attackers, but the mental paralysis prevalent at all levels in Hawaii meant that this tactical warning—like that provided by the USS *Ward* in sinking a submarine at 6:40 AM—also was missed.

© 2004 NavPublishing, LLC

7. Admiral Kimmel and Rear Admiral Bloch (Commandant, Fourteenth Naval District) and their subordinates failed to understand that the sinking of an unidentified submarine at the entrance to the harbor at 6:40 a.m. might be a prelude to a full-scale attack. (141)
8. Finally, the lack of mental preparedness for war was reflected in the general disbelief that the planes in the skies over Oahu could be hostile. Almost without exception, those who saw attacking aircraft were certain that they were observing another Navy or Army exercise. Golfers looked up but then played on. Sometime after 8 a.m., one group of officers playing on the Schofield Barracks course ran into a soldier firing his rifle at airplanes flying above them. "Get out of here and play your war games somewhere else!" said one of the officers. Those on their way to church heard the deafening sound of engines overhead, but continued on. A lifeguard beginning what he expected to be an uneventful Sunday watched a plane pass at low altitude over a freighter and then saw a column of water shoot upward from a bomb dropped by that plane. A second bomb then exploded 200 yards up the beach. The lifeguard "thought to himself that such war 'exercises' were 'very dangerous for the swimmers.'" (142)

Soldiers and sailors were just as mentally unready. Staff Sgt. David H. Wagner, a soldier with the 27th Infantry at Schofield Barracks, heard heavy gunfire while standing outside his house, looking in the general direction of Pearl Harbor. Wagner simply thought it was "unusual to be having AA [Anti-Aircraft] practice on Sunday." (143) Aviation Machinist Mate First Class Otto Horky was adjusting an engine on a Navy seaplane when he spotted "a brightly polished fighter plane from nowhere and his machine gun tracers plowing into" another seaplane in the water. Horky and his fellow sailors were sure that a drunk American pilot was at the

> controls until they saw the red "rising sun" painted on the attacking plane's wing. (144)
>
> Officers were no more alert: Lt. Cdr. Logan C. Ramsey, on duty in the Ford Island command center, was sure that a plane diving over the station was "flathatting"—showing off at low altitude—and he and the staff duty officer were discussing the difficulty of getting plane fuselage numbers (to report the offending pilot) when a bomb dropped from the aircraft exploded. (145)

Had Kimmel and Short instilled a sense of urgency in their commands, results might have been different.

Thus the crucial question becomes: *in the certain knowledge that the United States and Japan were moving inexorably and ever more rapidly toward war but not knowing exactly where, when, or how Japan would strike, what did Admiral Kimmel and General Short do to resolve their uncertainty?*

By his actions, General Short assumed he would have at least four hours warning of an air attack. (146) Since he employed none of his assets in reconnaissance or surveillance, he could get that warning only from the Navy or from Washington. Under the agreement in place in Hawaii, the Navy was responsible for long-range reconnaissance. Admiral Kimmel conducted no long-range air reconnaissance out of Oahu. Thus on December 7th he could get warning only from Washington.

This exclusive reliance on Washington for both tactical and strategic warning is at the heart of the failure at Pearl Harbor, and of the debate about the failure. The record suggests that officials in Washington believed they had provided strategic warning with their messages of November 27th; neither Admiral Kimmel nor General Short read the messages that way. The debate over the handling of Japan's 14-part message (147) on December 6th and the morning of the 7th is about tactical warning. Admiral Kimmel and General Short did not get tactical warning.

The Dorn Report is incorrect on this point: there was sufficient tactical warning on 7 December 1941. It occurred at 6:40 a.m.—more than an hour before the first bombs fell over Oahu—when a Japanese midget submarine tried to infiltrate the harbor before the air attack, and the USS *Ward* sank it. The skipper, Lt. Cdr. William W. Outerbridge, immediately radioed to the Fourteenth Naval District: "We have attacked, fired upon, and dropped depth charges upon submarine operating in defensive area." That message, sent in the clear and not using code as wrongly claimed by one Kimmel apologist (148), was received at 6:54 a.m. Most battleships at anchor, and other vessels maintaining routine radio guard, also heard the *Ward* transmission. But there was no sense of urgency in Hawaii; the radioman on duty recorded the dispatch, then laid it aside. About 7:15 a.m., the *Ward*'s message finally arrived on the desk of the naval district watch officer, who then informed the district commandant, Rear Adm. Claude C. Bloch, by telephone about 7:30 a.m. that the *Ward* had sunk an unidentified submarine at 6:40 a.m. Kimmel also learned about the *Ward*'s dispatch about the same time. Instead of recognizing it for what it was—a clear and unambiguous tactical warning—Kimmel, Bloch, and their staffs were still arguing over its significance when the first Zeros appeared in the skies over Oahu.

In testimony before Congress in 1946, Kimmel explained why he missed this warning: "we had so many . . . false reports of submarines in the outlying area, I thought, well, I would wait for verification of the report." (149) Kimmel's mental paralysis made him unable to see this as a likely prelude to a full-scale attack, and this mindset was reflected in the command inertia of his subordinates. And it explains why Kimmel and Bloch never told Short about the *Ward*'s unambiguous report of combat: why inform the Army that a submarine had been depth-charged when they themselves did not believe the report? Although the historical

THE REPORT

**ENTRANCE TO PEARL HARBOR
6:40 AM**

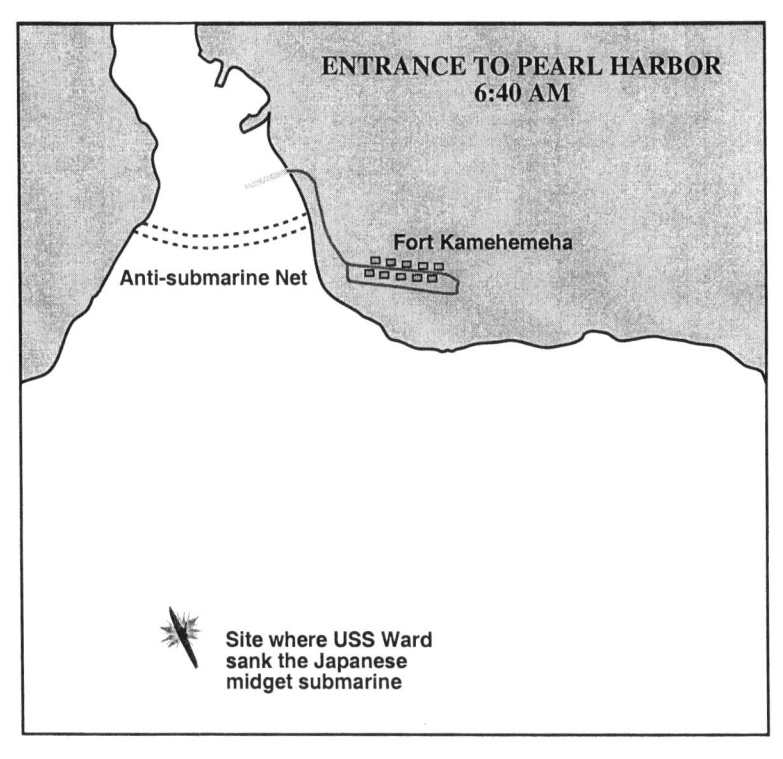

Fort Kamehemeha

Anti-submarine Net

Site where USS Ward sank the Japanese midget submarine

When the USS *Ward* radioed in the clear that she had sunk a submarine at the entrance to Pearl Harbor at 6:40 AM, this was a clear tactical warning of the impending Japanese attack. Unfortunately, Kimmel and his staff were still debating the significance of the *Ward*'s action when the first bombs fell over Oahu at 7:55 AM.
© 2004 NAVPUBLISHING, LLC

accuracy of the *Ward*'s fight with the submarine has not been seriously doubted, the discovery of the enemy submarine in late 2002 fully substantiated the truth of this event. (150)

Had Kimmel and Short better integrated their commands, and had they been mentally prepared for an aerial bombardment, this tactical warning would have given the Army

and Navy more than an hour to set any defensive plans in motion.

Later, Admiral Kimmel argued, "This lack of action on the part of both the War and Navy Departments must have been in accordance with high political direction. These two agencies were responsible only to the President of the United States. It is impossible to believe that both these agencies of such proved reliability and competence should simultaneously and repeatedly fail in such a crisis." (151) Although Admiral Kimmel did not know late in 1941 that he was not getting all the Magic product, he knew of Magic's existence. (152) He had sought and extracted from Admiral Stark a promise to provide all the warning available. (153) Thus, as a practical matter Admiral Kimmel effectively placed total faith—and the security of the forces in Pearl Harbor against air attack—in Washington's ability to obtain and provide to him timely and unambiguous strategic and tactical warning from the Magic and other intercepts alone. This faith was not justified, nor was it consistent with his assessment of other technological developments of the time, or since. Even with today's satellite intelligence and instantaneous world-wide communication, it still is not prudent to depend exclusively on Washington for timely and unambiguous information.

Figure 2 sets out, with explanatory notes, specific items known in Washington, and by Admiral Kimmel and General Short. The record of 1941 is filled with urgent requests from Admiral Kimmel and General Short for more resources, especially fighter and reconnaissance aircraft, to buttress Hawaii's defenses against air attack. American resources were stretched thin, and American strategy consciously gave priority to the Atlantic and to buttressing the even weaker defenses in the Philippines. Nevertheless, Admiral Kimmel and General Short were not without resources for defense against air attack on Hawaii.

Together, Admiral Kimmel and General Short had 49 serviceable Catalina long-range patrol aircraft, and six serviceable

B-17 long-range bombers useful for reconnaissance. They also had a significant force of cruisers with embarked scout-observation floatplanes, destroyers, several land-based radar stations capable of detecting aircraft at substantial ranges, (154) coast watch stations, nearly a hundred P-40 fighter aircraft (the most modern in the American inventory), and several hundred anti-aircraft guns on land and on ships in the harbor.

There were significant competing demands on the delicate Catalinas and practical limitations on the employment of each of the other resources. Nevertheless, if properly employed in an integrated and coordinated fashion at a reasonable state of readiness, these resources could have made an enormous and perhaps critical difference in the events of December 7.

The Dorn team identified Kimmel's decision to tell the Army that the Navy would do long-range reconnaissance, but subsequently do no long-range reconnaissance, as one of the major deficiencies in his performance. Not surprisingly, Kimmel and his supporters have vociferously maintained that not conducting long-range reconnaissance was the correct decision. (155) Kimmel insisted that the Army and the Navy "had no means to conduct distant air reconnaissance."(156) Additionally, as Kimmel's primary mission was to prepare for war with Japan, if he borrowed Fleet patrol planes for distant searches, those aircraft would be unready "for operations thousands of miles from Hawaii should war come." That is, if he used his aircraft for long-range reconnaissance, training would suffer, the planes would be worn out, and consequently, when war came, the Fleet would be critically short of flight-ready planes. Additionally, Kimmel maintained that even if he had decided to do aerial patrolling, he did not have planes "in sufficient number to cover in distant searches more *than one fourth of the area through which a hostile force could approach Pearl Harbor.*" (157) In sum, Kimmel balanced what he believed was the

need to conserve his aerial resources for the coming war against the need for warning of an approaching enemy fleet. Deciding that the risk of attack was nil, and that reconnaissance was an "all or nothing proposition," he elected to do no long-range patrolling.

The Dorn Report concluded that Kimmel's decision to do no long-range aerial reconnaissance was a poor choice, chiefly because this meant that there was no possibility of detecting an attack. But the report also pointed out that Kimmel compounded his bad choice by failing to inform the Army that the Navy had elected to do no long-range searches, despite having agreed with the Army to do them. Significantly, however, the report also pointed out that even if Kimmel was correct that the Navy had insufficient aircraft to conduct long-range reconnaissance, his conclusion that this meant no reconnaissance was simply wrong. On the contrary, the report stressed that Kimmel could have used picket ships as long-range-warning platforms. Even a Kimmel defender like Michael Gannon admits that Kimmel missed this viable option. In *Pearl Harbor Betrayed,* Gannon quotes at length from Admiral Stark's 10 February 1941 message to Kimmel, in which Stark "urged" Kimmel to deploy small surface ships as sentinels. Stark wrote:

> It is noted that no provision is made in the Local Defense Force plans of the 14th Naval District for the employment of vessels as part of an aircraft warning net in the waters to the northward and southward of Oahu. It is suggested that in coordinating the plans of the Commander-in-Chief, U.S. Pacific Fleet [Kimmel] and the Commandant, Fourteenth Naval District [Rear Admiral Claude C. Bloch, USN], this matter be given consideration. It is possible that large sampans equipped with radio might prove useful for this purpose during the war. (158)

Kimmel could—and should—have used sampans (a flat-bottomed skiff), submarines, old destroyers, minesweepers, and Coast Guard cutters as a picket patrol. As Gannon notes, these vessels "sat low on the water [and] thus would have limited radius of vision, but they still had the practical potential of sighting by chance a carrier's tall island on the horizon." (159) Whether such a picket patrol would have sighted the Japanese attackers on 6 or 7 December will never be known, but by failing to follow Stark's recommendation, Kimmel ensured that the Japanese carriers would not be seen until it was too late.

In any event, history shows clearly that the use of surface ships for long-range reconnaissance was both feasible and wise: on 18 April 1942 Japanese fishing boats stationed 650 nautical miles east of Japan spotted the U.S. Navy task force carrying Jimmy Doolittle's soon-to-be-famous Tokyo bombing raiders. As the Americans feared that these enemy pickets had radioed their sighting to Japan, this forced Doolittle to begin his B-25 raid earlier (so that the attack now had to be made during daytime instead of at night) and at a greater distance (650 miles instead of 500 miles) from his targets. While the Doolittle raiders were successful, the added flight time jeopardized the mission, and some aircraft ran out of fuel before reaching landing fields in China. (160)

For Kimmel, long-range reconnaissance was an all-or-nothing proposition. Despite having agreed with the Army that the Navy would conduct long-range aerial patrols, Kimmel decided to conserve his aircraft, rejected Stark's suggestion for picket ships, and did nothing. When questioned before the Army Board in 1944 about this decision, Kimmel claimed that "the use of surface craft for distant reconnaissance against an air attack would have required so many ships that their use was considered entirely impracticable for this purpose."(161) Given that Kimmel did not believe in his heart that a Japanese attack was possible, this comment makes sense. But others took a different view. On 21 December 1945 Adm. Kelly Turner testified

ROUTE OF THE JAPANESE TASK FORCE

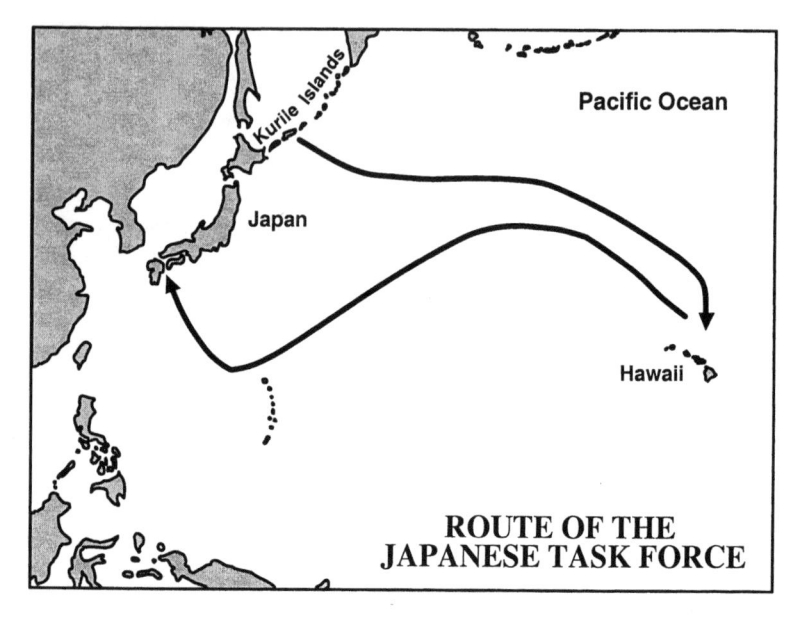

The Japanese attack was brilliantly conceived and flawlessly executed. It involved a bold new use of carriers, and meant crossing four thousand miles of ocean undetected—which explains why the Japanese took the storm-tossed northern route where there was little commercial shipping.
© 2004 NavPublishing, LLC

before the Joint Congressional Committee that Kimmel had been told "in at least three official communications during 1941" to use surface ships as early-warning platforms. (162) Senator Ferguson then asked Turner why the Navy did not use these surface assets as picket boats. Replied Turner: "I do not know sir." (163)

Only the guns on the ships were able to respond in significant numbers on December 7. However, not all were able to respond immediately. (164) The reconnaissance aircraft were being conserved for other tasks. The use of destroyers and cruisers and their float planes in reconnaissance apparently was not considered. The radars were used only for training, and not during the hours of the attack. (165)

The coast watch stations were not manned. The fighters were on four-hour alert. (166) Mobile land-based antiaircraft guns were not deployed, and ammunition was kept separate from the guns. And, despite the existence of agreements and plans for cooperation in air defense, the air defense system was not coordinated between the Army and the Navy.

Finally, passive defense measures were available which might have mitigated the effect of the raids that did occur. First, training patterns could have been altered in response to heightened tensions. The Navy trained hard during the week, but its ships generally were in port on Saturdays and Sundays. The touchstone of Japanese planning was this predictable ship location.

The Japanese also knew that ships moored at Pearl Harbor would have cold boilers. As the technology of the day required one to two hours to bring boilers on line and build sufficient steam pressure to get under way, ships without a head of steam would be unable escape from Battleship Row.

While the Japanese could not have known that many U.S. ships in port on Sunday morning would also have their hatches open for inspection, this factor meant immediate flooding when the vessels were hit by Japanese torpedoes. Again, ships in port on Saturday and Sunday were simply unprepared for an air attack. (167)

Second, aircraft revetments had been constructed but were not used because the fear of sabotage was greater than the fear of air attack. Had some aircraft been in revetments, rather than lined up wing-to-wing, losses in material would have been mitigated. Third, anti-torpedo baffles or nets could have been used within Pearl Harbor for protection against torpedo plane attacks. These items were not furnished to Admiral Kimmel, but they might have been requested. (168) Fourth, Admiral Kimmel and General Short could have used barrage balloons in selected areas to restrict the most dangerous air approaches to "battleship row." (169)

Although the commanders in Hawaii failed to make adequate preparations in light of the information they had, more information was available in Washington but not forwarded to them (Figure 2). Army and Navy officials in Washington were privy to intercepted Japanese diplomatic communications (notably the "bomb plot," "winds," "pilot," and "fourteen part" messages (170)) which provided crucial confirmation of the imminence of war. Read together and with the leisure, focus, and clarity of hindsight, these messages point strongly toward an attack on Pearl Harbor at dawn on the 7th.

However, it is not clear that they were read together in 1941. The "bomb plot" message—the only one that points clearly to Pearl Harbor—seems not to have been correctly interpreted or widely disseminated at the time. (171) The "winds" message points to increasing imminence of attack, a point that the "war warning" messages of November 27 attempted to convey. The "pilot," "fourteen part," and "one o'clock" messages point, by the evening of December 6th, to war at dawn (Hawaii time) on the 7th—not to an attack on Hawaii—but officials in Washington were neither energetic nor effective in getting that warning to the Hawaiian commanders.

For more on Washington's "failure" to hear the signals (like the bomb plot and winds messages) that pointed to an attack on Pearl Harbor, see Roberta Wohlstetter's *Pearl Harbor: Warning and Decision*.

Various conspiracy theories (172) have been advanced, but no evidence has been offered to support those theories. Rather, the evidence of the handling of these messages in Washington reveals some ineptitude, some unwarranted assumptions and misestimates, limited coordination, ambiguous language, and lack of clarification and follow-up at higher levels.

Republican Party candidates seeking gains in the 1944 elections are in large part responsible for various conspiracy theories, all permutations of the claim that Roosevelt knew that the Japanese would attack Hawaii, but did nothing to stop it. If the Republicans could prove—or at least present some evidence—that President Roosevelt had baited the Japanese into attacking Pearl Harbor or, alternatively, that he had known about the impending attack but had not warned Kimmel or Short, the Republican National Committee would have "the perfect campaign issue." While Pearl Harbor ultimately did not emerge as the emotionally charged campaign issue the Republicans had hoped it would be, their whispering campaign against Roosevelt ensured that more than a few Americans would forever believe that the president, seeking to break America's isolationists and propel the country into war, was somehow culpable, and that Kimmel and Short were "an American Dreyfus case." (173)

Even a cursory examination of this claim, however, shows that it is nonsense. First, as a former assistant secretary of the Navy, Roosevelt loved the naval service. It is impossible to believe that he would intentionally take any action to harm it. Second, if Roosevelt knew in advance about the Japanese attack plans, then he would have known about them through decrypted radio traffic. But teams of cryptologists were decoding Japanese diplomatic and military message traffic, and they passed their work on to admirals and generals, who then took the intelligence to the president. These men would have needed to join Roosevelt in a conspiracy—a totally improbable course of action since it meant that these same admirals would have allowed their ships to be sunk. Moreover, if Roosevelt knew the Japanese were going to attack—and truly wanted that attack to succeed—then Kimmel and Short would need to be in on the conspiracy to ensure that U.S. forces were not sufficiently alert to detect the Japanese carriers.

A more sophisticated claim is that Roosevelt squeezed the Japanese with an oil embargo, thus leaving them with no choice but to attack the United States. This too is nonsense. Roosevelt did not want war with Japan in 1941. On the contrary, war on a second front was the last thing he wanted since the U.S. Navy had been fighting an undeclared war against German forces in the Atlantic since 1941. Roosevelt, if he truly wanted war, wanted a fight with Hitler's Germany—not with imperial Japan. It follows that permitting a Japanese surprise attack would likely thwart this goal, as Americans would shift their focus away from the struggle in Europe to the Pacific. Additionally, starting a war with Japan when U.S. forces were already fighting in the Atlantic would open up a two-front war—an ill-advised and risky venture. Note that when President Roosevelt on 8 December demanded that Congress declare war, he sought only a declaration of war against Japan—and Congress only declared war on that nation. Despite the Axis partnership with Japan, Hitler was in no way obligated to declare war on the United States. Consequently, it seems likely that if Hitler had not declared war against the United States on 11 December 1941—on his own initiative—the United States might very well have stayed out of the European war. Had America instead focused solely on defeating Japan, Roosevelt's desire to join the struggle against fascism in Europe would not have been fulfilled. In sum, the conspiracy theory is simply illogical. (174)

While there is absolutely no evidence of a Roosevelt conspiracy, virtually every Kimmel and Short defender insinuates that FDR, Marshall, Stark, and others in Washington plotted against Kimmel and Short. Ned Beach, for example, insists that Roosevelt "did all he could" to cause a war with Japan. (175) Additionally, he peppers his book with quotes from a variety of conspiracy theorists, thus insinuating that there was a plot of some sort. For example, Beach writes that William J. Casey, director of the CIA under Reagan, claimed that the "British had sent word [to Roosevelt] that a Japanese fleet was steaming east toward Hawaii."(176) Similarly, Beach refers approvingly to John Toland's *Infamy: Pearl Harbor and Its Aftermath,* James Rusbridger and Eric Nave's *Betrayal at Pearl Harbor: How Churchill Lured Roosevelt into World War II,* and other revisionist works. (177) While Beach admits that the conspirators are short on evidence, his sympathetic treatment of them reflects his own suspicion that Roosevelt, working with Marshall, Stark, and other senior leaders in Washington, lured Japan into war with the United States; and that after Pearl Harbor, they covered up their own actions and allowed the Hawaii commanders to be scapegoated. (178)

John Toland, cited approvingly by Beach and other Kimmel defenders, claimed in *Infamy* that Roosevelt and his inner circle knew in advance about the Japanese attack. Toland insisted that the Dutch army in Java had passed on to the United States intercepted Japanese messages predicting the attack on Pearl Harbor. He also claimed that Roosevelt knew days before the attack that a Japanese carrier task force was steaming toward Hawaii. In support of this last assertion, Toland wrote that an American steamship had picked up radio traffic from the Japanese carriers, and had reported it to the FBI; that a sailor (identified only as "Seaman Z") working in the Navy's intelligence office in San Francisco had likewise intercepted the Japanese carrier signals and, using triangulation, had discerned that the ships were heading toward Oahu; and that the diary of a Dutch naval attaché stationed in Washington, D.C., disclosed that he had learned from the Office of Naval Intelligence that the Americans knew a carrier task force was on its way to Hawaii. Recent scholarship, however, has disproven Toland's claims: there is no evidence that any reports were received by the Dutch in Java; it was impossible for "Seaman Z" to have intercepted Japanese carrier signals as there is no doubt that they maintained radio silence—a fact confirmed by the surviving Japanese themselves. As for the Dutch naval attaché, it is now clear that Toland misinterpreted the written diary entries. (179)

Two recent conspiracy claims come from Daryl S. Borgquist and Robert B. Stinnett. Borgquist published an article in *Naval History Magazine* in which he insists that shortly before the attack, Roosevelt informed one of America's top Red Cross officials that he knew the Japanese were planning to attack Pearl Harbor. (180) Stinnett in *Day of Deceit: The Truth about FDR and Pearl Harbor* (181) claims that a vast government conspiracy—including Roosevelt, Marshall, Stark, the press, and other military and civilian officials in the War and Navy Departments—lured Japan into war. According to Stinnett, the conspirators succeeded because the United States was decoding and reading Japanese Navy operational ciphers from September 1940 on—decrypted messages that clearly revealed the Japanese attack on Pearl Harbor. Stinnett also claims that the Japanese carriers on their way to Oahu did not maintain radio silence; that their transmissions reflecting an imminent attack on U.S. forces in Hawaii were intercepted, decoded, and forwarded to the White House; and that FDR knew about the Japanese plan to attack Pearl but did nothing to prevent it.

Stinnett's claims, however, are totally false as U.S. codebreakers had not deciphered Japanese naval messages. On the contrary, the Purple machines used to produce Magic were reading diplomatic codes—embassy message traffic that did not convey current military details. (182) Additionally, no serious student of Pearl Harbor now doubts that the enemy carriers maintained radio silence—if for no other reason that to prevent the Americans discovering their location through triangulation of radio signals. Stinnett's book is riddled with misstatements, inaccuracies, and falsehoods. No wonder a reviewer writing in the prestigious *Journal of Military History* described *Day of Deceit* as

"a bad book ... [that] relies on distortion and ignorance to fabricate a case." (183)

Conspiracy theorists never give up. (184) Roosevelt's alleged perfidy even finds expression in recent fiction, like Gore Vidal's novel *Golden Age*. (185) More Pearl Harbor conspiracies are certain to be "revealed" to the public in the coming years.

Together, these characteristics resulted in failure by senior Army and Navy leadership to appreciate fully and to convey to the commanders in Hawaii the sense of focus and urgency that those intercepts should have engendered. The Service reports and the Joint Congressional Committee properly recognized and criticized those failures as errors of judgment which must take their place alongside the errors of judgment by Admiral Kimmel and General Short.

Advocates for Admiral Kimmel and General Short argue, in effect, that the failure of Washington officials to provide the critical intercepts to the Hawaiian commanders excuses any errors made in Hawaii. It does not. No warfighting commander ever has enough information or enough resources. It is the job of the commander to carry out his or her mission as best he or she can with the information and resources available to him or her. Indeed, placing exclusive reliance on Washington for tactical as well as strategic warning of air attack was an act of misplaced faith.

The Dorn Report states clearly that Washington could have done a better job in sharing information with Kimmel and Short; leaders in the War and Navy Departments also could have done a better job in following up after issuing guidance to the commanders in Hawaii. However, nothing that Washington did or did not do was the proximate cause of the disaster at Pearl Harbor. On the contrary, the direct cause of the greatest defeat ever suffered by U.S. maritime forces was Kimmel's and Short's failures to appreciate Japanese capabilities and to prepare to counter them.

Stated differently, even if Washington had shared all available information, and had checked up on the activities of Kimmel and Short prior to 7 December 1941, the Japanese attack could not have been prevented—and given the lack of mental and physical preparedness in the Hawaii, the result would have been the same.

In summary, this review of the Pearl Harbor investigations and of the available evidence provides no reason to reverse the conclusions of the Services and the Joint Congressional Committee that Admiral Kimmel and General Short made errors of judgment in the use of the information and the employment of the forces available to them.

Advocates for Admiral Kimmel and General Short also suggest that they were held to a higher standard than their superiors. A full reading of the proceedings and reports of those panels suggests clear recognition of the faults at all levels. That said, Admiral Kimmel and General Short were the highest ranking commanders at Pearl Harbor; it was appropriate to subject their actions to closer scrutiny and accountability. Additionally, the decisions affecting Admiral Kimmel and General Short were tailored to their individual situations; what did or did not happen to others is not an appropriate consideration. Finally, the catastrophe at Pearl Harbor remains a distinct and unique historical event in US history, and this explains in part why Admiral Kimmel and General Short were uniquely affected by it.

Michael Gannon, for example, argues that Kimmel's conduct should be excused for two reasons. First, he was deprived of the Magic intercepts. Second, he could never have mounted a successful defense because of the great superiority of the attacking Japanese forces. (186) The chief problem with Gannon's view is that it misses the mark: the issue is not whether Kimmel could have defeated the Japanese, but only whether he and Short could have done a better job in configuring their existing forces to mit-

igate the huge—and lopsided—American losses that occurred.

Advocates for Kimmel and Short also insist that blaming the two Hawaii commanders was unfair when Douglas MacArthur's debacle in the Philippines resulted in his receiving a Medal of Honor. In their view, it was unfair for Roosevelt to bestow the nation's highest military award on MacArthur when his command failures in the Philippines resulted in a disaster arguably worse than Pearl Harbor, and this "wrong" should now be righted. There is no question that MacArthur "bears overall responsibility for the dismal events of December 8, 1941, especially his failure to protect U.S. air assets at Clark Air Field after he learned of the successful Japanese aerial attack on Oahu." (187) It is also clear that the decision to award MacArthur a Medal of Honor was highly political. General Marshall, who recommended MacArthur for the medal, saw it as a way to "offset any propaganda by the enemy" about the disaster in the Philippines, and as a way to boost morale in the United States. Roosevelt clearly did not think the medal was awarded for heroism. On the contrary, Roosevelt viewed MacArthur's performance in Corregidor and Bataan as "more a rout than a military achievement," and told Supreme Court Justice Frank Murphy that his actions in approving the award were "pure yielding to Congressional and public opinion." (188) In any event, that MacArthur received undeserved praise is an insufficient reason to hold Kimmel and Short blameless.

Finally, advocates for Admiral Kimmel and General Short argue that the Pearl Harbor investigations were conducted in a manner unfair to those officers. Yet none of these investigations was a judicial tribunal, and none had the power to impose sentences or otherwise punish an individual, much less bring charges against anyone. Rather, the investigations were for fact-finding. There is generally no right to "due process"—in the sense of a right to have counsel and to cross-examine witnesses—at a fact-finding investigation. And General Short stated at the time that the record of the Joint Committee, if not its findings, provided vindication of his position. (189) Interestingly, no new discoveries have emerged since publication of the Joint Committee's report that would radically change the *facts* contained in the source material it published. Indeed, the 39 volumes of hearings and exhibits have provided the factual basis for almost all of the modern interpretations.

Kimmel's argument that he was denied due process is ludicrous. U.S. courts have interpreted the "due process" clause of the U.S. Constitution as giving a defendant in *criminal* proceedings the right to be represented by a lawyer, to present evidence, and to call witnesses in *criminal* proceedings. The nine investigations conducted between 1941 and 1946, however, were not criminal proceedings. They were not conducted with a view toward punishing either Kimmel or Short. On the contrary, all were fact-finding bodies that sought to learn the facts and circumstances surrounding the Japanese attack and U.S. unpreparedness. Consequently, when Kimmel's defenders insist that the 1944 Navy Court of Inquiry found him "not guilty" of wrongdoing at Pearl Harbor, they fail to understand that this court had been convened only to gather information, and that its recommendations or opinions were advisory only, and not binding in any way. In any event, while Kimmel and Short were not legally entitled to present evidence to those conducting these fact-finding inquiries, they did have full opportunity to present their version of events at the Navy Court of Inquiry, the Army Pearl Harbor Board, and the JCC hearings.

Advocates for Kimmel in particular lament that he was never court-martialed, and point to this fact as a "wrong" perpetrated by the Navy's leadership. In their view, Kimmel had a "right" to clear his name at a court-martial. The U.S. Supreme Court decided in 1909, however, that the secretary of the Navy was not required to convene a court-martial "to clear the name of any officer." (190) It follows that Kimmel had no right to a court-martial. Moreover, what might have happened at a court-martial is pure speculation. Under the Articles for the Government of the Navy as they then existed, Kimmel could have been charged with "negligence or carelessness in obeying orders" and "culpable inefficiency in the performance of duty." He might have been convicted.

What Kimmel's defenders rarely admit, however, is that Kimmel was offered a court-martial. After reading the 1944 Army Pearl Harbor Board and Navy Court of Inquiry reports, President Harry S. Truman announced that the "public must share blame for Pearl Harbor." Truman also stated that while he did not intend to order courts-martial for any officers involved in the debacle, he would "see to it that any one of them could have a fair and open trial if they wanted one." (191) Consequently, Secretary of the Navy Forrestal wrote to Kimmel in August 1945 that he would "order your trial by General Court-Martial in open court in the event you still desire to be so tried." Kimmel declined the offer. He decided that the upcoming joint congressional investigation would provide him with a better forum than any criminal proceedings. (192). It is disingenuous for Kimmel's defenders to continue to insist that he was deprived of the court-martial that would have exonerated him. Rather, it is important to remember that no adverse action *of any kind* was ever taken against Kimmel and Short.

IV. THE COURT OF PUBLIC OPINION

The families of Admiral Kimmel and General Short are concerned with the "stigma and obloquy" flowing from early charges

Figure 2. Information Known in Washington and Hawaii, October 9–December 7, 1941

Date	Item	Washington	Kimmel	Short
Oct. 9	"Bomb plot" message (193)	x (194)		
Nov. 26–28	"Winds" message (195)	x (196)	x (197)	
Nov. 27	"War warning" message	x	x	x
Dec. 1	Carrier call sign change	x (198)	x (199)	
Dec. 2	"Lost carriers"	x (200)	x (201)	
Dec. 3–6	Code destruction	x (202)	x (203)	x
Dec. 4–6	"Winds execute" message (204)			
Dec. 6	"Pilot" message (205)	x (206)		
Dec. 7	"Part 14" message (207)	x		
Dec. 7	"One o'clock" message (208)	x		

(209) and their persistent effect on public opinion. Because it is not sufficient to review the personnel actions and investigations which constitute the Government's formal actions in these cases, this Section of the review addresses accountability, responsibility, and fairness in the "court of public opinion."

The Record

Three periods must be distinguished: (1) the early war years, (2) the period of response to the reports of the Service boards and of the Joint Congressional Committee, and (3) the post-war period.

THE EARLY WAR YEARS

The national response to the Japanese attack on Pearl Harbor took two forms. The first was the national rage at Japan for the surprise attack, captured, echoed, and perhaps led by President Roosevelt's characterization of December 7th as "a date which will live in infamy" in his speech to Congress.

The second response, following almost immediately, was shock and disbelief at the extent of the devastation, the one-sidedness of the battle, and the obvious unreadiness of the American forces. These sentiments turned rapidly to incessant demands, that continue to this day, for explanation and for identification of those responsible. "[T]he American citizenry . . . were less interested in why the Japanese had attacked Pearl Harbor than in how they got away with it." (210)

Interest immediately and inevitably focused on the officials in command in Pearl Harbor. Admiral Kimmel said, "The flood of abuse and misrepresentation began immediately after the attack. My court-martial was demanded on the floor of the House of Representatives on Monday, December 8, 1941." (211)

That same day, Secretary Knox left for Pearl Harbor. After he returned and reported to the President, the full text of his report (212) was released to the public on December 15th. The relief of Admiral Kimmel and General Short was announced on December 17th. Although the press releases merely announced their relief without comment and Secretary Stimson explained that the action "avoids a situation where officials charged with the responsibility for the future security of the vital naval base would otherwise in this critical hour also be involved in the searching [Roberts] investigation ordered yesterday by the President" (213), the plain language of the Knox report and the juxtaposition of that report with the relief of the Hawaiian commanders naturally focused attention on those individuals. Admiral Kimmel saw a more sinister interpretation: "After the Secretary of the Navy, Mr. Frank Knox, reported to the President the result of his inspection at Pearl Harbor, additional statements were released which augmented the campaign of vilification." (214)

The Roberts Commission report, containing the "dereliction of duty" language, was presented to the President on January 24, 1942, and released to the press that same day. The Commission's findings do not indicate a determined effort by the Commission to single out Admiral Kimmel and General Short as scapegoats to bear all of the blame for the disaster at Pearl Harbor. However, the harm to Admiral Kimmel's and General Short's reputations began almost immediately. The headline on the front page of the *New York Times* the next day read: "ROBERTS BOARD BLAMES KIMMEL AND SHORT; WARNINGS TO DEFEND HAWAII NOT HEEDED." A sub-headline added: "Stark and Marshall Directed Hawaii Chiefs to Prepare—Courts-Martial Likely." (215) Admiral Kimmel found that "[w]hen the Roberts report was published a veritable hurricane of charges were hurled indiscriminately at Short and me." (216)

Although the President stated that that he did not intend to order courts-martial or take any other action personally (217) and the Services took no further action, the accusation of "dereliction of duty" remained unchallenged in public, and the announcements of the retirements of Admiral Kimmel and General Short made public the reservation "without condonation of any offense or prejudice to any future disciplinary action." This had the effect of leaving the issue unresolved in the public sphere. Admiral Kimmel complained to Admiral Stark on February 22, 1942:

> I stand ready at any time to accept the consequences of my acts. I do not wish to embarrass the government in the conduct of the war. I do feel, however, that my crucifixion before the public has about reached the limit. I am in daily receipt of letters from irresponsible people over the country taking me to task and even threatening to kill me. I am not particularly concerned except as it shows the effect on the public of articles published about me.
>
> I feel that the publication of paragraph two of the Secretary's letter of February 16 [accepting Admiral Kimmel's retirement "without condonation of any offense"] will further inflame the public and do me a great injustice. (218)

The need to keep secret the Magic intercepts (of which Admiral Kimmel had some knowledge but General Short did not) effectively precluded informed and objective public discussion during the war years of the Pearl Harbor issue, or final resolution of Admiral Kimmel's and General Short's role. The need to keep Magic secret precluded even explaining to the public the necessity of keeping it secret.

Nevertheless, the public clamor for fuller investigation of fault in Washington began almost immediately after the publication of the Roberts Commission report. On January 27th, the *New York Times* reported that members of Congress from both parties were demanding a full Congressional investigation, asserting that officials in Washington had been remiss in failing to follow up on actions being taken at Pearl Harbor, and charging that there had not been proper coordination between the Army and Navy. (219) The debate in Congress immediately took on a partisan political tone, as reported in the press. (220) After the initial blaze of interest in additional investigation into responsibility for the disaster at Pearl Harbor in early 1942, Admiral Kimmel and General Short appeared from time to time in the press in 1943 and 1944 in connection with the extension by federal law, or waiver, of the statute of limitations on courts-martial. Debates in Congress over courts-martial also took on a partisan tone as the 1944 election neared. (221)

THE SERVICE BOARDS AND THE JOINT
CONGRESSIONAL COMMITTEE

Suggestions that the Army Pearl Harbor Board and the Navy Court of Inquiry would clear General Short and Admiral Kimmel began to appear in November and December 1944. (222) Admiral Kimmel's counsel, Charles B. Rugg, stated publicly that the findings of the Roberts Commission had been corrected by the Court of Inquiry:

Kimmel Cleared, Says Lawyer

BOSTON, Dec. 1—Charles B. Rugg, counsel for Rear Admiral Husband E. Kimmel, declared here tonight that "the statement of Secretary of the Navy Forrestal means that Admiral Kimmel has been cleared" of charges of dereliction of duty at Pearl Harbor. (223)

Final release of the reports made front page news in August 1945, with reports that Marshall, Secretary of State Cordell Hull, Stark and Lieutenant General Leonard Gerow (224) had also been cited for various failures. (225)

After the war, the veil of secrecy was lifted from the intercepts, and, with the permission of President Truman, (226) the Joint Congressional Committee explained the Magic intercepts and published the full texts of the critical messages. Again, issues associated with the Congressional investigation stimulated lively partisan debate, with accusations that Democrats on the Committee would control the proceedings. (227) In July 1946, the Joint Congressional Committee's findings were described in the press as exonerating Roosevelt and determining that "the overshadowing responsibility . . . lay with the Navy and Army commanders in Hawaii," Admiral Kimmel and General Short. (228) While neither Admiral Kimmel nor General Short was happy with the Commission's findings, General Short at least could argue that ". . . I am satisfied that the testimony presented at the hearings fully absolved me from any blame and I believe such will be the verdict of history. As I have stated before, my conscience is clear." (229) Testimony to the completeness of the Commission's review is the fact that the many analyses and interpretations published since 1946 have drawn primarily on the primary sources published in the JCC hearings record.

THE POST-WAR PERIOD

On the other hand, sober analysis in the years since the publication of the Joint Congressional Committee's report has produced a number of works of nuanced and balanced scholarship which constitute the beginnings of the verdict of history. Those works, based on a careful reading of the entire record of the Joint

Congressional Committee and of other primary sources that have come to light in the intervening years, are creating a responsible and increasingly accurate and just understanding of the tapestry of failure at Pearl Harbor. Ultimately, in a free society this must be the function of the academic community, and it is one that the academic community is performing well in this case.

Assessment

Without question, Admiral Kimmel and General Short got "bad press" in the war years, especially in the immediate aftermath of the attack and of the publication of the Roberts Commission's report. The critical contribution of Magic and purple to the war effort meant that questions could not be answered while the war raged, and in that sense to some degree Admiral Kimmel and General Short's reputations were sacrificed to the war effort. While concentration on them deflected attention away from others, perhaps conveniently, there is no evidence of organized efforts to make Admiral Kimmel and General Short into "scapegoats" and little evidence of efforts to vilify them personally. In particular, there is no evidence of official government actions directed only against their reputations. There is, however, also no evidence of government actions to deflect criticism from Admiral Kimmel and General Short.

Pearl Harbor occurred in the midst of a spirited debate between isolationists and interventionists. The energies of those debates were not stifled by Pearl Harbor, but redirected. To a certain extent, Admiral Kimmel and General Short became causes celebres in that partisan rivalry. This was, and occasionally is today, the result of the politically charged world in which officers holding three-star and four-star positions become involved by virtue of their high public offices, often with consequences out of all proportion to one's talents or standing as a military professional. Indeed, Admiral Kimmel willingly and even eagerly entered that fray, keeping the issue of his reputation before the public; his autobiography details his efforts, some of which have been cited in this report. (230)

With the publication of the Joint Congressional Committee's report—a gold mine of primary sources—and the growing body of valid scholarship, a responsible and increasingly accurate and just understanding of the nature of the failure at Pearl Harbor is emerging. In this process Admiral Kimmel and General Short are taking their rightful place—certainly not solely to blame for the disaster at Pearl Harbor but also certainly not entirely innocent of error. There is nothing that government can or should do to alter that process.

V. OPTIONS FOR FURTHER ACTION

Promotion Based on Performance

No significant error was committed in any of the three personnel actions. (231) Their cumulative effect placed Admiral Kimmel and General Short in their current two-star rank on the retired list. Relief and retirement were all but inevitable, and not unfair under the circumstances.

Promotion is based on potential, and not on past performance. That is, promotion is based on expectation of performance at the level to which the individual is being considered for promotion. At the time of the Japanese attack on Pearl Harbor, Admiral Kimmel and General Short had been promoted to four-star and three-star rank, respectively, based on their potential for performance at that level of command. Their relief on December 16, 1941, reflected the Service Secretaries' assessment that their potential for continued service at those grades had changed.

By the end of 1946, the Services and the Joint Congressional Committee had independently concluded that Admiral Kimmel and General Short had adequate information to suggest placing their forces in a higher state of readiness to defend against an air attack on Pearl Harbor. They had sufficient forces to put up an effective as well as spirited defense had those forces been alerted and coordinated. Government officials at the highest levels reached similar conclusions over the next 50 years. This DoD study—after examining all the facts and circumstances anew—finds no basis to change the conclusion reached by the Services, Joint Congressional Committee and others—that Admiral Kimmel and General Short made "errors of judgment."

This report concludes that Admiral Kimmel and General Short were not solely responsible for the disaster at Pearl Harbor. Others made significant errors of judgment. In particular, senior Army and Navy leaders failed to appreciate fully and to convey to the commanders in Hawaii the sense of focus and urgency that intercepted Japanese messages should have engendered. That they did not do so does not excuse the errors of Admiral Kimmel and General Short. The scope of the disaster at Pearl Harbor and the lofty ranks of Admiral Kimmel and General Short set them apart from others who served in World War II. The decisions not to promote or advance them on the retired list, or otherwise restore their temporary ranks, were not unfair. There is no basis to require reversal of those decisions.

While concluding that Kimmel and Short were not solely responsible for the Pearl Harbor disaster, the Dorn Report did not identify all those other individuals whose errors of judgment contributed to the catastrophe. The reason for this is clear: Secretary Dorn and his team concluded that mistakes made by others—in both Washington and Hawaii—were not the proximate cause of the lopsided U.S. losses on 7 December. Since any errors made by other persons did not absolve Kimmel and Short of responsibility, much less indicate that their posthumous advancement was appropriate, there was no relevant reason for the Dorn Report to detail the faults made by others. However, in concluding that responsi-

bility for the disaster should be broadly shared, the authors of the Dorn Report agreed with many of the conclusions contained in Henry C. Clausen's *Pearl Harbor: Final Judgment.* During a seven-month period in 1944 and 1945, Major Clausen interviewed more than one hundred Army, Navy, civilian, and British personnel as part of a one-man investigation authorized by Secretary of War Stimson. On a scale of 0 to 10, with 0 indicating "no blame" and 10 reflecting the "high end" of culpability, Clausen identified fourteen men whose "negligence" made them "responsible" for Pearl Harbor. However, as Clausen's scale is subjective, as some of his analysis is flawed, and as more than one of his conclusions are pure speculation, the Dorn Report did not cite *Pearl Harbor: Final Judgment,* except in an endnote on an unrelated matter.

Bearing these comments in mind, however, Clausen's observations are worth summarizing for two reasons. First, as a lawyer by profession, Clausen was trained to evaluate evidence in reaching a conclusion. Whether examining written documents or weighing the credibility of witnesses, Clausen's legal skills made him ideally suited to sift through the varied and often conflicting stories of the many participants. Second, as a one-man investigation answerable only to Stimson, Clausen was free of the institutional bias and partisan politics that influenced the Army Pearl Harbor Board and Naval Court of Inquiry.

Major Clausen identified Short and Kimmel as the most culpable actors; of the fourteen men he held responsible, they alone received the maximum score of 10. There were twelve individuals whom Clausen "charged with contributory negligence," identifying and assigning scores to them as follows:

Col. Carlisle C. Dusenbury (9)
Lt. Col. Kendall J. Fielder (8)

Lt. Col. George Bicknell (8)
Capt. Edwin T. Layton (8)
Rear Adm. Richmond K. Turner (8)
Capt. L. F. Stafford (7)
Capt. Irvin H. Mayfield (7)
Col. Rufus S. Bratton (7)
Cdr. Joseph J. Rochefort (6)
Brig. Gen. Leonard T. Gerow (6)
Lt. Cdr. Alwin D. Kramer (6)
President Roosevelt (5)

Colonel Dusenbury, an Army intelligence officer in Washington, failed to deliver the fourteen-part message to General Marshall on 6 December. This message made clear that diplomatic relations between the United States and Japan were about to be broken—a clear indicator of imminent hostilities—and Clausen believed that if Marshall had seen this Magic on Saturday evening, "he would have sent a special alert to Short in time to blunt or repel the Japanese attack."

Colonel Fielder, in charge of Army intelligence in Hawaii, "shunned responsibility" and "failed to find out what was really going on in the intelligence world" in Hawaii. While Fielder's failures were sins of omission rather than commission, this did not absolve him of blame.

Colonel Bicknell, the Army's assistant intelligence officer in Hawaii, failed to tell Short that Kimmel knew that Japanese embassies and consulates were burning their codes—a sign that war was both imminent and unavoidable.

Captain Layton did not obey Kimmel's direct order to personally deliver the 27 November war warning message to Short. When Kimmel learned on 3 December that the Japanese were burning their codes and destroying their Purple decoding machines, Layton failed to tell Kimmel that this meant war was upon them. Finally, Layton failed to keep his Army counterpart (Fielder) informed of intelligence matters, as required by the Joint Action Agreement under which Kimmel, Short, and their commands were to cooperate in the defense of their commands. The existence of the Purple decoding machines, about which Layton learned on 3 December, was the type of intelligence that Layton should have shared with Fielder and his staff.

Admiral Turner erroneously believed that Kimmel was receiving Magic when he was not. In fact, while Kimmel knew Magic existed, he was not getting it—and Kimmel knew nothing about the Purple machines producing it. Turner's arrogance, however, prevented him from asking Kimmel, or anyone else, what decoded message traffic was being transmitted to Hawaii. In Clausen's view, Turner's failure to discover that Kimmel was not getting Magic was "contributory negligence."

Captain Safford, head of the Navy's security intelligence section in Washington, was culpable because he was "pretty sure that something was going to pop" on 6 or 7 December, yet Safford was home having breakfast when the Japanese attacked.

Captain Mayfield, a naval intelligence officer in the Fourteenth Naval District, was to blame because, after illegally tapping the telephones of the Japanese consulate in Hawaii for twenty-two months, "he broke off the taps" five days before the Japanese attack—without telling anyone. Clausen believed that the taps, if they had continued, "might have been yet another opportunity to avoid Pearl Harbor."

Colonel Bratton, in charge of the Far Eastern Section of Army Intelligence (G-2) in Washington, D.C., having ordered his subordinate, Colonel Dusenbury, to deliver the fourteen-part message to General Marshall on the evening of 6 December, then failed to ensure that this order was obeyed.

Clausen awarded a score of 6 to three other military personnel. Commander Rochefort, chief of communications security in the Fourteenth Naval District, was negligent because, having learned on 3 December 1941 that the Japanese consulate in Hawaii had destroyed all but one code system, he failed to relay the importance of that development to Captain Layton. Brigadier General Gerow, as head of the Army's War Plans Division, was at fault in failing to follow up on Short's ambiguous reply about the state of alert in Hawaii. Finally, Lieutenant Commander Kramer, working in the translation section of the Navy's communication division in Washington, was negligent because he was at home asleep in the early hours of 7 December instead of being on duty. Since the Navy had the responsibility to translate decrypted messages on 7 December, and since Kramer was the only man in the Navy responsible for such translation, his absence meant that the fourteenth part of the Japanese diplomatic message, announcing that relations with the United States were at an end, was not translated—and hence was not delivered to Roosevelt— prior to the attack. While Clausen believed that timely delivery of the message might have given Hawaii advance warning, this is very speculative.

Finally, President Roosevelt received a score of 5 from Clausen. Major Clausen concluded that Roosevelt did not know that Pearl Harbor would be attacked, and dismissed any claim that Roosevelt conspired "to force a war with Japan." But Clausen argued that "it is only fair that Roosevelt share the guilt" because he failed "to take prompt and effective action to bring his subordinates together to achieve a decision about what should be done." Since Roosevelt knew that war was certain, Clausen faulted him for failing to exercise leadership at that crucial moment. (232)

As noted earlier, three- and four-star grades are "positions of importance and responsibility" requiring individual Senate confirmation. As earlier sections of this review suggest, though perhaps at times they were unfairly characterized, Admiral Kimmel and General Short were not entirely blameless in connection with Pearl Harbor. They were the men in charge at the site of the worst military disaster in U.S. history, and their errors of judgment were of sufficient magnitude to lead to the conclusion that their overall performance did not compare favorably to that expected of other three-star and four-star officers of their era.

Promotion Based on Other Considerations

Article II, Section 2 of the Constitution gives the President broad power, with the advice and consent of the Senate, to appoint officers in the Armed Forces. (233) The President may use that discretionary authority to appoint an officer independently of the statutes that otherwise govern the promotion process. (234) Thus, the President has the power to nominate Admiral Kimmel and General Short for posthumous advancement on the retired list.

Because of their unique positions as the commanders on the scene in Hawaii, it was inevitable that much of the weight of public dismay over the Pearl Harbor disaster focused immediately on Admiral Kimmel and General Short. The need to keep secret the nation's codebreaking capabilities prevented knowledgeable officials from correcting the record during the war years. The families of Admiral Kimmel and General Short are concerned today with the lingering effects of reports published over fifty years ago. They argue that the "stigma and obloquy" from that era persist, and demand official government action, saying "the vehicle we have chosen" (235) to restore those officers' reputations is advancement on the retired list.

Advancement on the retired list is not an appropriate vehicle with which to remedy damage to reputation. With the end of the war and the publication of the reports of the Services and the

Joint Congressional Committee came official public determinations that Admiral Kimmel and General Short were not solely responsible for the disaster at Pearl Harbor, clear public affirmations that their errors of judgment did not rise to the level of dereliction, and that others also made errors of judgment. There the official public record stands, as it should.

It is indisputable that Admiral Kimmel and General Short got more than their fair share of bad press in the early war years, and that the errors of others, whose errors contributed to the disaster at Pearl Harbor, generally escaped censure. Posthumous advancement in rank, however, necessarily would be based on the judgment that, at a minimum, they had served satisfactorily at the three- and four-star level. Their superiors at the time decided that they had not, and there is no compelling basis to contradict this earlier decision.

As already noted, some commentators point to General MacArthur's failures in the Philippines on 8 December. (236) Assuming for the sake of argument, however, that MacArthur's errors in judgment led to the loss of U.S. lives and materiel in the Philippines, what happened to General MacArthur is irrelevant to any decision to posthumously advance Kimmel and Short on the retired list.

To use posthumous advancement to compensate for harsh treatment in the media, as a form of official apology or as a symbolic act, would not be appropriate. Additionally, there is no precedent for such an advancement. Finally, using advancement or promotion for such purposes would be manifestly unfair to those who earned advancement based on performance, and would imply a double standard for advancement in the armed services. The highest retired grades to which an officer may aspire should not be conferred on anyone as an apology. Rather, those grades should be reserved for those officers whose performance stands out above others.

Conclusions

An examination of the record does not show that advancement of Admiral Kimmel and General Short on the retired list is warranted.

A final point: Admiral Kimmel, who while alive worked tirelessly to restore his reputation, *never requested advancement to his highest rank;* it is his surviving family members who have seized upon this remedy. If Admiral Kimmel never thought it necessary to request the return of his stars, perhaps this indicates that he believed retirement at four-star rank was neither necessary nor appropriate.

3

Aftermath

What has happened in the years following the first and only Defense Department inquiry into responsibility at Pearl Harbor? From 1995 to 2003, the Kimmel family—joined by the Shorts to a lesser degree—have continued to wage their campaign for Admiral Kimmel's exoneration. After Senator Thurmond provided the families with a copy of the Dorn Report, the Kimmels and Shorts responded with a written rebuttal authored by Vice Adm. David C. Richardson, USN (Ret.). Portions of this rebuttal, written by Richardson in July 1997, are reproduced in Appendix C, but a brief summary of the major points is appropriate here. First, Richardson insists that "the disaster at Pearl Harbor was rooted in and caused by" failures in Washington: Roosevelt adopted a military strategy that weakened the Pacific Fleet; the chief of naval operations withheld "crucially important tactical (as distinct from strategic) intelligence information"; Washington failed to collect information and accurately assess the threat from the Japanese. Second, Kimmel did everything he could under the circumstances: "there was no lapse of foresight nor evidence of faulty judgment on his part." Third, Washington's failure to keep Kimmel and Short "fully and continuously informed" about Purple and the Magic derived from it was "a grievous error" that "increased the scale and scope of the damage to the fleet and to other military objectives." In short, Richardson's rebuttal, reflecting the prevailing view of those defending Kimmel and Short, maintains that Roosevelt and military and naval leaders in Washington are the true culprits. Underlying Richardson's view, not surprisingly, is the belief that President Roosevelt "knew that the Japanese were about to attack Pearl Harbor." Admiral Richardson is sufficiently cautious to hedge on this point, but the detailed discussion about it in his rebuttal leaves no doubt that he believed that Roosevelt had advance warning that Pearl Harbor was to be attacked. Richardson's belief in Roosevelt's perfidy is an important factor in understanding his rebuttal, for it explains why he is so adamant that Kimmel and Short were scapegoats. (1)

After providing Richardson's rebuttal to the Defense Department, the Kimmels and Shorts redoubled their political lobbying. These efforts bore fruit on 15 April 1999 when Senator Bill Roth and sixteen other senators, joined by Rep. Smith and four congressmen, introduced Senate Joint Resolution 19. (2) That resolution made the following claims:

Kimmel and Short had "excellent and unassailable" records.
"[N]umerous investigations" had "documented" that Kimmel and Short "were not provided necessary and critical intelligence that was available."
The 1944 Naval Court of Inquiry had "exonerated" Kimmel.
The 1944 Army Pearl Harbor Board's conclusions were similarly favorable to Short.
Kimmel and Short were both denied the right to defend their actions at courts-martial.
The 1946 Joint Congressional Committee had cleared Kimmel and Short of any dereliction of duty.
The majority of the members of the 1991 Army Board for Correction of Military Records concluded that Short "was unjustly held responsible for the Pearl Harbor disaster."

While the Dorn Report did not support advancement of Kimmel or Short, it did conclude that "responsibility for the Pearl Harbor disaster should not fall solely on the shoulders of Admiral Kimmel and General Short."

Kimmel and Short are the only two World War II officers excluded from the list of retired officers advanced to their highest wartime ranks.

"[T]his singular exclusion serves only *to perpetuate the myth* that the senior commanders in Hawaii were derelict in their duty and responsible for the success of the attack on Pearl Harbor, *a distinct and unacceptable expression of dishonor toward two of the finest officers who have served in the Armed Forces of the United States.*" (emphasis supplied)

On 25 May 1999 the Senate voted 52 to 47 in favor of this joint resolution, and on 7 October 1999 similar legislation was introduced by Representatives Spratt, Spence, and Skelton in the House. (3) On 30 October 1999 Congress passed the 2001 Defense Authorization Act, (4) section 546 of which asked President Clinton to restore Kimmel's and Short's stars. Many observers believed Clinton would take favorable action prior to leaving office. But he did not, and when George W. Bush became president in January 2000, the issue moved to his desk. President Bush has taken no action in the matter. There are at least two probable reasons for this. First, Vice President Dick Cheney, who served as secretary of defense from 1989 to 1992, is very familiar with the Kimmel-Short controversy; he previously denied support to those clamoring for posthumous promotion. Consequently, it seems likely that Cheney has not altered his view of the matter and has conveyed this opinion to President Bush. Second, the events of September 11, 2001, may have affected the Kimmel-Short controversy. Allegations of American unpreparedness in anticipating and defending against the terrorist attacks on the World Trade Center and Pentagon—and the parallels drawn by the media and the public between these attacks and the Japanese attack on Pearl Harbor on 7 December 1941—make it unlikely that the president will take action tantamount to exonerating two long-dead officers who similarly failed to anticipate an attack and prepare a defense of U.S. soil.

Today, the Kimmels continue their efforts. The family's Web site, called "Kimmel Family Record—Admiral Husband E. Kimmel," states that "the families of Kimmel and Short are pushing for their advancement of rank." (5) Those contacting the Web site are encouraged to "support the cause by urging President Bush to initiate the posthumous promotions"; the site provides a "hotlink" to the White House Web site. "Not sure what to write?" asks the Web page. For those needing help, a copy of a letter "to the President written by [a] Kimmel supporter and crusader" is available as a model. (6)

While hundreds of pages of documents are available electronically at the Kimmel Web site, a letter written by Edward Kimmel to President Bush on 10 January 2002 is worth highlighting, for the insight it offers into the Kimmel family's perspective. After complaining that a Defense Department recommendation on the propriety of posthumous promotion is taking too long, Kimmel details at length the actions he, his family, and supporters have taken. "Ever since my brother [Tom Kimmel] and I started our efforts in 1987 to correct the wrong done our father by the government," he writes, "the DoD has opposed us at every turn." After explaining that the current president's father and Secretary Cheney had declined to promote Kimmel and Short, Edward Kimmel writes that "finally, in 1995, Senator Strom Thurmond came to our aid after we told him no one in the DoD would even meet or talk with us." Thurmond, "using his power as Chairman of the Senate Armed Services . . . commanded the DoD to provide representatives and to listen [*sic*] what the Kimmel [*sic*] had to say." Edward Kimmel concludes by acknowledging that the Dorn Report resulted from Thurmond's intervention, although he acknowledges that the report "recommended against promoting the Pearl Harbor commanders." But in Kimmel's words, this result was the work of "our entrenched hidden enemy, the DoD." In short, a conspiracy in the Defense Department is blocking truth and justice for Admiral Kimmel and Short. (7)

While the Kimmel and Short families have rejected the Dorn Report, what about its impact on the ranks of professional historians? A clear majority accept its overall conclusions. Those who have voiced their approval of the report by name include Donald Goldstein, Robert W. Love, Norman Polmar, and Dan van der Vat. Others, like Doris Kearns Goodwin, while not explicitly mentioning the Dorn Report, implicitly endorse its findings.

Goldstein, a professor of public and international affairs at the University of Pittsburgh, whose knowledge of Pearl Harbor made him ideally suited to edit Gordon Prange's *At Dawn We Slept,* has endorsed the Dorn Report's analysis and conclusions in a variety of academic forums. For example, at a symposium sponsored by the U.S. National Park Service to commemorate the sixtieth anniversary of the Japanese attack, Goldstein mentioned the Dorn Report as official support of his conclusions about the Japanese air attack. (8)

Love, a professor of history at the U.S. Naval Academy and editor of *Pearl Harbor Revisited,* stated at a 1999 colloquium that "the question of Kimmel's responsibility has long been settled in the scholarly publications that have examined Pearl Harbor." Love cited the Dorn Report as supporting this view. (9)

Polmar, a well-known naval analyst, historian, and coauthor of *Spy Book: The Encyclopedia of Intelligence,* quotes from the Dorn Report in a December 2000 article harshly critical of then secretary of defense William Cohen and then secretary of the Navy Richard Danzig. Polmar upbraided Cohen and Danzig for failing to publicly oppose efforts in the House and Senate to posthumously promote Kimmel and Short. He notes with approval that although "the pleas of Kimmel supporters" had resulted in a new Defense Department review, that review—the Dorn Report—had concluded that there could be no posthumous advancement for either man. (10)

Dan van der Vat, author of numerous works on modern warfare, including the highly acclaimed *Atlantic Campaign,* wrote the following on the eve of the sixtieth anniversary of the Japanese attack:

> In April 1995, Congress sanctioned another inquiry at the request of the Kimmel and Short families. Senator Strom Thurmond, chairman of the Senate Armed Forces [*sic*] Committee, and Representative Floyd Spence, chairman of the House Armed Services Committee, sat for a day and then asked the Department of Defense to conduct a speedy investigation. Undersecretary Edwin Dorn took seven months [*sic*] to reject the request for posthumous restitution of the commanders' rank and reputation. *With commendable brevity and clarity, Dorn declared: "As commanders, they were accountable."* (11)

Finally, Goodwin, a presidential historian and author of a number of bestsellers, including a biography of Franklin D. Roosevelt, appeared on television in a report about Kimmel and Short broadcast on NBC's *The News with Brian Williams.* While Goodwin did not mention the Dorn Report by name, she implicitly endorsed its finding that the posthumous advancement of Kimmel and Short was inappropriate. Commenting on recent legislative attempts to exonerate Kimmel and Short and restore their wartime ranks, Goodwin stated she was "not comfortable" with this approach. In her view, this was "rewriting history by congressional fiat," with Congress using its law-making powers to attempt to shift responsibility for Pearl Harbor to Roosevelt, Marshall, and other officials in Washington. (12)

Some historians, while apparently accepting the Dorn Report's factual findings, and endorsing its conclusion that Kimmel and Short were not alone responsible for Pearl Harbor, nonetheless argue that the two commanders should have their highest wartime ranks restored. Michael Gannon, a historian at the University of Florida and an accomplished author, falls into this category. In his book *Pearl Harbor Betrayed* Gannon refers approvingly to the Dorn Report's conclusion that "the War and

Navy Departments were guilty of mistakes . . . at Pearl Harbor." (13) He stated at a December 2001 symposium on Pearl Harbor that he was in favor of restoring Kimmel's stars. (14)

Apparently Paul Stillwell takes the same view. Kimmel and Short may have made mistakes while in command, but the fact that responsibility also falls upon others is sufficient mitigation to warrant restoring their wartime ranks. (15)

Finally, what about the public's acceptance of the Dorn Report? This is hard to measure but, to the extent the media reflects popular opinion, the Defense Department investigation is viewed positively. When NBC's *The News with Brian Williams* broadcast a segment on the Kimmel-Short controversy, it presented both views of the controversy. (16) Among those interviewed were Kimmel's grandson and Senator Roth. Both spoke of how the central issue was "honor": that Admiral Kimmel (and General Short) had been dishonored by the U.S. government, and that their good names should be restored with a posthumous advancement. Col. Fred Borch and Dr. Doris Kearns Goodwin advocated the status quo. The Kimmels have since complained to NBC that the Brian Williams broadcast was biased against them and Admiral Kimmel. (17)

What will the future bring for those who seek posthumous restoration of Admiral Kimmel's and General Short's ranks and reputations? At least one historian believes that the events of September 11, 2001, have had a major impact on the Kimmel-Short controversy. In *A Date Which Will Live: Pearl Harbor in American Memory,* Emily S. Rosenberg writes:

> The pro-Kimmel argument, with its implication of executive branch failure (or even conspiracy) to prevent a surprise attack in order to maneuver the country into war, was hardly a narrative that the new [George W.] Bush administration wanted to embrace after September 11, 2001. Congress' recommendation for presidential action remained unheeded by the White House, and the visibility of the Kimmel issue declined as the political constellation changed. After September 11 a

> Republican president had to confront another "day of infamy" and answer questions about intelligence capabilities and why America slept. (18)

Admiral Kimmel's son Edward seems to have reached a similar conclusion. As he told a reporter in December 2001: "I think the events of 9/11 have put [the recommendation for posthumous advancement] at the bottom of the pile." (19)

Whether the events of September 11, 2001, have altered the "political constellation" for Kimmel and Short is hard to say. What is known is that as the ten-year anniversary of the Dorn Report approaches, no action has been taken by the White House to alter the status quo or otherwise rewrite history.

Conclusion

There was no legitimate reason for the Defense Department to conduct a new investigation into responsibility at Pearl Harbor in 1995. In the face, however, of intense lobbying by the Kimmel and Short families—culminating in a personal request from Senator Thurmond to take a fresh look at the issue—the department acquiesced. Yet while the impetus for Defense Department involvement was intensely political, what resulted was truly a significant study—principally because it was an examination of Kimmel's and Short's performance by a new generation of civilian leaders. The participants in all previous investigations had lived through Pearl Harbor and World War II; Undersecretary Dorn and his team, however, had grown up after these events, and consequently had no preconceptions about Kimmel and Short. Additionally, they were unfettered by past Army or Navy inquiries, or other institutional prejudice or bias.

The Dorn Report is important for at least six reasons. First, it was the first independent, comprehensive official investigation into responsibility and culpability at Pearl Harbor to be conducted since the 1940s. Second, it is the only inquiry to be done outside the Army and Navy—the sole Defense Department look at Pearl Harbor. Third, it is the first official inquiry to conclude that Kimmel and

Short were not alone responsible for the crushing defeat suffered by U.S. forces at Pearl Harbor, but that others also were culpable. Fourth, it will continue to frame the ongoing debate about responsibility for Pearl Harbor. Historians, members of Congress, officials in the executive branch, and the Kimmel and Short families have all referred to it and quoted from it in support of their respective views about 7 December 1941. Fifth, the report is unique in addressing the propriety of restoring Admiral Kimmel and General Short to their wartime ranks. Those championing the Kimmel and Short cause insist that posthumous promotion is the only appropriate remedy, and claim that this will constitute official exoneration for any alleged wrongdoing at Pearl Harbor; this report contains the first official statement on this remedy. Sixth, and finally, the inquiry is the first investigation to examine the official treatment of Kimmel and Short—and to conclude that it was fair and proper.

In forwarding the Dorn Report to Senator Thurmond on 27 December 1995, Secretary White necessarily adopted the report's findings of fact as the official Defense Department position on Pearl Harbor. As these factual findings—and the Dorn Report's recommendations—are the first official statement by the civilian leadership of the Defense Department on Kimmel and Short, they are worth summarizing here:

- Admiral Kimmel and General Short knew that their primary mission—indeed, virtually their only mission—was to prepare for war with Japan.
- General Short's mission was to protect the fleet at Pearl Harbor; Admiral Kimmel had the duty to cooperate with the Army in defense of the fleet, and he also had the "general duty" to "take all practicable steps to keep the ships of his command ready for battle."
- Both men knew that war with Japan was highly likely; moreover, by 27 November 1941, when each received a "war warning" from Washington, both Kimmel and Short *knew* that the initial Japanese attack *could* occur within weeks or days.

CONCLUSION

Both Kimmel and Short knew that, if war came, Japan would strike the first blow, if only because the United States would not; the two men knew that a surprise attack would probably precede a declaration of war.

Kimmel and Short both knew that the initial Japanese attack *could* fall on Pearl Harbor (and the fact that they took vigorous measures to defend against submarine attack and sabotage testifies to their understanding that the war *could* come to Pearl Harbor).

Kimmel and Short knew that an attack on Pearl Harbor could come in the form of an attack from aircraft carriers.

Both officers knew from their own staffs of the danger of surprise air attack.

Kimmel and Short knew from recent events that the idea of a carrier air attack on Pearl Harbor was not new.

Both men made statements prior to 7 December 1941 that acknowledged the possibility of an air attack on their forces. Kimmel, for example, in a letter to Admiral Stark on 18 February 1941 stated, "I feel that a surprise attack (submarine, air, or combined) on Pearl Harbor is a possibility." Similarly, the 14 August 1941 *Honolulu Advertiser*, in an article titled "General Short Sees Danger of Oahu Air Raid," quoted Short as saying that "an attack upon these [Hawaiian] islands is not impossible and in certain situations it might not be improbable."

Admiral Kimmel was briefed on 2 December 1941 that American intelligence had lost track of the Japanese carriers.

Having accepted these facts as true, the Defense Department further agreed with the Dorn Report's resolution of this question: *In the certain knowledge that the United States and Japan were moving inexorably and ever more rapidly toward war, but not knowing exactly where, when, or how Japan would strike, what did Admiral Kimmel and General Short do to resolve their uncertainty?*

Secretary Dorn agreed with his research team's unanimous conclusion that Kimmel and Short failed to make adequate defensive preparations in light of the information they *had* available to them. Dorn further agreed with the team members that this meant there was no reason to reverse the conclusions of the services and the Joint Congressional Committee that Admiral Kimmel and General Short made errors of judgment in the use of information and the employment of the forces available to them. Secretary White's letter to Senator Thurmond makes clear that the Defense Department explicitly endorsed this conclusion—and that this was now the official Department position on the issue.

It must be underscored, however, that the Dorn Report also contained an official acknowledgment that while the two Hawaii commanders had made "errors of judgment," responsibility should be "broadly shared." Others had made errors of judgment in the days, weeks, and months leading up to Pearl Harbor. In particular, military leaders in Washington, D.C., should have followed up their instructions to Hawaii—especially after the war warning messages of 27 November—to ensure that Admiral Kimmel and General Short had taken appropriate action and were aware of each other's defensive posture. Washington also should have shared more intelligence information with Admiral Kimmel and General Short. But, while finding that some fault lay with civilian and military leaders in Washington, the Dorn team— and Secretary Dorn himself—also concluded that any failure in Washington was not the proximate or direct cause of the lopsided U.S. losses. In sum, Kimmel and Short were not wholly to blame. Their errors, however, were sufficiently grievous that restoration of their stars was not warranted.

As for shortcomings, the Dorn Report mistakenly concluded that Kimmel and Short did not get tactical warning on 7 December 1941. This was not true: the sinking of an unidentified submarine by the USS *Ward* at 6:40 a.m. was sufficient tactical warning of an imminent attack. That the Army and the Navy missed this warning goes to the heart of the nature of the disaster at Pearl Harbor. It also drives home a point that the Dorn Report perhaps should have emphasized more: that Kimmel and

Short and their subordinates were mentally unprepared for a surprise air attack. Despite all that they knew, and their recognition that an aerial bombardment of Oahu was possible, Kimmel and Short simply did not believe in their hearts that the Japanese would attack. This failure to anticipate the unexpected—part of their duties as the senior Army and Navy commanders in Hawaii—was reflected in all Kimmel and Short did in the days, weeks, and months leading up to that disastrous Sunday morning. That their subordinates were no better mentally prepared does not excuse their unpreparedness. It does explain, however, more than any other single factor, why U.S. losses were so lopsided in comparison to those suffered by the Japanese fleet.

The Kimmels, Shorts, and their advocates, will never be satisfied with the Dorn Report—or any other inquiry that does less than result in the posthumous advancement of Admiral Kimmel and General Short. Underlying the Kimmel-Short crusade is a firm belief that Roosevelt, Marshall, Stark, and others in Washington are somehow responsible for the disaster—and that blame has been unfairly shifted to the two commanders in Hawaii. Given the efforts of the Kimmels and Shorts in the aftermath of the Dorn Report, it appears unlikely that the families will cease their efforts to rewrite history.

Pearl Harbor, wrote the late Gordon Prange, "demonstrated one enduring lesson: The unexpected can happen and often does." (1) Husband E. Kimmel and Walter C. Short, as the senior officers in command in Hawaii in 1941, were expected to understand this self-evident truth, and to defend against it. But their mental limitations, and their preconceptions about the form that the coming war would take, caused them to fail. As a result, America suffered the greatest single military defeat in its history. Given their errors in judgment, and the death and destruction that followed from these mistakes, the loss of a few stars is not much to ask of them.

Appendix A

Photocopy of Memorandum for the Deputy Secretary of Defense, Signed Edwin Dorn

APPENDIX A

UNDER SECRETARY OF DEFENSE
4000 DEFENSE PENTAGON
WASHINGTON, D.C. 20301-4000

DEC 1 5 1995

PERSONNEL AND
READINESS

MEMORANDUM FOR THE DEPUTY SECRETARY OF DEFENSE

SUBJECT: Advancement of Rear Admiral Kimmel and Major General Short

This review was undertaken in response to a commitment that former Deputy Secretary Deutch made to Senator Thurmond in April 1995. You assigned me to conduct it. In essence, you asked me to advise you whether actions taken toward General Short and Admiral Kimmel some 50 years ago were excessively harsh, and if so, whether posthumous advancement to three- and four-star rank is the appropriate remedy.

These issues are immediate and highly emotional to the descendants of Admiral Kimmel and General Short.[1] Family members feel that the Pearl Harbor commanders were scapegoats for a disaster that they could neither prevent nor mitigate, and that others who were blameworthy escaped both official censure and public humiliation. They argue that advancement (or, as they put it, restoration to highest rank held) is the best way to remove the stigma and obloquy.

More is at stake here than the reputations of two officers and the feelings of their families. The principle of equity requires that wrongs be set right. In addition, we owe it to posterity to ensure that our history is told correctly.

With support from a small team of DoD civilians and military officers, I studied the performance of the two commanders, the procedures that led to their relief and retirement and the reports of the several Pearl Harbor investigations. I also tried to understand the basis for the families' claim that General Short and Admiral Kimmel were unfairly denied restoration to three-star and four-star rank when that action became legally possible in 1947. The team reviewed thousands of pages of documents, read a number of secondary sources, visited Pearl Harbor and interviewed members of the families.

My findings are:

1. Responsibility for the Pearl Harbor disaster should not fall solely on the shoulders of Admiral Kimmel and General Short; it should be broadly shared.

  a. The United States and Japan were pursuing policies that were leading inexorably to war. Japan had occupied Manchuria, was threatening much of Asia and had joined in a tripartite alliance with Italy and Germany. The US reaction was to stop selling Japan

---

[1] On December 7, 1941 Admiral Husband E. Kimmel was Commander in Chief, United States Fleet and Commander in Chief, United States Pacific Fleet -- the Navy's second-highest officer after the Chief of Naval Operations. Lieutenant General Walter C. Short was Commander of the Army's Hawaiian Department.

strategically important materials including oil (Japan bought most of its oil from the US) and, in the summer of 1941, to freeze Japanese assets in the US. Negotiations in the summer and fall of 1941 failed to break the impasse. By late November 1941, civilian and military leaders in the US had concluded that conflict was imminent; the only questions were when and where it would occur.

b. Admiral Kimmel and General Short were both sent "war warning" messages on November 27. They were advised that negotiations were stalemated and that Japan might take hostile action at any moment. Admiral Kimmel was ordered to execute a "defensive deployment" consistent with the US war plan in the Pacific; General Short was ordered to undertake "reconnaissance and other measures...", but his instructions were muddied somewhat by advice to avoid actions that would "alarm [Hawaii's] civil population or disclose intent."

c. Admiral Kimmel and General Short discussed the November 27 war warning, but concluded that an attack would occur in the Western Pacific, not in Hawaii. Indeed, the November 27 messages had mentioned the likelihood that the attack would occur in "the Philippines, Thai or Kra Peninsula or .... Borneo." Washington also did not expect Hawaii to be attacked. Further, it appears that Admiral Kimmel and General Short were depending on timely tactical warning from Washington, should Hawaii become a target. Military leaders in Washington, on the other hand, appear to have felt that the November 27 war warning would lead Admiral Kimmel and General Short to heighten their vigilance, and failed to examine closely what they actually were doing.

d. Officials in Washington did not send Admiral Kimmel and General Short other information, derived from the *Magic* project that broke the Japanese code, that might have given them a greater sense of urgency and caused them to surmise that Hawaii was a likely target. For example, Washington did not tell them that Japanese agents in Hawaii had been instructed to report on the precise location of ships at Pearl Harbor. (The Japanese attacked Hawaii, the Philippines and several other targets on the same day.)

e. Information-sharing and operational cooperation were hampered by bureaucratic rivalries. The Army and Navy were separate executive departments reporting directly to the President, and only the President could ensure that they were working together. Admiral Kimmel and General Short had cordial personal relations, but felt it inappropriate to inquire into one another's professional domains. This apparently was the standard at the time. General Short's mission was to defend the fleet in Hawaii; Admiral Kimmel apparently never asked in detail about General Short's plans. Admiral Kimmel's mission was to prepare for offensive operations against Japan. Early in 1941 the Navy also had assumed from the Army responsibility for conducting long-range aerial reconnaissance. Even after receiving the war warning, General Short apparently did not ask Admiral Kimmel whether the Navy actually was conducting long-range air patrols. Nevertheless, General Short assumed that he would receive the advance warning needed to launch Army Air Corps fighters, which were on four-hour alert, and to ready his anti-aircraft guns, whose ammunition was stored some distance from the batteries. Just as

Washington did not provide the Hawaii commanders with all the intelligence that was derived from *Magic*, so it also appears that Admiral Kimmel had more intelligence than he chose to share with General Short. For example, Admiral Kimmel learned on December 2 that several Japanese carriers were "lost" to US intelligence; their radio signals had not been detected for more than two weeks. He did not tell General Short.

f. The run-up to Pearl Harbor was fraught with miscommunication, oversights and lack of followup. In his November 27 war warning message, Army Chief of Staff Marshall directed General Short to "undertake such reconnaissance and other measures as you deem necessary..." General Short assumed this order was misworded, because he believed General Marshall knew that the Navy had taken over the reconnaissance responsibility from the Army. He also assumed that the Navy was doing it. General Short's response to General Marshall described plans to defend against sabotage, but said nothing about reconnaissance. Apparently, no one in the War Department took note of the omission. The November 27 war warning from Admiral Stark, the Chief of Naval Operations (CNO), instructed Admiral Kimmel to undertake a "defensive deployment preparatory to carrying out the tasks assigned in WPL 46 [the war plan]." Exactly what Admiral Stark intended is not clear. Admiral Kimmel interpreted the CNO's guidance to mean that he (Admiral Kimmel) should continue what he had been doing for several weeks -- sending submarines and planes to patrol around Wake and Midway, and patrolling outside Pearl Harbor for Japanese submarines. Carrier task forces en route to Wake and Midway were doing aerial reconnaissance as part of their normal training, thus covering a portion of the Pacific west and southwest of Hawaii. "Deployment" also could have meant to sortie the fleet from Pearl Harbor. Admiral Kimmel did not do that. Instead, he kept his ships in port, but pointed their bows toward the entrance so that they could leave quickly if the need arose. Moving several dozen warships through Pearl Harbor's narrow channel and into fighting posture on the high seas would have taken several hours. No one in the Department of Navy took issue with Admiral Kimmel's interpretation of the CNO's instructions.

g. Resources were scarce. Washington didn't have enough cryptologists and linguists to decode all the Japanese message traffic, so the analysts gave priority to dipomatic traffic over military traffic. The Navy in Hawaii was short of planes and crews. The Army in Hawaii was short of munitions.

h. Finally, the Japanese attack was brilliantly conceived and flawlessly executed. It involved a bold new use of carriers. It required crossing four thousand miles of ocean undetected, which meant taking the storm-tossed northern route where there was little commercial shipping. It required new technology -- torpedoes that could be used in the shallow, narrow confines of Pearl Harbor. And the attack required extraordinarily well trained air crews with commanders capable of coordinating more than 150 planes in each wave of attack. US Naval exercises during the 1930s and the British Navy's 1940 raid on the Italian fleet at Taranto had demonstrated the feasibility of carrier-based attacks. But the scale and complexity of the Japanese attack greatly exceeded anything envisioned before. American military experts underestimated Japanese capability.

PHOTOCOPY OF MEMORANDUM

2. To say that responsibility is broadly shared is not to absolve Admiral Kimmel and General Short of accountability.

a. Military command is unique. A commander has plenary responsibility for the welfare of the people under his or her command, and is directly accountable for everything the unit does or fails to do. When a ship runs aground, the captain is accountable whether or not he/she was on the bridge at the time. When a unit is attacked, it is the commander and not the intelligence officer or the sentry who is accountable. Command at the three- and four-star level involves daunting responsibilities. Military officers at that level operate with a great deal of independence. They must have extraordinary skill, foresight and judgment, and a willingness to be accountable for things about which they could not possibly have personal knowledge. Today, for example, the senior commander in Hawaii is responsible for US military operations spanning half the world's surface -- from the West coast of the United States to the east coast of Africa. His fleets sail the Pacific, the Indian Ocean, the China Sea, the Sea of Japan, the Arctic and the Antarctic. This, in the understated language of military law, is "a position of importance and responsibility."

b. It was appropriate that Admiral Kimmel and General Short be relieved. In the immediate aftermath of the attack, their relief was occasioned by the need to restore confidence in the Navy and Army's leadership, especially in the Pacific, and to get going with the war. Subsequently, investigations concluded that both commanders made errors of judgment. I have seen no information that leads me to contradict that conclusion.

c. The intelligence available to Admiral Kimmel and General Short was sufficient to justify a higher level of vigilance than they chose to maintain. They knew that war was imminent, they knew that Japanese tactics featured surprise attacks, and Admiral Kimmel (though not General Short) knew that the US had lost track of Japan's carriers. Further, they had the resources to maintain a higher level of vigilance. Admiral Kimmel believed that the optimum aerial reconnaissance would require covering 360 degrees around Hawaii for a sustained period. The Navy clearly did not have enough planes for that. This does not mean, however, that Admiral Kimmel had to choose between ideal aerial reconnaissance and no aerial reconnaissance. The fleet also had cruisers and destroyers that could have been used as pickets to supplement air patrols, but were not.

d. Different choices might not have discovered the carrier armada and might not have prevented the attack, but different choices -- a different allocation of resources -- could have reduced the magnitude of the disaster. The Navy and the Army were at a low level of alert against aerial attack. Shipboard anti-aircraft guns were firing within five minutes. The Army was not able to bring its batteries into play during the first wave of the attack and only four Army Air Corps fighters managed to get airborne. US losses included 2,403 dead (1,177 of whom are entombed in the Arizona), 1,178 wounded, eight battleships, ten other vessels and more than 100 aircraft. Japanese losses were 29 aircraft, one large submarine and five midget submarines.

4

3. The official treatment of Admiral Kimmel and General Short was substantively temperate and procedurally proper.

a. Admiral Kimmel and General Short were the objects of public vilification. At least one Member of Congress demanded that they be summarily dismissed, stripped of rank and denied retirement benefits. They received hate mail and death threats. The public and Congress were clamoring for information about Pearl Harbor. The news media went into a feeding frenzy, gobbling up tidbits of blame and punishment. Under the circumstances, it is not surprising that information very hurtful to Admiral Kimmel and General Short -- information implying that they would be court martialed, for example -- was given to the press. These things happen, often not for the most honorable of reasons. This does not mean, however, that Admiral Kimmel and General Short were victims of a smear campaign orchestrated by government officials.

b. In contrast to their treatment by some of the media, their official treatment was substantively temperate. They were relieved, they reverted to two-star rank, and under the laws in force at the time, their retirements were at the two-star level. Although there was mention of court martial, no charges were brought. Indeed, official statements and investigations seemed purposely to avoid wording that would lead to court martial. For example, the Roberts Commission used the phrase "dereliction of duty" -- a stinging rebuke, but at the time not a court martial offense. The Roberts Commission avoided other phrases, such as "culpable inefficiency" and "neglect of duty", that were court martial offenses. Later investigations such as the Joint Congressional Committee report eschewed "dereliction" in favor of "errors of judgment."

c. Admiral Kimmel requested a court martial in order to clear his name, but the request was not acted on. There is an allegation that the government feared bringing charges because a court martial would have put other senior military and civilian leaders in a bad light. This is possible. But it is equally possible that there simply were not sufficient grounds to sustain a successful prosecution. A court martial almost certainly would have revealed the existence of *Magic*, a key US intelligence asset.

d. I do not find major fault with the procedures used in the investigations. Family members have complained that Admiral Kimmel and General Short were denied "due process"; that is, they were not allowed to call their own witnesses or to cross-examine witnesses. But the calling and cross-examination of witnesses is characteristic of trials, not of investigations. Some of the investigations may have been more thorough than others, but I do not see a convincing basis for concluding that Admiral Kimmel and General Short were victims of government scapegoating or of a government-inspired smear campaign.

4. History has not been hostile to Admiral Kimmel and General Short.

a. None of the official reports ever held that Admiral Kimmel and General Short were solely responsible for the Pearl Harbor disaster, although the Roberts Commission came close. Later reports exchewed the stinging "dereliction of duty" rebuke in favor of "errors of judgment."

b. Historians who write about Pearl Harbor seem to be divided into three camps: those who hold Admiral Kimmel and General Short partly (but not solely) responsible; those who believe they were scapegoats; and those who lay much of the blame on bureaucratic factors such as the lack of coordination between the Army and the Navy. National Park Service guides at the Arizona Memorial, for example, focus on the factors that led to war and on the tactics used in the attack, not on individual military leaders. A 30-minute film produced exclusively for use at the Arizona Memorial mentions Admiral Kimmel and General Short only once, and not at all disparagingly. Admiral Kimmel and General Short are not discussed prominently or disparagingly in history classes at West Point, Annapolis and the Air Force Academy. Of eight US history texts in use at the service academies today, one is critical of Admiral Kimmel. Thus, while their reputations may have been damaged in the years immediately following Pearl Harbor, the passage of time has produced balance.

5. There is not a compelling basis for advancing either officer to a higher grade.

a. Their superiors concluded that Admiral Kimmel and General Short did not demonstrate the judgment required of people who serve at the three- and four-star level. That conclusion may seem harsh, but it is made all the time. I have not seen a convincing basis for contradicting it in the instant case. It also is important to keep in mind that retirement at the two-star grade is not an insult or a stigma. Very few officers rise to that level of distinction.

b. Retirement at three- and four-star level was not a right in 1947 and is not today. Officers are nominated for retirement at that level by the President at the President's discretion and based on his conclusion that they served satisfactorily at the temporary grades. His nomination is subject to the advice and consent of the Senate. A nominee's errors and indiscretions must be reported to the Senate as adverse information.

In sum, I cannot conclude that Admiral Kimmel and General Short were victims of unfair official actions and thus I cannot conclude that the official remedy of advancement on the retired list in order. Admiral Kimmel and General Short did not have all the resources they felt necessary. Had they been provided more intelligence and clearer guidance, they might have understood their situation more clearly and behaved differently. Thus, responsibility for the magnitude of the Pearl Harbor disaster must be shared. But this is not a basis for contradicting the conclusion, drawn consistently over several investigations, that Admiral Kimmel and General Short committed errors of judgment. As commanders, they were accountable.

Admiral Kimmel and General Short suffered greatly for Pearl Harbor. They lost men for whom they were responsible. They felt that too much of the blame was placed on them. Their children and grandchildren continue to be haunted by it all. For all this, there can be sadness. But there can be no official remedy.

I recommend that you provide a copy of this memorandum and attachment to Senator Thurmond, the families of Admiral Kimmel and General Short, the secretaries of Army and Navy and other interested parties.

Edwin Dorn

Attachment: Staff Report

Appendix B

Photocopy of Letter to Strom Thurmond from John P. White

THE DEPUTY SECRETARY OF DEFENSE

WASHINGTON, D.C. 20301

27 DEC 1995

Honorable Strom Thurmond
Chairman
Committee on Armed Services
United States Senate
Washington, D.C. 20510

Dear Mr. Chairman:

Earlier this year, the Department of Defense agreed to examine whether Rear Admiral Husband E. Kimmel, USN, and Major General Walter C. Short, USA, should be posthumously advanced on the retired list to their highest temporary grades (Admiral and Lieutenant General, respectively). Pursuant to that commitment, I asked the Honorable Edwin Dorn, the Under Secretary of Defense (Personnel and Readiness), to conduct a review of this matter. The results of that review are reported in Mr. Dorn's December 15, 1995 memorandum to me and in a detailed analysis prepared under his direction. A copy of each of these documents is enclosed.

After thoroughly considering this issue, the Department has concluded that official governmental action, which would be required to advance Admiral Kimmel and General Short on the retired list, is not warranted. While I regret the necessity of disappointing their families, the historical record, as discussed in the attached documents, dictates this outcome.

On behalf of the Department, I express our appreciation for your interest in this important subject. Mr. Dorn is forwarding copies of the enclosed materials to the Kimmel and Short families.

Sincerely,

John P. White

Enclosures

Appendix C
A Critical Analysis of the Report by the Department of Defense Dated December 1, 1995, Regarding Advancement of Rear Admiral Husband E. Kimmel and Lieutenant General Walter C. Short on the Retired List[*]

VICE ADM. DAVID CHARLES RICHARDSON, USN (RET.)

Introduction

Acting on the request of the surviving sons of Admiral Kimmel, Senator Strom Thurmond, Chairman, Senate Armed Services Committee, held a meeting in the Senate Armed Services Committee Hearing Room on April 27th, 1995 to permit the Kimmel family to present to the Secretary of Defense reasons why their father, Rear Admiral Husband E. Kimmel, should have his four star rank restored to him posthumously. Senator Strom

[*]Spelling and language errors of the original document are preserved.

Thurmond conducted the meeting. Representing the Department of Defense were the Deputy Secretary of Defense, John M. Deutch, Secretary of the Navy, John H. Dalton and Navy General Counsel Steven S. Honigman. Those present in support of the Kimmel family were former Chairman of the Joint Chiefs of Staff, Admiral Thomas H. Moorer; former Chief of Naval Operations, James L. Holloway III; Admiral Harold E. Shear, Rear Admiral Donald M. Showers, Captain Edward L. Beach, author; John Costello, historian; Michael Gannon, historian; Mr. Anthony DeLorenzo, representing the Pearl Harbor Survivor's Association; Counsel for Admiral Kimmel, Edward Hanify; the sons of Admiral Kimmel, Edward R. and Captain Thomas K., Edward's son, Manning M. IV and Thomas's son Thomas K. Jr. Navy General Counsel Honigman presented the case against posthumous advancement. The attendees accompanying the Kimmel family spoke in favor of advancement. The Kimmel family spoke in favor of General Short. The outcome was a pledge by the Deputy Secretary of Defense to Senator Thurmond to review the matter of posthumous advancement objectively, and make a report. A transcription of remarks made in meeting is attached as Exhibit A. The report by the Under Secretary of Defense dated December 1, 1995, (the Dorn Report) is appended as exhibit B. The executive summary of the Dorn Report is exhibit C.

Shortly after the meeting in a letter to Senator Strom Thurmond dated 10 May, 1995, the Deputy Secretary of Defense, John Deutch, stated:

> As I pledged at the meeting, we will examine the matter without preconceptions so that a judgment can be reached on the basis of fact and fairness and the right action can be taken without delay. Like you, we seek to arrive at a closure that will be recognized as principled and fair.

Comment: In order to arrive "at a closure that will be recognized as principled and fair" Secretary Deutch's pledge "that a judgment can be reached on the basis of fact and fairness" is a pledge to identify what the errors in judgment were and when and by whom they were committed. To what extent did errors in judgment that occurred at seat of government impact on judgment errors that may have occurred in Hawaii? More specifically, were those that may have been committed by Kimmel and Short of a severity to affect in any significant way the outcome of the surprise attack, or warrant destruction of their reputations?

This paper will reexamine the events and related information that we now know was then available in Washington and in Honolulu, present an assessment of their significance when viewed in an operational context, and identify errors in judgment by the parties to that disaster. An additional purpose is to provide for the record information not previously known or, for whatever reasons, not permitted to be included in the several inquiries. The intent is creation of a contextual record of fundamental considerations that should apply in force commander relationships as revealed by errors committed in the days, weeks and months prior to Pearl Harbor in order that we not suffer needless losses in lives in future perilous situations.

In the Dorn Report an administration acknowledges for the first time that blame for Pearl Harbor does not rest solely on the shoulders of Admiral Kimmel and General Short. Others were also to blame. The others remain unidentified, their blame unexplained. The Dorn Report asserts that although neither commander is guilty of "dereliction of duty," as initially asserted in the Robert's Commission Report, both Admiral Kimmel and General Short were guilty of faulty judgment. They must therefore continue to bear blame for the disaster. But then, the Report notes, military commanders serve at the pleasure of senior command and may be relieved for no reason other than a loss of faith in their judgment. For this reason alone, the Report states, posthumous advancement of Kimmel and Short is inappropriate. The point is made that since the Pearl Harbor commanders' retirement in their permanent ranks are facts of history, violate no laws and are in accord with common practice they should stand.

It is, indeed, true, that military commanders serve at the pleasure of senior command. They may be relieved for any number of reasons. But we have here a major disaster, with enormous military and political consequences, and an issue of historical significance regarding which we need to set the record straight in order to not repeat past mistakes. The Dorn Report also notes the scope and depth of national criticism directed particularly at Admiral Kimmel. It makes clear that Kimmel's relief in particular was driven by considerations other than loss of confidence in his Judgment. In this regard the Report states;

> It is important to remember that the state of the allied cause in both the Atlantic and Pacific was extremely perilous in the dark days of early 1942. The greatest national need at the time was to prosecute the global war against both Germany and Japan.

Comment: The implication is clear. The nation's leaders at that critical juncture quite rightly feared the loss of confidence that would follow an admission that Washington authorities were in some degree at fault, an admission that in the context of the then existing military situation would have been irresponsible. Nor for several weeks did the extent of blame attributable to the mishandling of intelligence become increasingly apparent to those knowledgeable of the contents of that intelligence. There were needs to both preserve the secrecy of our codebreaking successes and our national political stability.

The public mood in the aftermath of the disaster was bitter, frightened. How could this happen? The view of the general public was that laxity and inattention by Admiral Kimmel and Lieutenant General Short had left the American fleet vulnerable. The public perception of life in Hawaii contributed to this suspicion. The reality was quite different, apparent to those of us who served there during 1940–41. As the war progressed, with victory clearly in sight, military reasons for blaming Kimmel and Short ceased to exist. But political reasons remained. Requests for posthumous advancement in rank of the Hawaiian commanders have been interpreted by some as an attack against the reputation of President Roosevelt. Is this consideration valid? While other injustices of that time have since been rectified, as for example, restitution made to Japanese Americans who were encarcerated in encampments during the war, the injustice done Kimmel and Short remains unadmitted. If then in the national interest to shoulder the Pearl Harbor commanders with the blame, does that interest apply today? Given that the attack was a Japanese initiative, and by any known measures American Intervention a prerequisite to Hitler's defeat, is there a valid basis today for reasoning that the reputation of President Roosevelt would be tarnished by an admission that blame for the damage inflicted lay in Washington? The circumstances then existing saw Great Britain, it's army devastated in it's retreat to and recovery from Dunkirk, fighting alone for survival against Hitler, Mussolini, Japan and, until the spring of 1941, Stalin's Soviet Union in uneasy alliance with Hitler.

Recorded history accurately notes the all out effort by President Roosevelt, supported by his key advisors, to assist Britain and, later, the Soviet Union in their defense against Hitler's aggression. The American public, on the other hand, was seemingly determined to avoid involvement, certainly not in a combat role. The President first initiated a buildup of our military strength and an increasing supply of military equipment to Britain. After Hitler's assault on the Soviet Union, and evidence that Stalin might succeed in his defensive efforts, Roosevelt initiated economic constraints designed to hold Japan in check to permit the Red Army to transfer military forces from Eastern Siberia for defense of Moscow. These constraints created conditions that the Japanese deemed unbearable. To the Japanese way of thinking, allied as they were to Hitler, achieving the Greater East Asia Prosperity Sphere and it's promise of economic freedom made war with America a necessity. On the other hand, the President knew that if America went to war, that could only occur if America were first attacked. Now this had come to pass. A well planned, superbly executed attack by six Japanese aircraft carriers stunned America and the world by the severity of damage the attacks achieved. In these circumstances an undermined national leadership would exacerbate an already dangerous situation. The course of action to be taken was clear and simple. Let Kimmel and Short shoulder the blame. This came naturally from pre-war mindsets and political self interest. Nor was it then clear that they weren't to blame.

Vice Admiral Frank E Beatty, ret. Aide to the late Secretary of the Navy, Frank Knox, in an Interview by U. S. News and World Report, date unknown, (enclosure X) states:

> I can say that prior to December 7th it was evident even to me, as I was reading the "magic" messages, that we were pushing Japan into a corner. I believe that it was the desire of President Roosevelt and of Prime Minister Churchill that we get into the war as they felt the allies could not win without us, and all our efforts to cause the Germans to declare war on us had failed. The conditions we imposed on Japan—to get out of China, for example—were so severe that we knew that nation could not accept. We did not want her to accept them. We were forcing her so severely that we should have known that she would react toward the United States. All her preparations in a military way—and we knew their overall import—pointed that way.

Although Admiral Beatty did not believe that Roosevelt knew of the impending attack, there is considerable evidence to the contrary. It is not conclusive, but not all the pertinent information has yet been released into the public domain. The evidence now known will be summarized. However, the matter of achieving justice for Kimmel and Short does not depend on any information beyond that now known. The known evidence is adequate.

Dorn Report Major Deficiencies

The Dorn Report findings are:

1. Responsibility for the Pearl Harbor disaster should not fall solely on the shoulders of Admiral Kimmel and General Short; it should be broadly shared.
2. To say that responsibility is broadly shared is not to absolve Admiral Kimmel and General Short of accountability.

3. The official treatment of Admiral Kimmel and General Short was substantially temperate and procedurally proper.
4. History has not been hostile to Admiral Kimmel and General Short.
5. There is not a compelling basis for advancing either officer to a higher grade.

While this presentation is directed at deficiencies in the Dorn Report, it is only fair and proper to point out that the Report, while lacking comprehension in some salient features of military operational life, is nevertheless exceptional in it's objectivity. While it has failed to include some highly pertinent and significant information that more thorough research would have revealed, we are nevertheless especially indebted for a presentation that permits a point counterpoint treatment of the case for posthumous advancement in rank for the two Pearl Harbor commanders. The Dorn Report is commendable also for recognizing that this subject cannot yet be put to rest. It states:

> On the other hand, sober analysis in the years since the publication of the Joint Congressional Committee's Report has produced a number of works of nuanced and balanced scholarship which constitutes the beginnings of the verdict of history. Those works, based on a careful reading of the entire record of the Joint Congressional Committee and of other primary sources that have come to light in the intervening years, are creating a responsible and increasingly accurate and just understanding of the tapestry of failure at Pearl Harbor. Ultimately, in a free society this must be the function of the academic community, and it is one that the academic community is performing well in this case.

Comment: An "increasingly accurate and just understanding" of the disaster's causes depends upon recognition of the essentiality of continuous intelligence inputs for effective command functioning and of the mutuality of command responsibility, one commander to another, in the command chain. As we shall see, Secretary Dorn reflects the general inability of non-professionals to distinguish between strategic intelligence, or statements of general warning applicable across a span of time, and tactical intelligence which provides minute-by-minute, hour-by-hour information updates that indicate change in the likelihood of a specific event occurring. This facet of the problem was clearly not understood in preparation of the Dorn Report.

Only recently has the general public learned from "other primary sources" the extraordinarily valuable information derived from codebreaking that inferred both time and place of the forthcoming attack. The importance of this information to Admiral Kimmel and General Short, but not provided them, as we shall see, was not comprehended in preparation of the Dorn Report. There are other basic faults. Given the risks being taken, both political and military, the President thought it expedient to take a more direct control of fleet operations. Dorn failed to take into account the added responsibility incurred by Washington as a consequence of that assumption of authority. More importantly, Dorn failed to recognize the essential relationship that must exist between conduct of foreign policy and employment of military force if we are to avoid disastrous consequences. The report's rationale with regard to important realities that guide and constrain force commanders in their conduct of operations is seriously flawed. Finally, in an assessment of fault, [we] must examine the operational options that were available to Kimmel and Short before the attack, and whether or not the arrangements that they made in the context of the information available to them reflected either bad judgment or omissions. That was not done.

Although we now have in the public domain much of the information available in Washington, but not in Hawaii, there remains one possibly crucial bit of evidence not yet released—the secure telephone conversation in which Churchill called Roosevelt early in the morning of 26 November, 1941, that may be central to the radical and sudden change in Roosevelt's attitude toward the then ongoing negotiations with Japan. Information from Secretary

Stimson concerning Japanese troop movements to the south most likely accounts for the war warning message sent Kimmel and Short November 27th. The coincidence of timing suggests this Churchill/Roosevelt conversation may also have played a role. Be that as it may, the case for restoring the reputations of Admiral Kimmel and General Short does not depend upon the content of that conversation.

We Must Understand Some Basic Premises and Fundamental Operational Realities

The commander assigning a mission to a subordinate commander is obligated to assign forces required for mission accomplishment. If force availability is deemed inadequate, the mission should be modified. The practice, and reality, in peacetime is that a force presence signifies intent, or will. Relatively small forces placed in harms way, when backed by clearly discernable national will, enjoy a degree of security and exercise influence beyond that inherent in the force itself. This can create a dangerous situation, however, when basic national interests are at issue, as was then the case with respect to Japan who imported 90% of it's oil from the United States.

Admiral Kimmel's forces were inferior to those available to the Japanese, substantially so. His predecessor. Admiral J. O. Richardson, was relieved of his command because of his unwillingness to keep the fleet stationed in Pearl Harbor because of it's vulnerability to surprise attack. Even so, several months after replacing Richardson with Kimmel, the President reduced Pacific Fleet forces a further 25 percent by transferring an aircraft carrier, three battleships, cruisers, destroyers and support ships to the Atlantic. Our President's strategy centered on providing all possible aid to Britain, including warship patrols in the western Atlantic. Since our military buildup was then in early stages, the President accepted the additional risk in the Pacific inherent in the transfer of major forces to the Atlantic.

Military events in the fall of 1941 caused the President to modify his strategy. The German Army was notably successful initially in it's invasion of the Soviet Union. The President foresaw a need to transfer Russian forces stationed in the Far East westward to assist in defense of Stalingrad and Moscow. To offset the possibility that Japan might attack a weakened Russian rear, he directed a strengthening of Army and Army Air Force forces in the Philippine Islands, diverting some forces otherwise destined for Britain. The B-17 bombers arriving Hickam Field, Oahu, the morning of December 7th were enroute the Philippines. These force movements themselves involved considerable chance taking by our national high command, since they could precipitate hostilities in the circumstances. No problem with that. The point is simply that in event of a miscalculation, a reverse or a defeat, a substantial amount of responsibility resides with the political and military leadership at the seat of government, since only that authority can orchestrate the necessary political and military interactions to reduce risks. If a miscalculation occurs, and for various (and good) reasons an admission of responsibility is unacceptable at the time of a disaster, acceptance is an obligation when those reasons no longer apply. The Dorn report took no account of the effect of force inferiority, especially in air power, and it's constraints on the operational options or initiatives that Kimmel could take. Dorn did not acknowledge that American policies and actions emphasizing support of Chunking and protection of the Soviet Union eastern provinces together with constraints on exports of oil served a strategic purpose, and were deciding factors in Japan's decision to initiate war with a surprise attack on the Pacific Fleet.

Admiral Kimmel was concerned at the weakened condition of his forces. He protested the transfer of the three battleships and the aircraft carrier *Yorktown* Battle Group to the Atlantic. Particularly significant was the loss of the *Yorktown*, as it left the Japanese navy with six large operational aircraft carriers a sizeable advantage in air strike power. Only three remained to Kimmel, the early carriers *Lexington* and *Saratoga,* and the more modern

Enterprise. Implicit in this transfer of forces was the degree of faith, existing in Washington, misplaced as we later learned, that Japan would not attack the Hawaiian Islands. Adoption by the administration soon thereafter of hardline policies toward the Japanese, as events soon proved, placed the Hawaiian commanders in untenable positions. A commitment further complicating, if not potentially compromising the President's domestic political situation, was his promise to the British and Dutch to come to their aid in event the Japanese initiated attack against their territories in the South Pacific. These actions were either miscalculations in Washington regarding the relative strengths of naval forces in the Pacific, a misplaced faith that the Japanese would not attack in Hawaii, or the President was willing to accept the risk of a Japanese attack somewhere in the Pacific.

I repeat for emphasis—the transfer of three battleships and an aircraft carrier to the Atlantic in the spring of 1941 left the Pacific fleet appreciably weaker than the Japanese fleet, especially in the all important carrier air strike aircraft category. This transfer severely constrained Kimmel's force employment options from that date forward.

The Role of Intelligence in the Application of Military Force

In all the books I have read about the disaster I find a common deficiency—they do not reflect an understanding of the essential interaction between fleet activity and operational intelligence. This is a major weakness in the Dorn Report as well. Even in "And I Was There" that interaction is taken for granted It is not explained. The reason is that assessing the significance of intelligence, then exploiting it, is a commander's responsibility, as is targeting of intelligence collection resources. The continuous presentation of intelligence, on the one hand, and exploiting it by redirecting ongoing fleet activity, on the other, makes clear that an extraordinary intimacy must exist between operations and intelligence. Smart command decisions depend upon an inflow of good, timely intelligence information.

One must understand the command need for a continuous accumulation of information from many sources for creation of a fund of knowledge that enhances command ability to function effectively. Within that information flow there is a category of time sensitive, operationally significant information (called opintel) that is pertinent to one's own situation and status at points in time. This "coin" has two sides: what one currently knows about a possible threat, and what one wants or needs to know, but doesn't. New information is continuously assessed in the light of other related information. A continuous appraisal is made of evolving situations in light of one's own activity as well as in the context of political developments and military activity elsewhere. The objective is to identify what to do in time so as to not lose control over evolving events, the imminence of which may be measured in minutes and hours. Often, information seemingly benign to recipients elsewhere, is viewed as quite significant when weighed in the context of other related information locally available and one's own activity at the time. For example: A submarine sighting near a port is interesting. If warships are about to depart, it is worrisome. In applying this process force commanders seek to control adversity by modifying ongoing operational activity to counter new developments. The demands of this process are why Admiral Kimmel held a meeting of key staff personnel at 3:00 PM, Saturday, December 6th, and asked the question about Japanese aircraft carrier locations that most authors mention.

A military historian whose name I have forgotten wrote that battles are won by commanders who make fewer mistakes. Mistakes occur when foresight is inadequate. At all points in time evolving military situations are characterized by uncertainty. Knowledge is imperfect. Seemingly minor occurances are often seen in retrospect to have set in motion a sequence of events that heavily influenced the outcome. The antidote to uncertainty is knowledge. Clearly, and importantly, Admiral Kimmel's 3:00 PM meeting that

Saturday afternoon. December 6th, was in search of a more perfect knowledge of the current situation, revealed by his comment about the location of the Japanese aircraft carriers. The story then unfolding in Washington, viewed in the context of intelligence from codebreaking during the previous several weeks, clearly foretold the likelihood of air attack against the fleet in Pearl Harbor that Sunday morning. But all of that information was withheld from Admiral Kimmel and General Short.

The central weakness of the Dorn Report is it's failure to understand the necessary intelligence/operational intimacy, and the potential consequences when lacking. Items two to ten, pages III-7 to III-11, inclusive, provide accurately what was known to Kimmel and Short. It does not identify operationally significant, time sensitive intelligence known in Washington, but not sent to Hawaii, that indicated both time and place of likely attack. Nor does it take into account the responsibilities of the Director of Naval Intelligence to ascertain and advise regarding possible enemy functional capabilities. Two quotes from the Dorn Report highlight this weakness.

> Despite this mass of evidence, the practical difficulties of conducting an aerial attack may have caused Admiral Kimmel and General Short to minimize its likelihood." (page III-10).

Comment: The practical difficulties referred to in this first quote, and the failure of naval intelligence to accurately assess the likely effectiveness of Japanese naval men and materials did, indeed, create an opinion that an air attack against Pearl Harbor might be damaging but not disastrous. This failure is attributable to the Director, Naval Intelligence, in Washington. As to the views of Kimmel and Short, any force commander is determined to defeat any attack, whether major or minor. The record is replete with information that neither Kimmel nor Short minimized the likelihood of an air attack. As to the "mass of evidence," the evidence that was both valid, timely and precise remained in Washington in intelligence withheld, as we shall soon see. There is no evidence that any military officer, Army or Navy, minimized the likelihood of a surprise air attack against Oahu. Throughout the 30's major fleet exercises drove that point home, and were the basis for the requirement for 120 B-17s for General Short (12 provided) and 100 naval patrol planes (none provided) for the Commandant, 14th Naval District. There is implied evidence that our civilian leadership in Washington minimized that likelihood in establishing national political and military priorities. All shared the belief that such an attack would have limited success. For example, of the two air weapons, torpedoes and bombs, and general recognition that torpedoes had the greater potential for damage where they could be used, that specific threat was dismissed. In response to Secretary of the Navy Knox's concern regarding a torpedo attack similar to that delivered against the Italian Navy, noting the greater depth of water in the south of Italy, the Chief of Naval Operations, Admiral Stark, in Washington in early 1941 provided detailed technical advice to the Pacific Fleet and the Commandant, 14th Naval District as follows:

> Consideration has been given to the installation of A/T (anti-torpedo) baffles within Pearl Harbor for protection against torpedo attack. It is considered that the relatively shallow depth of the water limits the need for anti-torpedo nets in Pearl Harbor. In addition, the congestion and the necessity for maneuvering room limit the practibility of the present type of baffles—a minimum depth of water of 75' may be assumed necessary to successfully drop torpedoes from planes. 150' of water is desired. The maximum height planes at present experimentally drop torpedoes is 250'. Launching speeds are between 120 and 150 knots. The desirable height for dropping is 60' or less. About 200 yards of torpedo run is necessary before the exploding device is armed but this may be altered.

Given the dimensions of water in Pearl Harbor, with depths less than 40', it was Washinton's assessment that discounted that danger. Nor was there capability in Hawaii to remedy that deficiency if Kimmel had reason to think otherwise.

The second Dorn Report quote states:

> This exclusive reliance on Washington for both tactical and strategic warning is at the heart of the failure at Pearl Harbor, and of the debate about the failure. The record suggests that officials in Washington believed they had provided strategic warning with their messages of November 27th; neither Admiral Kimmel nor General Short read the messages that way. The debate over the handling of Japan's 14-part message on December 6th and the morning of December 7th is about tactical warning. Admiral Kimmel and General Short did not get tactical warning.

Comment: This quote captures succinctly the single most significant area of disagreement in allocating blame for the disaster and does, indeed, go to the very heart of the problem. If, in fact, it is true that Washington thought it's responsibilities discharged by this last of several strategic warning messages, then we have an example of an egregious degree of ignorance by senior naval professionals that is hard to believe, hard to attribute to bureaucratic bungling, especially given the letter Admiral Kimmel gave Admiral Stark in June, 1941. The earlier assumption of authority by the Director of War Plans over distribution of intelligence, then his subsequent failure to assure that this intelligence went out was a most grievous error the net effect of which was to mislead Admiral Kimmel, and directly affect his assessment of the situation in the days and hours preceding the attack.

A more reasonable explanation for assertions that providing "strategic" warning was adequate is that it served the political purpose of diverting criticism. As to the Dorn Report, this quote also assumes adequacy of patrol plane resources and other long range surveillance means that simply were not available to Kimmel or to Short, but which means were, in fact, available from codebreaking in Washington. This quote drives home the point that Dorn has no understanding of the role of tactical intelligence in the operational decision process, which lack has also appeared in a number of books written about Pearl Harbor. As will be noted.

Admiral King stated a misuse by Admiral Kimmel of his patrol plane resources in his endorsement opposing the findings in the report by the Navy Court of Inquiry. That criticsm provided a convenient device to avoid a public relations debacle while the war was still in progress. It was also an endorsement Admiral King later retracted. See Exhibit K.

No one has stated the case better for complete and timely support by Washington regarding policy and intelligence updates than Admiral Kimmel himself. Having been informed by Vice Admiral Wilson Brown in February, 1941, that there was "confusion" in Washington regarding responsibilities for keeping him advised regarding intelligence, and having received in personal letters from Admiral Stark information that could have come only from codebreaking of Japanese message traffic. Admiral Kimmel handed the Chief of Naval Operations, Admiral Stark, a letter during his visit in Washington in June, 1941, that contained the following:

> The Commander-in Chief, Pacific Fleet, is in a very difficult position. He is far removed from the seat of government, in a complex and rapidly changing situation. He is, as a rule, not informed as to the policy, or change of policy, reflected in current events and naval movements and, as a result, is unable to evaluate the possible effect upon his own situation. He is not even sure of what force will be available to him and has little voice in matters radically affecting his ability to carry out his assigned tasks. This lack of information is disturbing and tends to create uncertainty, a condition that directly contravenes that singleness of purpose and confidence in one's own course of action so necessary to the conduct of military operations.
>
> It is realized that, on occasion, the rapid development in the international picture, both diplomatic and military, and, perhaps, even the lack of knowledge of the military authorities themselves, may militate against the furnishing of timely information, but certainly the present situation is susceptible to marked improvement. Full and authoritative knowledge of current poli-

cies and objectives, even though necessarily late at times, would enable the Commander-in-Chief, Pacific Fleet, to modify, adapt, even re-orient his possible courses of action to conform to current concepts. This is particularly applicable to the current Pacific situation, where the necessities for intensive training of a partially trained Fleet must be carefully balanced against the desirability of interruption of this training by strategic dispositions, or otherwise, to meet impending eventualities. Moreover, due to this same factor of distance and time, the Department itself is not too well informed as to the local situation, particularly with regard to the status of current outlying island development, thus making it even more necessary that the Commander-in-Chief, Pacific Fleet, be guided by broad policy and objectives rather than by categorical instructions.

It is suggested that it be made a cardinal principle that the Commander-in-Chief, Pacific Fleet, be immediately informed of all important developments as they occur and by the quickest secure means available.

Several years later, after Admiral Kimmel had learned of all the information held in Washington that could, and should, have been provided him, he wrote:

> The Navy Department thus engaged in a course of conduct which definitely gave me the impression that intelligence from important intercepted Japanese messages was being furnished to me. Under these circumstances a failure to send me important information of this character was not merely a withholding of intelligence. It amounted to an affirmative misrepresentation—This failure not only deprived me of essential facts. It misled me.

The stage for the disaster was set in April, 1941, by the Director of War Plans when he took control of distribution of any intelligence that might prompt a fleet commander to move forces. He did this with the concurrence of the Chief of Naval Operations. It rmust be noted that this new arrangement was without precedent. It represented a change in a procedure that was doctrinal in nature.

Nor was any explanation of the change, or of the reasons therefor, made known to the fleet commanders. The then subsequent failure to keep Kimmel properly informed of obviously important intelligence was an error in judgment of major proportion. This decision increased enormously the responsibility of authorities in Washington for any consequent disaster if, as happened, the flow of essential information ceased. The record is clear that very significant information from codebreaking, essential to a proper exercise of command, was denied Kimmel and Short.

Commanders of forces then and now have no choice but to rely on Washington for wide area surveillance. During WWI "radio intelligence" first exploited enemy use of radio transmissions for their control of forces. This exploitation included codebreaking, which also had great political import, so collection, analysis, security protection and prioritization became located at seats of government. Dissemination of information thus derived became the responsibility of top level military authority. Since a commander can only make sense in his force employment if he possesses related intelligence, top commands at seats of government took on a shared responsibility for force effectiveness and security. As noted above, this obligation was ignored by the Director of War Plans and the Chief of Naval Operations in the months preceding Pearl Harbor. Kimmel and Short were denied, despite their many complaints, information they needed to properly employ their forces.

With regard to Kimmel's state of mind, note that when the carriers *Lexington* and *Enterprise* departed Pearl Harbor in the days preceeding the Japanese attack with reinforcements for Wake and Midway, Halsey placed his forces on a full wartime basis, with authority to shoot. Every senior force commander knows that a direction of this sort is done only with the compliance, or by direction, of the next higher authority. No complacency there! No indication there of an unlikelihood of attack mentality!

The Dorn Report criticised Admiral Kimmel for not using his cruiser based amphibious aircraft to augment his search coverage. Consider the search problem. To reach the Japanese air strike launch point 275 miles from Pearl Harbor at daybreak, December 7th, the attacking group would be about 550 miles at sunset , December 6th, and 800 miles at sunrise, December 6th. Presumably cruiser searches would have started November 27th. There were few cruisers, their search capabilities very limited. This would have presented severe logistical problems, and logistics support was very limited, an impediment already to even sustained local operations. The comment does reveal the lack of depth of inquiry into the limitations that constrained fleet operational activity represented by the researchers and preparers of the Dorn Report.

Dorn's assertion that exclusive reliance on Washington for tactical warning was at the heart of the failure at Pearl Harbor assumes adequacy of reconnaissance resources when their availability was but a small fraction of the requirement. To criticise the admiral for not using his cruiser aircraft for long range search is reaching for straws.

As to the likelihood of a Japanese air attack against Pearl Harbor, as distinct from it's expected effectiveness, throughout 1940 and until departure of *Yorktown* in April, 1941, as a fighter pilot in VF-5, the *Yorktown* fighter squadron, I personally flew dawn and dusk patrols against that possibility of an air attack whenever the ship was in Pearl Harbor. There was never any lack of "strategic warning" in the sense used in the Report, nor of awareness of the possibility of a surprise air attack. An attribution otherwise is uninformed and unwarranted. This failure, of course, presumes a degree of ignorance of the intelligence process at top levels of navy command in Washington that may not be true. There may be another explanation, one having to do with the degree to which direct control of fleet operational activity in both oceans was being exercised by Washington. Given the course of international developments on the one hand, and domestic political determination to avoid involvement in the conflict on the other, the Director of War Plans action is understandable. What is not understandable is his failure to then discharge the responsibilities he so eagerly sought. The subsequent severity of the Pearl Harbor attack made it indiscreet to admit this confused state of affairs. The Dorn Report neither recognizes nor admits to this.

Along time, common practice, one that was increased in numbers of units involved in the weeks before the disaster, was protection from submarine attack while warships egressed or ingressed Pearl Harbor. Detection equipment in those days was technically weak, especially as to reliability of identity of contacts. As a result, more whales than submarines were reported as submarines and destroyed in the early days of the war.

There is another facet to the problem of balancing risk versus maintenance and training, in which dependence is placed on incoming intelligence. One must understand that deployed naval forces are fully occupied 24 hours a day, seven days a week, in numerous "housekeeping" chores, including maintenance, and training in pursuit of mission assignment. Nor must command neglect the mental and physical needs of personnel that include athletics and recreation after periods at sea. A command, thusly, is always engaged in more or less essential activity, defined in operating schedules, from which one departs as made necessary by incoming intelligence or direction from above. A commander of deployed forces is continuously and directly involved in assessing the significance of incoming information to the end that "harmful" disruptions of ongoing activity within the force occur as seldom as a changing situation warrants or avoidance of surprise mandates. We all know the loss of confidence in command that attends "cry wolf" nervous Nellies. We who served in warships moored in Pearl Harbor in the late thirties before air conditioning came along also know why ships were not buttoned up to resist until evidence existed of a high probability of an attack. In sum, incoming intelligence triggers operational initiatives in a dynamic process on a twenty-four hour, seven days a week basis. The Secretary of the Navy message providing strategic warning simply acknowledged something Pacific fleet commanders had known for several years. For that matter, so did I.

So, what was known in Washington that Kimmel needed to know, but didn't? There follows information known in Washington, but not sent Hawaii, from October 9 to December 7, 1941, Some of them highlight Japanese interest in detailed information regarding ships in Pearl Harbor. They can be compared for completeness with that presented in the Dorn Report (page III-18).

—Dorn cites the "bomb plot "message, translated October 9th, as available in Washington but not in Hawaii. Dorn makes no further reference to this important indicator of interest in detailed information needed by Japan to plan air assaults against ships in port there. Nor does Dorn mention other related information held in Washington. The first such evidence originated with "Tricycle," a German double agent. The Federal Bureau of Investigation informed Navy of Japanese interest in harbor details and warship locations in Pearl Harbor. Navy responded with information then passed to "Tricycle" by the FBI to preserve his credentials as a spy working for the Axis powers. Kimmel was not informed of any of this information exchange. Details are provided in Exhibit D.

Comment: The bomb plot messsage was sent September 24th, 1941 to the Japanese consul-general in Honolulu. It divided Pearl Harbor into five areas, and specified that reports were to be made regarding identity of ships within each area, including those at anchor, those that were moored and those moored alongside others. This information was of a specificity that made plain it's purpose—planning for an air attack! When Admiral Kimmel learned of this message years later, he remarked to his family that with this knowledge, given his limited force availabilities, he would have been much more forceful in his dealings with the Navy Department.

—November 15th J-19 code # 111 (translated 12/3) Tokyo to Honolulu states as relations between Japan and the United States most critical make ships in harbor report irregularly at least twice weekly.
—November 18th J-19 code #113 (translated 12/5) Tokyo to Honolulu Special report on ship locations requested.
—November 18th J-19 code #222 (translated 12/6) Honolulu to Tokyo Reports additional ship locations
—November 29th J-19 (Navy translated 12/5) Tokyo to Honolulu We are getting your ship movement reports. Now report even when ships not moving.

See Exhibit E for text of decoded messages revealing sustained and detailed interest in Pearl Harbor, and the identity and location of major warships when moored in the harbor. Their timing in relation to the "purple" diplomatic traffic increases their significance, a point also missed by the preparers of the Dorn Report. In this regard, a factor in assessing the significance of information contained in any intercept is the review of earlier, related information and consideration of other activity that is ongoing in the same time frame as the intercept being read. This observation of a thought process is so obvious that it is a given that Washington based analysts using the intelligence intercepts then available were doing just that. It is in this context that the most significant of all the intercepts, the 14 part message received December 6th and in a separate message, it's delivery instructions, should be interpreted. An attack on Pearl Harbor early on the morning of December 7th was highly probable.

While these messages were being decoded and distributed, so were other messages then being sent to Japanese embassies world wide directing destruction of codes and provision of alternative methods for providing information.

A second category of Japanese message traffic, that being sent the Japanese Ambassador in Washington in the Purple, or diplomatic code, was being translated by our Army and Navy codebreakers and distributed, but only in Washington. None of these were provided Kimmel or Short. As noted above, when viewed in the context of the other intercepts held in Washington, the diplomatic code messages clearly indicated the time and place of the surprise attack. The more significant ones follow.

—November 5th Purple (Diplomatic) code #736 (translated 11/5) Tokyo to Washington states that because of various circumstances, it is absolutely necessary that all arrangements for the signing of this agreement be completed by the 25th of this month.
—November 16th Purple code (translated 11/17) Tokyo to Washington Refers to #736 above Advises. ". . . In your opinion we ought to wait and see what turn the war takes (refers to German assault on Russia) and remain patient. However, I am awfully sorry to say that the situation renders this out of the question. I set the deadline for the solution to these negotiations in 736 (ie, 25 November) and there will be no change" and "You see how short time is, therefore do not allow the United States to sidetrack us and delay the negotiations any further. . . ."

Comment: The implications of this message must be assessed knowing that the Japanese are witnessing the buildup of our B-17 bomber forces in the Philippine Islands, and that this change in military posture is very recent.

—November 22nd #812 purple code Tokyo to Washington Another reference to #736 "It is awfully hard for us to consider changing the date we set in my #736. . . . There are reasons beyond your ability to guess why we wanted to settle Japanese-American relations by the 25th, but if within the next three or four days you can (settle satisfactorily) we have decided to wait until that date." "This for information of you two ambassadors alone."

Comment: Reasons beyond your ability to guess? and, in the preceeding message above ". . . therefore do not allow the United

States to delay the negotiations any further." Something big is imminent. Look for clues!

—November 30th #985 purple code instructs the Japanese ambassador to inform Hitler of British and American provocativeness, and that the Empire faces a "grave situation and must act with determination," that there is extreme danger that war may "come quicker than anyone dreams" and that this information must be held in the most absolute secrecy.

—December 1st Purple #865 (translated 12/4) Tokyo to Washington Situation continues increasingly critical however, to prevent U. S. from being unduly suspicious, we advising press and others in Japan negotiations continue.

Comment: "However, to prevent the United States from becoming unduly suspicious"— Suspicious? of what? We (Japan) will employ deception for "reasons beyond your ability to guess."

—December 2nd Purple #867 (translated 12/3-4) Tokyo to Washington directs specific code destructions.
—December 6th Purple #901 (translated 12/6) Tokyo to Washington Extremely sensitive message in 14 parts coming. Await specific instructions by separate message as to when to present it.
—December 6th Purple #902 first 13 parts (translated 12/6) Tokyo to Washington. This message reviews entire sequence of negotiations, notes the hardening of the U S proposal of November 26th "as a result of frequent consultations with Great Britain, Australia, The Netherlands and Chunking," concludes these nations are as one in ignoring Japan's position.

Comment: When read by the President and close advisor, Harry Hopkins about 07:30 on the evening of December 6th, the President exclaimed: "This means war."

—December 7th Purple #902 14th part (translated by Navy about midnight 12/6) . Tokyo to Washington States U. S. and Britain

conspired to thwart Japan. Not possible to reach agreement through further negotiations.
—December 7th Purple #907 (translated by Army during night of 12/6-7) Tokyo to Washington Directs Ambassador to present 14 part message to Secretary of State at 1300 Washington time, December 7th.

The Japanese decoded message traffic is taken from the appendix in "Pearl Harbor, Final Judgment" by Clausen. The complete messages from which the above are gisted are provided in Exhibit F.

Another mishandled, significant indicator of an early surprise attack by the Japanese against either the Philippines or Hawaii was the so-called Winds Instruction message, translated November 26th and provided to Admiral Kimmel, not by Washington, but by the Commander, Asiatic Fleet, and the Winds Execute, or enemy identification message. The Winds Instruction message alerted various Japanese authorities of a possible initiation of hostilities against either Russia, the British and Dutch or the Americans, the choice to be indicated later in the form of a plain language weather report. This arrangement assumed previous orders to destroy codes will have been implemented. This message was intercepted November 19th, J-19 code numbers 2353 and 2354 and translated Nov 26th and 28th. The Dorn Report indicates that Kimmel was informed of this advisory of a soon-to-be-sent identity of who the enemy would be. In an overstatement of it's significance he records as an error of judgment and evidence of an unacceptable state of cooperation between Kimmel and Short, Kimmel's failure to pass this information to General Short.

More interesting, and far more significant, is what occurred following receipt in Washington of the execute message in which the United States was identified as the enemy. Why was that information not provided Kimmel and Short? This second message, the Winds Execute message, was erroneously claimed to have not been received in Washington. We now know that the Winds Execute message was intercepted by Naval Communications

Station Cheltenhelm late on December 4th and immediately relayed to the Navy Department. It made it's way partially through the Navy bureaucracy, and then "disappeared." Details and sources are described in CRYPTOLOGIA in Exhibit G to this presentation. Confirmation was also provided by Army Brigadier General Clarke, an intelligence specialist, who saw the message. Admiral Kimmel was not informed of this development, nor was General Short. This message stated that the outbreak of hostilities would occur against American territory and/or forces. If Kimmel's failure to inform Short of the earlier Winds Instruction message was a significant error in judgment, what harm resulted from that failure? How much more grievous is Washington's failure to inform either Kimmel or Short of the execute message?

At least one principle cause of the extent of the Pearl Harbor disaster was clearly understood to have it's roots in Washington. There is a quite remarkable admission by Henry Clausen and Bruce Lee in "Pearl Harbor, Final Judgment" since their comments otherwise are the most critical of Admiral Kimmel in any book on that subject known to me. In an astonishing inconsistency, they attribute the disaster to the foulup in and by Washington in managing highly sensitive, relevant intelligence information, and conclude that had the intelligence been properly handled, the disaster could have been prevented. Their comments are provided in Exhibit H. Secretary of War, Henry Stimson, also suspected the real cause to be mishandled intelligence information. In "Marching Orders" author Bruce Lee states that on January 19, 1942, Stimson charged Alfred McCormack, a trusted associate, to recommend new procedures for handling and disseminating information derived from breaking enemy codes, overruling army opposition in the process. Referring to the decoded message traffic disseminated within Washington prior to Pearl Harbor, (but not sent Kimmel) McCormack writes Stimson that "it became apparent that the event had been clearly foreshadowed in the Japanese traffic of 1941. By his action Stimson makes clear his concerns regarding management of decoded messages.

Also in "Pearl Harbor, Final Judgment" author Clausen cites Stimson in equating Kimmel and Short to sentries. Stimson used that analogy in describing the magnitude of delinquency he attributed to the two Hawaiian commanders. But, who were the real sentries, the ones with eyes to see and ears to hear? They were the code breakers in Washington.

Why, then, did Stimson later refer to Kimmel and Short as sentries? The reason is clear. Stimson entertained two different explanations for the disaster; one for political reasons given the gravity of the military situation we then faced, the other to prevent additional disasters.

Realities in Command Relationships. Constraints on Command Authority

Another major contributing factor to the disaster was, as noted earlier, a migration of authority from the fleet commanders-in-chief to the Directorate of War Planning in the offices of the Chief of Naval Operations commensurate with the President's assumption of a more detailed control of fleet operations. Again, no problem, that is, until something goes wrong, for the President was very personally engaged in the two-pronged, dangerous endeavor of constraining Japan in it's aggressions while continuing to provide the greatest possible direct support to Britain. When the President replaced Admiral Richardson (no kin) in the fall of 1940, for attempting to move the Pacific Fleet away from Pearl Harbor, where it had been basing since about March, 1940, every fleet and force commander knew that the President was now exercising a degree of personal control over fleet activity. Henceforth, any significant force movement would, first, have to be cleared with Washington. By his action the President also transferred a degree of responsibility for fleet security from Hawaii to Washington. This is not an error in judgment by the President. As noted previously, the decision to keep the fleet in Hawaii was a move calculated for it's political effect.

The potential for disaster arose later, with the subsequent movement of three battleships and the carrier *Yorktown* to the Atlantic in April, 1941, an action that substantially weakened the Pacific Fleet, especially in air power. As noted, these movements left Japan with a substantial advantage in air strike power and Admiral Kimmel with fewer operational options available to him. This was a risk taken, later proved to be an error in judgment, with it's origin in Washington in the administration.

Senior Navy force commanders were further reminded of the migration to Washington of an increased degree of operational control by another event that occurred in January, 1941. "A Well Kept Secret" is an article written by Admiral Robert B. Carney published by *Shipmate* in the June, 1983 issue. The admiral (then a commander) recounts receiving a telephone call from BUPERS on January 31st, 1941, advising that he would receive orders within hours detaching him from Executive Officer of the battleship California, in Hawaii, to report to the Chief of Naval Operations in Washington "without delay." Asking to detour via Coronado to see his wife, he was told "no." Upon his arrival, Admiral Bristol, to whom the CNO directed Carney to report, informed him that (Exhibit I):

> the President had decided to form a special force for protection of shipping in the Atlantic, and that certain ships and aircraft would be allocated to the force. Because of still-existing popular aversion to U.S. involvement in the war, the innocuous title of Support Force was assigned. Bristol would be responsible to the President, not to the Navy's Atlantic Command—a most unusual arrangement.

When Carney submitted to Bristol a budget proposal for $10 million, Bristol replied:

> We would spend that in a week: we will seek $100 million." Thereafter "we" applied the Bristol Factor—multiply by 10.

Thus, in the immediate aftermath of the firing of Richardson, we have the President taking direct control of the soon to be "engaged" naval forces in the Atlantic. Control was moved from the commander-in-chief in Norfolk, VA, in this specific instance to Washington. Domestic opposition to an involvement in the European war was strong. This arrangement likely could better assure accommodation to domestic political realities. And, of course, assumption of control of distribution of significant current intelligence, ie operational, or tactical intelligence, by the Director of War Plans in Washington to avoid unanticipated initiatives by a fleet commander, as noted earlier, further diminished the authority of Admiral Kimmel, limiting his operational options or freedom to act.

Observations and Assessments

Having explained that operational options are identified and/or implemented depending upon the degree of knowledge available at the time, is it not ironic that literally within minutes of the time Kimmel and his staff were engaged in assessing his situation in Honolulu, the President in Washington, upon completing reading the Japanese 13 part message to Nomura, remarked; "This means war," then upon return to his dinner guests, "We will be at war tomorrow." See Exhibit S. What possible supposition can explain Washington's failure to advise the Hawaiian commanders of an appraisal of this magnitude, based on information available in Washington but not in Hawaii? On the basis of diplomatic message codebreaking alone the likely location of an attack was indicated at about midnight, December 6th, when the 14th part of PURPLE was received, as were instructions for delivery. The Japanese choice of time for effecting delivery when assessed in the context of the decoded J-19 and Purple message traffic recorded in this presentation, surely indicate an enormous likelihood that war will commence at about 07:30 AM, Hawaiian time. The Japanese penchant for initiating combat with a surprise attack was fully understood by military officers. And time was a strong indicator of place.

Diplomats, if anything, are knowledgeable about and deferential to the well known habits of their counterparts. Thus, Washington's knowledge that Ambassador Nomura was receiving instructions to seek a meeting with Secretary of State Cordell Hull at 1:00 PM, Sunday, December 7th, did, indeed, raise very loud alarm bells. That was 07:30 Hawaiian time. Given the then widely known capabilities of carrier based aircraft—that launches took place at first light to accomplish join up, and so that as much time remained during daylight to increase extent of damage—identified Hawaii as the likely target of a surprise attack. As we would now say, it takes no rocket scientist to draw that conclusion. So here, again, the failure to notify Kimmel and Short immediately was another grievous error in judgment. There exists evidence that a meeting of principal advisers with the President took place in the White House around midnight on the 6th. Navy secretary Knox expressed surprise to Admiral Kimmel during his visit to Pearl Harbor following the attack that he had not been alerted to the events of December 6th, an item presumably discussed during that meeting. However, for whatever reasons, Kimmel was not informed.

An anomaly among many, one that appears to reflect the tightness of control being exercised in Washington over fleet activity, occurred at about 10:30 Sunday morning, two and a half hours before the attack. The CNO, Admiral Stark, was being briefed on the 14 part Purple message and it's delivery instructions. The briefer pleaded with Admiral Stark to pickup the phone and call Admiral Kimmel. Stark picked it up, thought a moment and put it back down, saying he would "call the President instead." Had he called as requested, Kimmel would have had what he needed to implement his one remaining operational option—setting General Quarters, an action that can be completed in fifteen minutes.

In his statement to the attendees assembled in the Senate Armed Service's Hearing room on April 27th, 1995, Admiral

Moorer, former Chairman of the Joint Chiefs of Staff, notes the strange behavior of the Chief of Staff, U S Army General George C. Marshall and Chief of Naval Operations, Admiral Stark, during the night of December 6th and the following morning. Seemingly, neither was available at a time both they and the President well knew was exceedingly dangerous. (Exhibit A, pages 32, 33.) Admiral Moorer notes that in his view Admiral Kimmel used the forces available and the capabilities available to their extreme. On another occasion he has stated that if Nelson and Napoleon had been in command in Hawaii, the results would have been the same. Admiral Moorer stated to the assembled group:

> So I think in all justice, anyone that has to make a decision on this problem should make certain that they are completely aware; A) of the military situation in Hawaii and the Pacific Ocean and B) the political situation and the information that was available here in Washington. And I believe if one really gives that a thorough look, and uses common sense in his judgment, he will see that the fair thing to do is to restore the rank of 4 stars to Admiral Kimmel.

Courses of Action Available to the Administration in Washington

A too often overlooked parallel to the relationship of intelligence to military initiatives is it's relationship to initiation of diplomatic actions. Diplomatic initiatives can also be taken in the course of evolving situations in reaction to incoming intelligence. We had a situation that December 6th where the President and his military leaders in Washington had an operational option, an initiative available to them, that Kimmel, lacking that information, did not. It matters not that Stark was at an opera and Marshall was who knows where—the intelligence judged by the President as indicating war was available in Washington sixteen hours before the attack. The President could have directed notification of the

Japanese embassy, or the Japanese in Tokyo, of his "suspicions," thereby eliminating in Japanese minds any benefit to be derived from surprise. Such notification could have been accomplished in ways that would not have involved a breach of security. His other option was to make sure Kimmel knew. He did neither.

Courses of Action Available to Admiral Kimmel and General Short

The Dorn Report asserts that the fact that others were also at fault does not absolve Admiral Kimmel and General Short from accountability. If Kimmel and Short were derelict, as the Robert's Commission judged, or used faulty judgment as the Dorn Report claims, that issue is properly resolved by considering the courses of action (operational options) available to Kimmel and Short but not used, or not properly used. Where was judgment faulty, and what resulted therefrom? Did failures by others create or lead to faulty decisions by Admiral Kimmel and General Short? Was it within their combined capabilities to have initiated actions that would have thwarted the Japanese attack, or substantially reduced the scale of deaths and damage? Is not this the crux in an assessment of their blame?

Both aircraft carrier battle groups, the *Enterprise* and *Lexington,* departed Pearl during the two weeks prior to the surprise attack pursuant to orders from Washington with reinforcements for Wake and Midway Islands. When not engaged in gunnery and other fleet exercises at sea, units of the fleet were moored in Pearl Harbor. When in port, crews were required to be aboard in adequate numbers day and night to set General Quarters and to man all (repeat, all) antiaircraft guns. Ammunition was placed in ready ammunition boxes at all AAA gun sites. The orders in effect required one fourth to one half of the antiaircraft guns, depending on the type of ship, to actually be manned at all times when in port. Small ships had the lower requirement. The specified condition of readiness required that ships watertight integrity be maintained except where necessary for regular access by the crew. Is it not noteworthy that these orders remained in effect throughout the year following the surprise attack? These arrangements assured that the full defensive capabilities of the ships in Pearl Harbor could be employed, a fourth to a half of the ship-based anti-aircraft guns instantly, the balance in minutes. Admiral Inglis testified that on the morning of the attack, all (repeat, all) antiaircraft batteries were manned and firing within four to seven minutes.

The 3:00 PM Saturday staff meeting convened by Admiral Kimmel reviewed the general situation and current fleet status. In the absence of air support, ordering the ships to sea would be unwise, pointless. Apart from his plans for conducting surveillance, his only option was to set General Quarters, thereby making his ships more resistant to damage from air and submarine attack. For this he needed indications that an attack was imminent. The discussion during the 3:00 PM meeting that referred to the lack of knowledge of the location of the Japanese aircraft carriers did not warrant any initiative beyond that indicated the day before, or the day before that. Nor was there reason to take exception to General Short's interpretation of the war warning message in the absence of indicators of imminent attack, indicators that even then were being distributed and read in Washington, and interpreted as "We will be at war tomorrow."

However, force commanders remain responsible for making sound decisions governing their force employment whether or not the available intelligence is adequate. To further clarify what Kimmel could have done to greater advantage December 6th, let us assume that Washington had kept Kimmel fully informed, and Kimmel had concluded that an attack was likely the next morning. Or, assume that despite long odds his reconnaisance aircraft had spotted the Japanese attack force during daylight, December 6th. What could he have done that would have defeated the attack, or reduced the extent of damage?

If the admiral had ordered the fleet to sea, what would have been it's purpose? To seek and destroy, pitting battleships against carriers in a venture ad absurdum? To hide? The prevalent professional view at the time was that pitting 18 knot battleships armed with 15 mile turreted guns against 30 knot aircraft carriers with 275 mile air strike ranges was foolish. Given the six carrier strength of the attacking force, even with full information the only prudent option available to Admiral Kimmel was to remain in port and set general quarters at sunrise in preparation for an attack. Presumably he would have done that. Although we are dealing here with conjecture, the point is that Admiral Kimmel did the only sensible thing, which was the same with or without intelligence, and no one has yet identified what he should have done differently that can withstand critical scrutiny. That challenge stands open. Given the relative strengths of Japanese naval forces and those available to Admiral Kimmel, it is clear that the Japanese were in complete control of events. The idea that it was within Kimmel's power to have somehow thwarted or overcome the attack is nonsense.

The Navy Court of Inquiry convened in 1943 to inquire into the Pearl Harbor disaster was composed of three very senior naval officers. Their reasoning was that of experienced force commanders. The realities enumerated above were known, and their significance understood, by these three gentlemen. This court found Admiral Kimmel blameless. Pertinent also is the fact that this court knew of the decoded Japanese messages, including those recorded in this paper, that were distributed in Washington, but not sent to Admiral Kimmel. Their finding, however, was reversed at the political level, first by the CNO, Admiral King, who cited misuse of Kimmel's surveillance resources as his reason, and by further endorsement by the Secretary of the Navy, who cited misuse of his patrol aircraft Kimmel's "most grevious fault." As previously noted, Admiral King in a July 14th, 1948 letter to the Secretary of Defense withdrew his endorsement.

Also pertinent in this regard is that in an earlier appeal by the Kimmel family, the then Chief of Naval Operations, Admiral Carlyle Trost, relying on a report by the naval historian who also cited misuse of Kimmel's patrol planes, recommended against approval. Upon reading the recent, thorough analysis of Admiral Kimmel's use of his patrol planes by Mr. Gannon (exhibit T), Admiral Trost advised the Secretary of the Navy that he no longer supported the position he had taken, and requested that his adverse endorsement on the Kimmel family request be withdrawn. See Exhibit L. The Gannon analysis convincingly demonstrates that Kimmel simply did not have aircraft in anywhere near the numbers required for even sustained 180 degree coverage. It is noted that Admiral Kimmel sought and followed the advice of his top air commanders in employing his patrol aircraft. His decisions were not arbitrary.

It should be noted here that all forces assigned the Pacific Fleet in war plans approved in Washington were for employment at sea away from Pearl Harbor. War plans at war's outset envisioned fleet operations toward Midway to the northwest and the Japanese controlled Marshall Islands to the west and southwest. Patrol aircraft would patrol this operating area to permit a more secure and effective employment of Pacific Fleet's three aircraft carriers (one of which was on the West Coast at the time of the attack) and nine battleships in offensive and defensive operations pending reinforcement. The pace of employment of patrol aircraft prior to war's outbreak was constrained by the needs of that operational readiness requirement.

Ships of the fleet when in Pearl were placed in Army plans for coordination of anti-aircraft defenses, with the Commander 14th Naval District the designated adviser to the Senior Officer Present Afloat in implementation of those plans. The 14th Naval District Commander maintained liaison with the Army in effecting those arrangements. Defense of Hawaii was an Army responsibility. Readiness status of Army forces in Hawaii were matters under control of Lieutenant General Short and General Marshall in Washington. Here an error of significance occurred. The war warning message to General Short was interpreted to mean the principal danger was sabotage. Short ordered his fighter aircraft placed in the center of his airfields, with guards to prevent their being sabotaged and, as directed in the Army war warning message (Exhibit J), reported the action he was taking to Army headquarters in Washington. In subsequent testimony General Marshall admitted his opportunity and failure in this instance. The Army Pearl Harbor Board generally criticised the conduct of the Secretary of Army, the Chief of Staff, the then Chief of War Plans Division and General Short, but made no recommendations.

Was Kimmel derelict in not objecting to General Short's action? Had he been in possession of the intelligence available in Washington and not done so, he would have been. His interjection, however, would have been limited to an expression of an opinion. The authorities and responsibilities of force commanders in the field were specified and allocated by the respective chiefs of services in Washington, with approval by the President, not by Admiral Kimmel, who was devoid of authority to change plans that were arranged between Generals Short and Marshall.

Despite the pledge by the Deputy Secretary of Defense to "examine the matter without preconceptions so that a Judgment can be reached on the basis of fact and fairness," it is obvious that the Dorn Report relies instead primarily on information contained in earlier hearings and inquiries that were designed to deflect criticism from Washington. Statements and accusations that we now know are inaccurate, or false, that appeared in the congressional inquiry reappear in the Dorn Report, and are included with comment in exhibit M.

Conclusions

1. In summary, the disaster at Pearl Harbor was rooted in and caused by:
    A. The adoption in Washington of a military strategy that weakened the forces allocated to the Pacific Fleet substantially below those available to the Japanese during a time and in an area of likely conflict, while

B. Incrementally increasing the economic, political and military pressures on the Japanese government by limiting sales and shipment of scrap steel and oil products, then shortly before the attack, adoption of a hard line negotiating position including the demand that Japan relinquish it's conquered territories on the Asian continent, and
C. For a variety of reasons transfer of a degree of control over the operational activity of fleet forces, taking it away from their titular heads, the Commanders-in-Chief, to the Director of War Plans within the office of the CNO. which he then exercised imprudently by denying transmission to the fleet Commanders-in-Chief crucially important tactical (as distinct from strategic) intelligence information.
D. The failure of intelligence in Washington to collect information, analyze and distribute throughout Washington and the fleets in the years preceding the attack accurate threat assessments listing the capabilities of Japanese military equipment and personnel performance in combat, and lastly,
E. The thoroughness of planning and excellence of execution by the Japanese attack force.

2. The first three of the above actions, possibly even including the failure to provide current intelligence, were risks deemed required and acceptable by our national leadership given the extent of deteriorating worldwide political and military situations, complicated by our inadequate force structure, in light of our Presidents overall strategic objective, the defeat of Hitler.
3. There was no reasonable course of action available to Admiral Kimmel during the several days preceding the attack, other than to preset General Quarters the morning of the attack, that would have enabled him to thwart the Japanese attack, or limit the extent of damages, and there was no lapse of foresight nor evidence of faulty judgment on his part.
4. Washington's failure to keep Admiral Kimmel and Lieutenant General Short fully and continuously informed regarding

intelligence being derived from codebreaking was a grievous error that may have prevented Admiral Kimmel presetting General Quarters, and did eliminate fighter defense of Oahu. This failure increased the scale and scope of damage to the fleet and to other military objectives, with attendant larger losses in lives of Army and Navy personnel.
5. Rear Admiral Kimmel and Major General Short should have their reputations restored, and should be advanced posthumously in retirement to their pre-Pearl Harbor disaster ranks.

The Story Still Unfolding

When asked do I believe President Roosevelt knew that the Japanese were about to attack Pearl Harbor, my answer is: "Yes. A qualified yes." To the query "why the hedge," my answer is that while a considerable body of evidence supports the view that he knew, it does not yet seem beyond reasonable doubt. It is my observation that when a series of apparently dumb actions are taken across a span of time by otherwise highly competent individuals, there is more to the story. If a reason common to all of them can be deduced that makes sense in light of the situations of the moment, then that reason is likely the real reason. The two alternate reasons, protecting our code breaking successes and bureaucratic bungling fit too few of these troubling situations. Then, some evidence is unequivocal.

William Casey, a former head of the CIA, in his book "The Secret War against Hitler" makes the flat out statement that Churchill had alerted Roosevelt of the impending attack. Note the last sentence from the following quote, page 7 (Exhibit O):

> The months before Pearl Harbor showed the bureaucratic problems Donovan would encounter. As the Japanese storm began to gather force in the the Pacific, the most private communications between the Japanese government and it's ambassadors in Washington, Berlin, Rome and other major capitals were being read in Washington. Army and Navy cryptographers

having broken the Japanese diplomatic cipher, were reading messages that foretold the attack. The British had sent word that a Japanese fleet was steaming east toward Hawaii.

Casey does not explain the basis for his claim.

Joseph Leib was a reporter for United Press in Washington, and a confidant of Cordell Hull. Before he died, on numerous occasions he said that he was told on November 28th, 1941, by Cordell Hull that the Japanese were planning an attack on Pearl Harbor within a few days. He tried to get his boss to publish that information, but his boss refused. He was able to persuade an underling to do so. The only paper to pick it up was the *Honolulu Advertiser.*

Constantine Brown was a reporter for the *Washington Star.* In his book entitled "The Coming of the Whirlwind" he tells of a friend, whom he does not identify, that came to see him on December 5th in a state of ill-suppressed excitement. "This is it," he exclaims, "The Japs are ready to attack. We've broken their code, and we've read their orders." Brown states that he was referring to the "Winds" execute message. The informant brought the word to him in person because he did not trust a messenger. Brown considered the story too hot to publish, reasoning that it might reveal code-breaking successes, and in any event it would already have been read by the President. According to recorded testimony the Winds Execute message was first reported as never having been received in the Navy Department. Later, in the face of direct evidence to the contrary, the Winds Execute message was declared "lost." It identified the enemy as the United States. As noted elsewhere in this analysis, this is another extremely important message that was not provided Admiral Kimmel or General Short. The Winds Execute message did not indicate a time for attack. The time of attack was strongly implied by the delivery instructions that accompanied the 14-part Purple diplomatic code message broken around midnight, two days later, on December 6th.

Brigadeer General Elliott Thorpe was a military attache in Dutch-controlled Java in 1941. Admiral Layton in "And I Was

There," advises that we now know the Dutch were also reading the JN-25 Japanese Navy operational code. According to the newspaper account of Thorpe's death at age 91, (Exhibit Q) the Dutch informed Thorpe of the impending attack against the Philippines, Thailand and Hawaii. General Thorpe immediately cabled the information to Washington, but his warning allegedly was not taken seriously. A week later the Japanese attacked Pearl Harbor. Admiral Edwin Layton was Intelligence Officer first to Admiral Kimmel, then to Admiral Nimitz.

Major General Bonner Fellers in a letter to Admiral Kimmel dated March 6, 1967, (Exhibit P replicates the entire letter) advised:

> About 10:00 AM Friday, December 6th, 1941, I walked into the Royal Air Force Headquarters in Cairo. Air Marshall Lonmore who was then in command of the RAF Middle East, sat at his desk. Immediately he opened with: "Bonner, you will be in the war in 24 hours." He continued: "We have a secret signal Japan will strike the US in 24 hours."

In letters to both President Clinton and Senator Thurmond, Helen E. Hamman of Frankfurt, Ohio, reported that her father, in 1941 head of Disaster Services of the Red Cross, had been called shortly before the attack by President Roosevelt, and told that his intelligence staff had informed him of a pending Japanese attack against Pearl Harbor, and that her father should be prepared to deal with expected casualties. I am advised that a recent review of Red Cross files corroborates that story.

Predominant in the many inexplicable occurances that continue to intrigue researchers is the strange, out-of-character behavior of General Marshall, who seemingly, could not be reached the evening before, or found the morning following the President's exclamations "This means war" and "We will be at war tomorrow." His unavailability compounded by his subsequent dilatory handling of the alert message to the Hawaiian commanders suggest more at work than a casual state of mind. If on the other hand, events were proceeding along an anticipated course, with our leaders awaiting an expected event, it made sense. His conduct suggests a desire to avoid initiating an alert based on Purple Magic information received during 6 December.

Marshall's behavior continued to haunt those who were intimately involved with him during that troubling time. On May 4th, 1961 Brigadier General Bonner Fellers had as his guests for lunch Brigadier General Carter Clarke and a Dr. Charles G. Tansill. Dr. Tansill was a professor of history at Georgetown, and an author of an excellent book about FDR's entrance into the war and Pearl Harbor. General Clarke was a central figure in War Dept. intelligence, directly involved in the analysis and distribution of decoded Japanese message traffic before and after Pearl Harbor. Clarke stated (additional confirmation that the Winds Execute message was distributed in Washington) that on December 4th, the "East Wind Rain" message was received. As already noted, this device to inform Japanese worldwide that war had been decided upon, had been revealed by our codebreakers. "East" meant war with America was imminent. Clarke noted that this information was greeted with no apparent surprise, that senior Army and Navy officers were seemingly unconcerned. This changed, taking on a comic opera quality, according to Clarke, upon receipt of the Japanese diplomatic traffic, December 6th. The record of the meeting is contained in Exhibit R. The unstated but completely obvious implication is that the senior officers to whom he referred knew what was to be, but only on Dec. 6th did they know when. Since the time of delivery of the diplomatic traffic was to occur on a Sunday at 01:00 PM, ie, 07:30 AM in Hawaii, that would be the optimum hour to commence air strike operations. What is equally clear from this report of meeting is that the over three thousand deaths at Pearl Harbor were still very much on their minds twenty years later.

The recorded views of as well as actions taken by many who served on the staffs in Washington of the chiefs of service in positions charged with analysing, distributing and briefing information derived from codebreaking in the days prior to December 7th, make clear they understood the meaning and significance of that intelligence. The idea that the chiefs of service, the service secretaries, the Secretary of State and other key advisers to the President did not understand is beyond believeability. Why would Admiral Stark not complete the call to Kimmel he started to make at the urging of the briefing officer three hours before the attack? The significance of the requested 01:00 PM meeting with the Secretary of State was not lost on Stark's briefer. Why would he put the phone down, saying he would call the President instead? (page 303, "And I Was There"). According to Admiral Layton the call was made, however. Stark was told the President was occupied. What state of mind, or administrative process, then prevented him from calling Kimmel? Does this behavior pattern not resemble that of General Marshall? Again, the purpose being served makes sense if the objective was to not cause change in the flow of events at that point in time.

The evidence is persuasive enough that Churchill knew the time, probably the place, of the attack. Several possible sources existed. Soviet agents under control of Richard Sorge had penetrated top level Japanese authorities including a member of the Imperial Family and the Moscow and Bangkok Japanese embassys. Stalin had transferred seven divisions of troops from the Far East to the defense of Moscow, leaving that area defenseless, and was desirous of Japanese force involvement elsewhere. Stalin is therefore a possible source. Another possible source was British penetration of Soviet cipher message traffic. Still another, and the most likely, British and Dutch penetration of the Japanese JN-25 five cipher naval operational code. According to "Betrayal at Pearl Harbor" by James Rusbridger and Eric Nave, the British codebreakers in Singapore succeeded in breaking the JN-25 code. Nave is credited as having lead that effort. The code, itself, was not exceptionally difficult, but success required collecting an unusually large amount of radio transmissions. Singapore intercepted Japanese message traffic being sent the

Pearl Harbor Strike Force, was able to decode and determine the strike force's mission, and so informed London, with request that Hawaii be informed. According to Nave "must climb Nitakayma on 8 December, Tokyo time," was the final message sent. This was 7 December, Hawaii time. Nitakayma was the highest mountain in the Japanese empire. What Churchill may have told Roosevelt based on this and other sources remains conjectural. Of interest is the fact that the JN-25 code was also broken by Mrs. Driscoll, a codebreaker in OP-20-G, working under Captain Safford, but had not advanced to an exploitative stage by that time.

Eric Nave allegedly reported to London that a Japanese fleet of 6 carriers, 2 battleships, 2 heavy cruisers, 1 light cruiser and 9 destroyers had departed the Kuriles for Hawaii and refueled December 4th. London was asked to inform Hawaii. These figures are a match with those contained in the alleged German decrypt of the Churchill/Roosevelt November 26th conversation described by Gregory Douglas.

The information that Churchill advised Roosevelt that a Japanese naval force was enroute Pearl Harbor, it's purpose to attack the fleet, is alleged in "Gestapo Chief : The 1948 Interrogation of Heinrich Muller" by Gregory Douglas, a specialist in intelligence research. He states that this conversation took place on an AT&T created scrambler radio-telephone known as the A-3 system that was commercially available. This system was in use in Germany from before the war. I am informed by a former high official in the National Security Agency that the A-3 system was easily broken. Douglas states that this conversation was descrambled and distributed within Germany. According to Douglas, Heinrich Muller brought it and many other intercepts with him to this country, where he lived for 14 years, occupied at least initially, in informing the U S what Germany knew about Stalin and the USSR. A copy of the alleged intercept is provided as Exhibit W. Of special interest is the Churchill question: "What about Chiang Kai-Shek? Is he not having a very thin diet?" which appears elsewhere as well. There is a view that this document may have been a fake, planted after war's end in the German archives. If this were so, what purpose was served, and why did not it's "planters" make use of it? Why did it lay fallow for decades? We do know that the Germans were efficient, successful codebreakers.

Admiral Layton cites these same words in indication that news of Japan's treachery had come directly to the President from Churchill. The cover note to the American Embassy in London of 26 November that enclosed Churchill's "thin diet for Chiang Kai-shek" "telegram" was marked Most Secret. It apologized for the lateness of the hour of it's delivery—yet nothing is contained, at least as it is now presented, that could have warranted waking up top level embassy personnel at 03:00 AM Had it been sent at daybreak, it still would have reached Washington early that morning. Layton believed that another communication took place that date, one not in the record, for which the "thin diet" message serves as a convenient cover.

Navy's chief codebreaker. Captain Laurence Safford, expressed outrage that Admiral Kimmel was surprised by the attack, exclaiming "But they knew. They knew." When Safford anticipated that he would be called as a witness in any Pearl Harbor investigation, he began looking for relevant documents. It was then that he discovered that none of the codebroken messages had been sent Admiral Kimmel. He became incensed then, on February 22, 1944, went by train to New York, met with the admiral and acquainted him with the contents of those messages.

Safford was called before the Admiral Hart Inquiry where he testified as to the existence and substance of the decoded messages. He was not asked for and did not provide copies to the Hart Inquiry. It became necessary for Admiral Kimmel to request permission of the Secretary of the Navy to provide to the Navy Court of Inquiry the decoded messages. Secretarial stonewalling of his request ended when Admiral Kimmel threatened to hold a press conference to publicise the fact that the Navy court was being denied important information.

Later, in his appearance before the Army board, after Admiral Kimmel had answered all questions regarding the performance of General Short, he was asked if he had further information relating to the disaster. Kimmel then revealed to them the information derived from codebreaking, leaving them "astonished." There were rumors, according to an Army Board member, that such messages existed and that they had been purged from Army files. But for the coincidence of Captain Safford's desire to refresh his memory, their removal from their proper location in Navy files as well by Commander Kramer would have prevented their being seen by Admiral Kimmel's designee, Captain Lavender. Why Kramer did this improper and unusual action is conjectural. It does, however, suggest a coordinated attempt higher up to prevent these messages from being made known to both Army and Navy Inquiries.

The date of November 26th, 1941, continues to intrigue many inquirers into the circumstances leading to the disaster. Chapter 18, entitled "Negotiations Off" in Rear Admiral Edwin T. Layton's book, "And I Was There" addressed most issues surrounding that date, both known and as yet unexplained. Pertinent paragraphs are replicated in exhibit N. Why, he asked, did Secretary of State Hull confront the Japanese ambassadors on the afternoon of November 26th with the hardline position the Japanese referred to as an ultimatum when, until then, the agreed strategy was to seek accommodation until the buildup of our forces in the Philippines could be completed? Why would Secretary Hull declare the sudden shift in strategy in the course of it's implementation as his decision when there was no doubt whatsoever that the President was in direct control of all our actions then being taken? In Hull's memoirs he claimed as his reason for so advising the President that even a temporary modus vivendi with Japan would undermine Chinese morale, and quotes an extract from a communication from Churchill to Roosevelt that states: "What about Chiang Kai-shek? Is he not having a very thin diet?" How frequently we encounter these words!

Of interest is an extract from the report of a recent symposium held at the Admiral Nimitz Foundation in Fredericksburg, Texas, as reported in *Naval Intelligence Professionals* quarterly, entitled "The Gathering Storm, page 4: (Exhibit V) which states:

> In mid-November Stimson abandoned his hard-line position because of continual warnings from Marshall and Stark. . . . Tokyo would not endure three more months of diplomatic procrastinations while their oil reserves drained away. . . . On 17 November Hull and Secretary of the Treasury, Morganthau proposed a six months truce in the oil and rice embargo, provided Japanese troops left IndoChina. On 25 November Stimson, Knox, Stark and Marshall agreed to a new "modus vivendi" with Japan. But if they do not accept this compromise, said Roosevelt, how then can we get them to make the first aggressive move? (on that same day a Japanese task force put to sea for Hawaii). Two days later Hull gave Ambassador Nomura and Special Envoy Kurusu an uncompromising ultimatum. We do not know why this came about. We know only that Hull did it with the greatest reluctance, and he did it on instructions from Roosevelt.

There was, indeed, a mindset that a Japanese attack in SE Asia was imminent. Navy's war warning message specifically mentioned the Philippines, Kra Peninsula, or possibly Borneo as likely choices for an amphibious assault. Army's war warning message stated that if hostilities could not be avoided, the United States desired that Japan commit the first overt act. The expected amphibious attack, however, did not rule out a concurrent attack against Hawaii. Nor can it be ruled out that despite evidence to the contrary, Roosevelt just refused to believe the Japanese would attack Hawaii. There is another possibility. He may have underestimated Japanese air strike effectiveness, as did many at that time, and reasoned that an attack against Pearl Harbor would have had only minor success, and would have served his purpose. In that case the surprise at Pearl Harbor was the extent of damages received.

The altogether regretful thing is that because damages in Hawaii were so extensive, the issue became politicised. Admissions of Washington miscalculations would not only become indicators of presidential incompetence, but would also jeopardise all that he had risked in pursuing his objective - the defeat of Hitler. The consequence is misjudgment of all three principals, President Roosevelt, Admiral Kimmel and General Short.

President Roosevelt went to war personally about the time of the fall of France. Aid to Britain in his view was a mandatory first step, our entry into the war an essential later action, and it was clear that an initial offensive combat action by Germany or Japan was prerequisite. His actions taken in defense of his authority and effectiveness before this nation entered the war should be judged in light of his objective—the defeat of Hitler, and of his immediate purpose—to induce an attack on our forces or territory in order to get us into the war. To remind us of the magnitude of the problem he faced, we need only recall that our rearmament after war's outbreak in Europe passed in the congress by a one vote majority. There are numerous examples of presidential deceptions. In war deception, when successful, is a virtue. The many initiatives he subsequently took, both political and military, the deceptive among them, were designed to achieve his wartime aims while hampered by our own vastly inferior forces.

The Dorn Report asserts that "The official treatment of Admiral Kimmel and General Short was substantially temperate and procedurally correct." Now, withholding significant information, or attempting to do so, in a duly constituted judicial procedure, if not criminal, is most certainly prejudicial to achieving a just outcome. There is simply no question but that there was a consistent, concerted effort to keep knowledge of the existence of the vitally important intelligence derived from codebroken Japanese messages from the many inquiries into the Pearl Harbor disaster. Was it for the purpose of maintaining security of this capability that was of such crucial importance to the conduct of military operations? Not believeable. The fact is we were more open with our British allies than with our own senior military officers designated to head the Army and Navy courts. In 1941 we gave the British two "purple" diplomatic code deciphering machines that had been purchased for Admiral Kimmel's use, and did not reorder. Another decoder was given the Commander, Asiatic Fleet. Given this background, and the intimacy of our mutual codebreaking arrangements with the British, security could not be the real motivator for the denial to the Army and Navy courts. Then what was? The real reason was the desire to hide the fact that crucially important information held in Washington had not been provided Kimmel and Short. Withholding information on the one hand while employing "substantially temperate treatment" of the Hawaiian commanders by avoiding sworn testimony in courts martial that would inevitably reveal information embarrassing to the administration on the other, is anything but substantially temperate treatment.

Many senior naval officers during and after the war knew that Admiral Kimmel and General Short had been scapegoated. Two references serve to make that point. Admiral Raymond Spruance answered naval historian Samuel Eliot Morison who had written him regarding the disparate treatment meted out to Kimmel and Short as compared to that of General MacArthur. MacArthur's delinquencies included a direct disobedience of orders from General Marshall plus loss of his aircraft to Japanese attack nine hours after the attack on Pearl Harbor because he refused to allow General Brereton to launch them against Japanese forces in Formosa. Admiral Spruance replied:

> I have always felt that Kimmel and Short were held responsible for Pearl Harbor in order that the American people might have no reason to loose confidence in their government in Washington. This was probably justifiable under the circumstances at that time, but it does not justify forever damning those two fine officers.

The point you raise about General MacArthur is well taken; but the Army would have lost a very able man if MacArthur had been dealt with as Kimmel and Short were.

Admiral Halsey expressed similar views in a personal letter to Admiral Kimmel. Admiral Halsey and Admiral Spruance were Navy's most experienced and honored naval combat commanders in World War II. It is pertinent also to note that both Admiral Stark and Admiral Turner, particularly Admiral Turner in numerous combat actions as the Amphibious Force commander, served with distinction throughout the war. Admiral Turner's resoluteness in his landing of Marines on Guadalcanal, and in his many support and resupply operations were enablers of our victory there. Although both were at the center of pre-war bungling in the Navy Department, they were significant figures in our subsequent victory, and were so recognized. Admiral Kimmel and General Short were denied further roles.

Epilogue

Divers initially engaged in rescuing entrapped personnel within compartments of ships sunk by bombs and torpedoes during the Japanese surprise attack on Pearl harbor, and in salvaging those ships, describe the murky conditions in the surrounding waters caused mainly by oil on the surface, some of it still burning as they worked. Numerous authors and other individuals who, for whatever reason, inquire into the events, actions and explanations that proceeded and followed that Day of Infamy have also struggled with a murkiness brought about by the potential political and military consequences that marked its aftermath. As information that was once highly classified has been released into the public domain, the popular belief that the commanders in Hawaii were to blame for their inattentiveness has steadily changed. Even though all pertinent information has not yet been released, the record is now clear that the errors then committed, and mistakes in judgment then being made, were being made in Washington, not in Hawaii.

In his oft repeated observation, eloquent in its simplicity, Robert Burns got it right. When dealing with uncertainty in military situations we see, or think we see, clearly in hindsight what should have been done in various combat actions. When assessing blame for what "Gang aft a-gley" in some military encounter, we must examine whether or not a commander was assiduous in his search for solutions, attentive to the advice of his subordinates, or heedless or unreasonable in one or more aspects of the encounter that were foreseeable. If a commander's decisions were thoughtfully arrived at, but for some unknown or even foolish action taken by an opponent, are seen in retrospect to be erroneous, that commander did not fail his obligations. A more perfect knowledge is the antidote, the distribution and exploitation of which is the obligation of every commander in a command chain. This is my basis for judging Admiral Kimmel.

My interest in the Pearl Harbor disaster commenced in about 1982, when I purchased in an estate sale a seven page, hand-written, letter by Admiral Kimmel to the movie star, the Rose of the Silent Screen, Corrine Griffith, which she then had mounted in a frame and displayed in her living room. He and Mrs Kimmel had been invited to one of her parties. His explanation in response to her question about what caused Pearl Harbor was frequently interrupted as other guests came up. So, upon their return home he wrote his explanation in the letter. In it he mentioned Captain Safford, then Navy's chief cryptanalyst, as the one who opened his eyes as to what had really taken place.

At that time I was a member of a subcommittee of the Naval Research Advisory Committee that specialized in matters associated with highly sensitive naval intelligence. This group was comprised mostly of scientists and technical experts who were outside advisers to the Naval Security Group, which is the offspring of Captain Safford's OP-20-G. I presented the Kimmel letter to Rear Admiral Dillingham, then Commander, Naval Security Group, for inclusion in the NSG museum in honor of Captain Safford. As an experienced operational commander I knew first hand command need for and dependence on intelligence support in applying force to greater advantage. As I inquired more into the circumstances surrounding the Pearl Harbor disaster, it became clear to me that political concerns, then and since, have served to preclude an honest appraisal of its causes. The price we paid was enormous. The lessons we should have learned are valuable as we look ahead.

In earlier times I was a fighter pilot aboard the carrier *Saratoga* during the Guadalcanal invasion then, subsequently, in September and October of '42, shorebased there on Henderson Field. I achieved four shootdowns of Japanese aircraft, and was myself wounded and shot down. During the Korean War I served as Executive Officer of a carrier with a Marine airwing aboard engaged in direct support of Marine troops ashore. During the Vietnam war I commanded the aircraft carrier task forces in the Gulf of Tonkin in 1966–67. I am a graduate of the U S Naval Academy, Class of '36, have also been a student at the Royal Navy Staff College, Greenwich, England, and both a student and staff member at our Naval War College in Newport, Rhode Island. My duties on the staff involved preparation of critical analyses of combat actions during WWII. I have served in the Strategic Plans Group on the staff of the Joint Chiefs of Staff and in Strategic Plans and Policy on the staff of the Chief of Naval Operations. These duties and combat experiences have made clear to me that an accurate historical record of our past political and military events and actions is a rich heritage, highly useful as we work our way through future difficult problems. The Pearl Harbor disaster is a perfect case in point for pressing the need for a proper management and exploitation of intelligence, by political as well as military authorities, and is the yet to be officially recognized lesson to be learned from that disastrous event.

A second reason developed as I became more knowledgeable of what had really transpired prior to December 7th. When viewed in the context of operational realities, it became clear that a terrible injustice has been done to the two Pearl Harbor commanders and, consequently, to the historic account of those momentous events. The record should be set straight.

David C. Richardson Vice Admiral, U S Navy (ret)
Julian, California August 4th, 1997

Notes

Introduction

1. The meeting was tape-recorded and a written transcript made. Copy in authors' files. All quotes are from this transcript. Transcript also available at: http://users.erols.com/nbeach/kimmel.html.

2. Letter, Sen. Strom Thurmond to Sec. William J. Perry, 17 May 1995.

3. Officer Personnel Act of 1947, 61 Stat. 795.

4. Husband E. Kimmel, *Admiral Kimmel's Story* (Chicago: Henry Regnery, 1955).

5. For more on the board and its authority, see http://www.hq.navy.mil/bcnr/bcnr.htm (19 April 2004). The Board for Correction of Naval Records was created by Congress in 1946 to provide a method for correcting errors or removing injustices from current and former Navy and Marine Corps members' records without the necessity for private legislation. The statutory authority for the board is codified in Title 10, United States Code, section 1552.

6. Letter, W. Dean Pfeiffer, Executive Director, Navy Board for Correction of Military Records, to Thomas M. Susman, Esq., Ropes & Gray, 9 June 1987.

7. Memo, Deputy Secretary of Defense William H. Taft IV to Secretary of the Navy George Ball, 19 January 1989.

8. Letter, Secretary of Defense Dick Cheney to Sen. William Roth, 13 June 1990.

9. See discussion of Edward L. "Ned" Beach's *Scapegoats* in chapter 2. Beach, a World War II submariner and recipient of the Navy Cross for extraordinary heroism, had a successful career as an author after retiring from the Navy. He wrote eleven books; his 1955 novel *Run Silent, Run Deep*

was a best-seller and was made into a movie starring Clark Gable and Burt Lancaster. Born in 1918, Beach died in 2002 at the age of eighty-four.

10. Letter, Sec. William J. Perry to Mr. Edward Kimmel, 7 September 1994.

11. Letter, Pres. Bill Clinton to Manning Kimmel IV, 1 December 1994.

12. Memo, Brig. Gen. Herbert D. Hoover to Director, Personnel & Administration (attn: Lt. Col. May), 19 January 1949.

13. Letter, Lt. Gen. Edward M. Brooks, 19 April 1949.

14. A pencil notation dated 6 September states simply "no action to be taken" at direction of the "Army Chief of Staff, s/ Stanley R. Larsen, Lt Col, Asst Secy, General Staff."

15. Letter, Col. Walter Short to Hon. Paul W. Stone, Secretary of the Army, 29 May 1990.

16. Memo from Judge Advocate General, for Office of Chief of Staff, General Officer Management Office, Subj: Request for Advancement on Retired List: MG Walter C. Short, 22 June 1990.

17. Army Board for Correction of Military Records Proceedings, Docket No. AC91-08788, Case of Short, Walter C. (Deceased), 13 November 1991, p. 6.

18. Ibid.

19. Memo from John W. Matthews, Dep. Asst. Secy. (DA Review Boards & Equal Opportunity), for Commander, U.S. Army Reserve Personnel Center, Subj: Short, Walter C. (Deceased), 19 December 1991.

20. Memo, West for Under Secretary of Defense (Personnnel & Readiness), Subj: Major General (MG) Walter C. Short, 30 November 1995.

21. Letter, Strom Thurmond to Hon. William J. Perry, 17 May 1995 (emphasis supplied).

Chapter 1. Approach and Methodology

1. Memo, Dorn for Deputy Secretary of Defense, subj: Advancement of Rear Admiral Kimmel and Major General Short, 15 December 1995.

2. Nicolas Timenes earned bachelor's and master's degrees from Yale University. In the 1960s he did weapons systems analysis for the U.S. Navy. From 1970 to 1985, he worked on energy and natural resources

issues at the Departments of Energy and Interior, and at the White House. Timenes came to the Pentagon in 1991 and retired from the Office of the Secretary of Defense in early 1996.

3. Roger D. Scott, B.A., Mary Washington College, 1977; J.D., University of Virginia, 1986; LL.M., University of Virginia, 1994; M.A., Naval War College, 1997; retired, commander, Judge Advocate General's Corps, U.S. Navy.

4. Borch, Memorandum for Record, subj: Initial Meeting with Mr. Dorn, Under Secretary of Defense re Kimmel-Short investigation, 24 October 95.

5. Ibid.

6. Ibid.

7. John R. Kuborn is the co-author (with Leatrice R. Arakaki) of *7 December 1941: The Air Force Story* (Hickam Air Force Base, Hawaii: Office of History, Pacific Air Forces, 1991). Thomas M. Fairfull is the director of Fort DeRussey Army Museum.

8. "General Short Sees Danger of Oahu Air Raid," *Honolulu Advertiser,* 14 August 1941, p. 2.

Chapter 2. The Report

1. Under the law in effect when Admiral Kimmel retired, he retired in his permanent grade as a Rear Admiral (Act of May 22, 1917, 65th Cong., 1st Sess., Ch. 20, Section 18 [40 Stat. 89]). Similarly, General Short retired in his permanent grade of Major General (Act of Aug. 5, 1939 [53 Stat. 1214]), as amended, Act of July 31, 1940 (54 Stat. 781); M.L. 1939, Supp. III, Section 286). A few months after Admiral Kimmel retired, however, a law was enacted permitting any officer of the Navy who had served one year or more in the grade of vice admiral or admiral to retire at that grade (Act of June 16, 1942 [56 Stat 370]). Admiral Kimmel was not eligible under this law because he had served less than one year as a four-star admiral. In August 1947, Congress removed the one-year requirement of the 1942 statute; this made Admiral Kimmel eligible for advancement on the retired list to four-star rank (Officer Personnel Act of 1947, Aug. 7, 1947, section 414, 61 Stat. 795). Although Admiral Kimmel has never been advanced to four-star rank, he began receiving retired pay based on the pay of a three-star admiral with the enactment of the Act of May 20, 1958 (72 Stat. 122, 130).

General Short was eligible for advancement on the retired list as a lieutenant general with the enactment of the Officer Personnel Act of 1947. Like the parallel Navy provision in the same Act, no minimum time of service in grade was specified. In June 1948, however, Congress enacted the Army and Air Force Vitalization and Retirement Equalization Act (P. L. 810, 80th Cong., June 29, 1948). A curious feature in this law (Section 203(a)) gave the Secretary of the Army the authority to advance any "commissioned officer of the regular Army . . . to the highest temporary grade in which he served satisfactorily for not less than six months while serving on active duty, as determined by the . . . Secretary." The provision, which only applied to World War II service, gave the Secretary of the Army the authority to advance General Short to lieutenant general on the retired list. This 1948 statute still is in effect, and recently provided the jurisdictional basis for the Army Board of Correction of Military Records (ABCMR) review of General Short's case. In that review (AC91-08788, 13 November 1991), the majority of the ABCMR recommended the advancement of General Short. The Deputy Assistant Secretary of the Army (DA Review Boards and Equal Employment Opportunity Compliance and Complaints Review), however, rejected the ABCMR's recommendation and denied the request posthumously to advance General Short on the retired list (memo SAMR-RB, 19 Dec 1991). The Secretary of the Army retains the authority to advance General Short. The Secretary of the Navy does not have any similar authority.

2. See, for example, letters from Secretary Cheney, October 23, 1989; President Bush, December 2, 1991; Secretary Perry, September 7, 1994.

3. Letter from President Clinton to Mr. Manning M. Kimmel, IV, December 1, 1994.

4. Letter from Sen. Strom Thurmond and Rep. Floyd Spence to Hon. William J. Perry, February 8, 1995.

5. Thurmond, Sen. Strom, and others, "Remarks at Meeting of the Office of the Secretary of Defense and Members of the Kimmel Family Dealing with the Posthumous Restoration of the Rank of Admiral for Rear Admiral Husband E. Kimmel, United States Navy, April 27, 1995, Washington, D.C.," Transcript, p. 7. Hereafter cited as "Thurmond transcript."

6. Ibid., p. 7.

7. Letter from Sen. Strom Thurmond to Hon. William J. Perry, May 17, 1995.

8. Letter from Hon. John White, Deputy Secretary of Defense, to Hon. Strom Thurmond, September 8, 1995.

9. Ibid.

10. U.S. Congress, Joint Committee on the Investigation of the Pearl Harbor Attack, Investigation of the Pearl Harbor Attack: Report of the Joint Committee on the Investigation of the Pearl Harbor Attack, Pursuant to S. Con. Res. 27, 79th Congress: A concurrent resolution to investigate the attack on Pearl Harbor on December 7, 1941, and events and circumstances relating thereto, July 20, 1946. Also reprinted by Aegean Park Press, Laguna Hills, CA, 1994.

11. U.S. Congress, Joint Committee on the Investigation of the Pearl Harbor Attack, Pearl Harbor Attack, Hearings, 39 volumes; hereafter cited as PHA.

12. Letter from Clifford G. Amsler, Jr., Assistant Director for Military Records, National Personnel Records Center, to Commander Rodger Scott, USN, November 3, 1995, with enclosures.

13. Kimmel, Husband E., *Admiral Kimmel's Story,* Chicago, Henry Regnery, 1955.

14. Beach, Edward L., *Scapegoats: A Defense of Kimmel and Short at Pearl Harbor,* Annapolis, Naval Institute Press, 1994.

15. Thurmond transcript, p. 67.

16. For example, Mr. Edward R. Kimmel has stated, "the Roberts Commission . . . dereliction of duty charge is the genesis of the injustice done to Admiral Kimmel." Thurmond transcript, p. 18.

17. Mr. Edward R. Kimmel, Thurmond transcript, p. 19.

18. Typically, relief and retirement of the most senior officers from the highest commands are handled personally and orally, and confirmed by very brief memoranda which do not give the reasons for the actions.

For a comprehensive examination of the legality of military personnel actions relating to Admiral Kimmel and General Short, see Roger D. Scott, "Kimmel, Short, McVay: Case Studies in Executive Authority, Law, and the Individual Rights of Military Commanders," *Military Law Review,* Vol. 156 (June 1998), pp. 52–199.

19. Franklin D. Roosevelt letter Nav-3-D of January 7, 1941 to Rear Admiral Husband E. Kimmel: "In accordance with the provisions of an

Act of Congress approved May 22, 1917, you are hereby designated as Commander in Chief, Pacific Fleet, with additional duty as Commander in Chief, United States Fleet, with the rank of admiral, effective on the date of your taking over the command of the Pacific fleet. In accordance with this designation you will assume the rank and hoist the flag of admiral on the above mentioned date." Documents in Rear Admiral Kimmel's service record indicate that he assumed duties as CincPac and CominCh on February 1, 1941.

20. Rear Admiral Kimmel's temporary designation as a four-star admiral was made under the provisions of existing law which allowed the President to designate six officers as Commanders of Fleets or subdivisions thereof with the rank of admiral or vice admiral. Act of May 22, 1917, 65th Cong., lst Sess., Ch. 20, § 18, 40 Stat 89. Such advancements to the rank of admiral or vice admiral were to be in effect only during the incumbency of the designated flag officer. Id. ("... when an officer with the rank of admiral or vice admiral is detached from the command of a fleet or subdivision thereof... he shall return to his regular rank in the list of officers of the Navy ...").

21. This had long been the case. For example, Admiral Charles Frederick Hughes, the Chief of Naval Operations from 1927–1930, retired in his permanent grade of rear admiral. William R. Braisted, "Charles Frederick Hughes," in *Chiefs of Naval Operations* (William Love, Jr., ed. 1980), p. 66. It is still the case today that retirement in a higher than 0-8 requires nomination by the President and confirmation by the Senate.

22. Secretary of the Navy Knox directed the relief of Admiral Kimmel on 16 December 1941 (PHA 5:2430), confirmed by SECNAV ltr 14358 of 3 January 1942.

23. PHA 3:1529.

24. *Chappell v. Wallace*, 462 U.S. 296, 300 (1983).

25. Ibid., quoting *Burns v. Wilson*, 346 U.S. 137, 140 (1953).

26. Over the years many officers relieved of command have challenged the discretion of senior officials in the chain of command to relieve and reassign them. In such cases the relieved officers have claimed a right to "due process" under the Fifth Amendment of the U.S. Constitution, which states, in pertinent part, that "nor shall life, liberty or property be deprived without due process of law." The federal courts, however, have consistently refused to invade the unre-

viewable discretion of senior officials to assign and reassign military personnel, noting that service members have no protected "liberty" or "property" interest in their assignments. See, e.g., *Orloff v. Willoughby,* 345 U.S. 83 (1953) (Army physician's assignment as laboratory technician not reviewable); *Sebra v. Neville,* 801 F.2d 1135, 1141 ("The policy behind the rule is clear; the military would grind to a halt if every transfer was open to legal challenge."); *Covington v. Anderson,* 487 F.2d 660, 665 (9th Cir .1973) (military duty assignments are unreviewable because "[a]ny attempt of the federal courts . . . to take over review of military duty assignments . . . would obviously be fraught with practical difficulties for both the armed forces and the courts" (quoting *Amheiter. v. Ignatious,* 292 F. Supp. 911, 921 [N.D. Cal. 1968], aff'd, 435 F.2d 691 [9th Cir. 1970]). See also *Crenshaw v. United States,* 134 U.S. 99 (1890) (no right to appointment) and *United States ex rel. Edwards v. Root,* 22 App DC 419, aff'd 195 U.S. 626 (1903) (no right to promotion). The President and subordinate officials in the chain of command have plenary authority to remove and replace subordinate commanders. See *Mullan v. United States,* 140 U.S. 240 (1891); *Wallace v. United States,* 257 U.S. 541 (1922). This authority is essential to the efficient functioning of a military organization.

27. U.S. Constitution, Article II, Section 2.

28. Naval Military Personnel Manual (MILPERSMAN) 3410105.7a.

29. MILPERSMAN 3410105.3. Other bases for detachment for cause of any officer include misconduct, unsatisfactory performance involving one or more significant events resulting from gross negligence or where complete disregard of duty is involved, and unsatisfactory performance of duty over an extended period of time.

30. MILPERSMAN 3410105.3d.

31. Secretary Stimson explained that relief "avoids a situation where officials charged with the responsibility for the future security of the vital naval base would otherwise in this critical hour also be involved in the searching investigation ordered yesterday by the President," quoted in Prange, Gordon W., *At Dawn We Slept,* New York, McGraw-Hill, 1981, p. 588.

32. Husband E. Kimmel, "Admiral Kimmel's Own Story of Pearl Harbor," *U.S. News and World Report,* December 10, 1954, p. 69 ("His [Admiral Richardson's] summary removal was my first concern. I was informed that Richardson had been removed from command because

he hurt Mr. Roosevelt's feelings by some forceful recommendations...").

33. James O. Richardson, *On the Treadmill to Pearl Harbor: The Memoirs of Admiral James O. Richardson, as Told to Vice Admiral George C. Dyer* (Washington, D.C.: Naval History Division, 1973) p. 455.

34. Memorandum, Edward B. Hanify to Director of Naval History, 23 December 1987.

35. In part as a courtesy to the officers, retirement of the most senior officers from lofty commands usually is handled personally and orally, and confirmed by very brief memoranda which do not give the reasons for the actions.

36. Prange, pp. 606–7.

37. Ibid.

38. PHA 17:2728.

39. 20 Act of May 22, 1917, 40 Stat. 89 (authorizing the appointment of six admirals and vice admirals).

40. PHA 7:3285–3300.

41. 10 USC 601.

42. On 25 November 1986 U.S. Attorney General Edwin Meese III identified Poindexter, Marine Lt. Col. Oliver North, and former national security advisor Robert C. McFarlane as the three men knowledgeable about the diversion of money from Iran to the Contras. Poindexter resigned that day. Some fifteen months later, on 16 March 1988, Poindexter was indicted on seven felony charges arising from his involvement in the Iran-Contra affair, as part of a twenty-three-count, multi-defendant indictment. He was named with North, retired Air Force Maj. Gen. Richard V. Secord, and Albert Hakim as a member of the conspiracy to defraud the U.S. government by means of the Iran-Contra diversion and other acts.

In April 1990 Rear Admiral Poindexter was tried and convicted of five felonies, including one count of conspiring to obstruct official inquiries and proceedings, two counts of obstructing Congress, and two counts of making false statements to Congress. U.S. District Judge Harold H. Greene sentenced him to a six-month prison term. In November 1991, however, Poindexter's convictions were overturned on appeal. In December 1992 the U.S. Supreme Court declined to review the case.

For more on Poindexter and the Iran-Contra affair, see "Report of the Congressional Committee to Investigate Covert Arms Transactions with Iran," H.R. Report No. 100-433, S. Report No. 100-216, 100th Cong., 1st sess. (1987).

43. E.g., Act of May 22, 1917, 40 Stat. 89 (Navy); Act of Aug. 5, 1939, 53 Stat. 1214 (Army).

44. Officer Personnel Act of 1947, section 414, 61 Stat. 795.

45. The rapid expansion of the Armed Forces in World War II led to the promotion of many officers to temporary grades, often significantly higher in rank than their permanent grades. Because of wartime exigencies, a large number of such promotions or "appointments" to a higher grade were made without the advice and consent of the Senate. Consequently, at the end of World War II, an officer might have a permanent rank of captain, but be serving as a colonel because of a temporary appointment. Congress recognized that it was unjust to those who had served in a higher grade, albeit without the advice and consent of the Senate, not to be able to retire in that higher grade. This recognition was a principal reason behind the enactment of the Officer Personnel Act of 1947 provisions relating to advancement on the retired list to the highest rank held.

46. Notice that the 1947 Act does not provide for "restoration" of the highest grade or rank held, a term used by the Kimmel family. "Restoration" implies the resumption of a right or entitlement, an individualized "property" interest in a rank or grade that has been taken away. Service in three- or four-star grade had always been a temporary privilege. The 1947 law provided for the discretionary grant of that privileged status de novo to members of that class of officers who had enjoyed it previously, should the President and the Senate so choose.

47. Many of these officers were U.S. Military Academy graduates: Carlos Brewer, USMA 1913; Ernest J. Dawley, USMA 1910; James P. Marley, USMA 1907; William McMahon, USMA 1917; James I. Muir, USMA 1910. For a general look at officers relieved from their commands in World War II, see Benjamin S. Persons, *Relieved of Command* (Manhattan, Kans.: Sunflower Press, 1997).

48. Martin Blumenson, *Salerno to Cassino: The U.S. Army in World War II* (Washington, D.C.: Government Printing Office, 1969), p. 152.

49. Robert H. Berlin, *U.S. Army World War II Corps Commanders: A Composite Biography* (Leavenworth, Kans.: Combat Studies Institute, 1989), p. 16, n.49.

50. See, for example, letters from Secretary Richard Cheney, October 23, 1989; President George Bush, December 2, 1991; Secretary William J. Perry, September 7, 1994, and from President William Clinton, December 1, 1994.

51. PHA 16:2429, SECNAV Forrestal's Fourth Endorsement of the 1944 Court of Inquiry. (James Forrestal became Secretary of the Navy after the death of Secretary Knox in April 1944.)

52. CNO First Endorsement on DIRNAVHIST memo of 5 Jan 88, CNO Ser 00/8US5000015 of 19 Jan 88, to SECNAV. Although he declined to do so in this January 1988 letter, Admiral Trost later recommended consideration of advancement of Admiral Kimmel on the retired list. His distinction between punitive action and privileges, however, is still apt.

53. Figure 1 in Section I diagrams the nine investigations, showing how each relates to Admiral Kimmel or General Short, or both. This Section, however, discusses only the five investigations most pertinent to this review.

54. Report by the Secretary of the Navy to the President, reproduced in PHA 5:2338–45 and 24:1749–56.

55. PHA 5:2338.

56. PHA 5:2342.

57. Secretary of the Navy Knox relieved Admiral Kimmel of his command on 16 December 1941. PHA 5:2430. That same day, Secretary of War Stimson relieved General Short of his command. Henry L. Stimson Diary, Yale Univ. Library, 17 December 1941. Both Knox and Stimson acted after consultation with President Roosevelt.

58. Executive Order 8983, 18 December 1941; reproduced in part in Roberts, Owen J., et. al., letter report to the President, January 23, 1942, p. 1, PHA 7:3285.

59. For example, Mr. Edward R. Kimmel has stated, "the Roberts Commission . . . dereliction of duty charge is the genesis of the injustice done to Admiral Kimmel." Thurmond transcript, p. 18.

60. Roberts, op. cit., p. 22.

61. Ibid., p. 2.

62. Secretary of War Knox announced on 26 February 1942 that "he had directed the preparation of charges for the trial by court-martial of General Short, alleging dereliction of duty." PHA 19:3811. The Office of the Judge Advocate General of the Navy also drafted charges and

specifications for use in general court-martial proceedings against Admiral Kimmel. PHA, 11:5495–97. Both the Army and the Navy later decided, however, that trial by court-martial was inappropriate. The Judge Advocate General of the Army, for example, opined that General Short's mistakes "were honest ones, not the result of conscious fault, and having in mind all the circumstances, do not constitute a criminal neglect of duty." PHA 39:253–54.

63. See, for example, Admiral Kimmel's letter to Admiral Stark dated February 22, 1942, quoted in Kimmel, op. cit., p.182. There is a useful chronicle of Admiral Kimmel's efforts in Prange, op. cit., Chapter 72.

64. Kimmel, op. cit., Preface, p. ix.

65. PHA 3:1358.

66. Appointed pursuant to the provisions of P.L. 339 (78th Cong.), approved June 13, 1944. By order of SECNAV Forrestal, the Navy Court held sessions beginning July 24, 1944, and concluded its inquiry on October 19, 1944.

67. Appointed pursuant to the provisions of P.L. 339 (78th Cong.), approved June 13, 1944. By order of The Adjutant General, War Department, the Army Pearl Harbor Board held sessions beginning July 20, 1944, and concluded its investigation on October 20, 1944.

68. Naval Court of Inquiry, p. 1–46.

69. This usage of "dereliction" is its plain-language meaning, and does not connote a court-martial offense.

70. "Culpable inefficiency" was a court-martial offense at the time; it is thus explicitly rejected here.

71. PHA 39:343–45; CNO to SECNAV, Second Endorsement, 6 November 1944, p. 3–15.

72. PHA 16:2429; SECNAV, Fourth Endorsement, 13 August 1945, p. 5–21.

73. After the war, Admiral King moderated his judgment somewhat. Letter to the Secretary of the Navy dated July 14, 1948, quoted in Kimmel, op. cit., p. 161.

74. PHA 3:1450–51.

75. PHA 3:1477 et seq.

76. JCC, p. 251.

77. Ibid. p. 252.

78. Ibid.

79. Ibid., p. 266-A.

80. US losses included 2,403 dead, 1,178 wounded, and 8 battleships, 3 light cruisers, 3 destroyers, and 4 auxiliary craft sunk, capsized, or damaged. Aircraft losses included 13 Navy fighters, 21 scout bombers, 46 patrol bombers, 4 B-17s, 12 B-18s, 32 P-40s, and 20 P-36s. Many other aircraft were damaged. Japanese losses totaled 29 aircraft, 1 large submarine, and 5 midget submarines. PHA 7:3069–70; 12:354–58; 22:60–61.

81. Prange, *At Dawn We Slept*, p. 344 (emphasis supplied). That the Japanese expected substantial resistance is also reflected by three decisions made by those planning the attack on Hawaii. First, the Japanese intended to call off the attack if the Americans sighted the Japanese task force before X-Day minus one. If, however, the Americans spotted only part of the fleet, then the Japanese would simply change course and proceed to Hawaii. Perhaps most important, if U.S. forces fired upon the Japanese, they intended to fight it out. Ibid., pp. 841–42.

82. PHA 15:1601–2.

83. PHA 17:2833, quoting "Navy Regulations Setting Forth the General Duties of a Commander-in-Chief," Art. 687.

84. Ibid., Art. 692.

85. PHA 32:219.

86. Admiral Kimmel, PHA 6:2498, 2518. General Short, PHA 7:2921–22; 2951, 1959.

87. The Navy's basic war plan, implemented in the Pacific by W[ar] P[lan] Pac[ific] 46, focused exclusively on Japan as the enemy. PHA 17:2571–2600. Admiral Kimmel wrote: "In the case of war ... [w]e must be in a position to minimize our own losses, and to inflict maximum damage to the Japanese fleet, merchant shipping, and bases." PHA 16:2252–53. Given that General Short's mission was to protect the fleet, he necessarily focused on Japan as the aggressor; General Short expected a Japanese invasion of Oahu. PHA 15:1626.

88. For more on pre–World War II planning for war with Japan, see Edward S. Miller, *War Plan Orange: The U.S. Strategy to Defeat Japan* (Annapolis, Md.: Naval Institute Press, 1991).

89. "Japan Mechanized Army Massed in Indo-China ..." *Honolulu Advertiser*, 3 December 1941, p. 1. "Foreign military intelligence reports from Saigon today said the Japanese are concentrating a mechanized striking force in southern Indo-China ... it [is] estimated that Japan has 75,000 troops in southern Indo-China."

90. President Roosevelt ordered an embargo on exports to Japan of high-octane gasoline and crude oil on 1 August 1941. This embargo complemented the earlier embargo on scrap iron and steel, announced by the President in September 1940. See also, Beach, op. cit., p. 20 ("Nearly all Japan's fuel oil came through the United States . . .").

91. "US–Japan War Emphasized by Spokesmen," *Honolulu Advertiser,* 10 November 1941, p. 1.

92. *Honolulu Star-Bulletin,* 22 November 1941, p. 1.

93. This was reemphasized in General Marshall's November 27, 1941 message to General Short. See also PHA 14:1328.

94. Major General Frederick Martin, Commander, Hawaiian Air Force, and Rear Admiral Patrick Bellinger, Hawaiian Based Patrol Wing (Martin's Navy counterpart), prepared the Report. It was a plan for joint action if Oahu or the Pacific Fleet were attacked. Martin was under General Short's overall command. PHA 22:349–54.

95. PHA 22:349.

96. PHA 4:1896.

97. His order 2CL-41 (Revised) October 14, 1941, reproduced in Kimmel, op. cit., p. 189.

98. Letter from Admiral Kimmel to Admiral Stark, PHA 16:2228.

99. See note 50, above, and accompanying text.

100. The "war warning" message of November 27th (text below) reinforced that view.

101. PHA 4:1939–40 and 23:1114; JCC, p. 76.

102. Letter of February 7, 1941. PHA 15:1601–2.

103. PHA 22:349.

104. See generally, Russell F. Weigley, *History of the United States Army,* New York, 1967, pp. 412–14.

105. See generally, Hawaiian Department, "Joint Army and Navy Maneuvers, Raid Phase, Jan. 29–31, 1933."

106. Newton, Don, and A. Cecil Hampshire, *Taranto,* London, 1959; Lowry, Thomas P., and John W. G. Wellham, *The Attack on Taranto* (Mechanicsburg, Penn.: Stackpole Press, 1995). The British attack was carried out by 21 biplanes operating from a single carrier.

107. Prange, *At Dawn We Slept,* p. 320.

108. PHA 16:2228.

109. "General Short Sees Danger of Oahu Air Raid," *Honolulu Advertiser,* 14 August 1941, p. 2.

110. PHA 10:4837–38.

111. PHA 10:4839; PHA 36:128; Prange, *At Dawn We Slept*, p. 440.

112. Among the factors making a carrier air attack unlikely were the large distance to be covered in sailing from Japan to Hawaii, the requirement to refuel any carrier task force during its voyage, and the difficulty of such a carrier force remaining undetected.

113. In his report to the President, Secretary Knox wrote that: "The Japanese attack . . . was a complete surprise to both the Army and the Navy." PHA 5:2338.

114. Special Naval Observer. PCC, p. 98 fn. 99.

115. Photocopy of original in Clausen, Henry C., and Bruce Lee, *Pearl Harbor: Final Judgment*, New York, Crown, 1992, following p. 262. See also PHA 14:1406; JCC, p. 98. Some of the copies in the literature contain transcription errors.

116. "Turner Describes Deployment," *New York Times*, 21 December 1945, p. 2, col. 3; see *The New Military and Naval Dictionary* (F. Gaynor, ed.), New York, 1951 ("deploy—(Navy) to change from a cruising or contact disposition to a battle disposition").

117. Photocopy of original in Clausen, op. cit. See also PHA 14:1328; JCC, p. 102.

118. JCC, p. 119–33.

119. See, for example, Beach, op. cit., pp. 165,171.

120. Dispatch CincPac to Pacific Fleet Info OpNav, November 28, 1941, 280355; PHA 17:496, quoted in Kimmel, op cit., p. 74, note 55.

121. Kimmel, op cit., p. 77.

122. William F. Halsey, *Admiral Halsey's Story* New York (1947), pp. 75–76.

123. PHA 27:156–58.

124. PHA 10:4680. This was the first time the Japanese changed call signs twice in a 30-day period.

125. PHA 36:138.

126. PHA 10:4839.

127. PHA 10:4839–40.

128. The "Purple" machines were electronic decoding machines that decrypted Japanese message intercepts. These messages were known as "Magic."

129. PHA 14:1408.

130. PHA 6:2764.

NOTES TO PAGES 57–67

131. PHA 6:2764–65.

132. For example, Admiral Kimmel's war plans officer, Capt. Charles McMorris, assured Admiral Kimmel on the 27th that there were no "prospects" of an air attack. PHA 27:412; 28:1497. See also, Prange, op. cit., p. 401.

133. Prange, *At Dawn We Slept*, pp. 125, 189–90.

134. PHA 23:696–97.

135. Stanley Weintraub, *Long Day's Journey into War: December 7, 1941* (New York: Truman Talley Books, 1991), pp. 243–44.

136. Prange, *At Dawn We Slept*, p. 527.

137. Joseph C. Harsch, "A War Correspondent's Odyssey," in *Air Raid: Pearl Harbor!* ed. Paul Stillwell (Annapolis, Md.: Naval Institute Press, 1981), p. 264 (emphasis supplied).

138. William W. Drake, "I Don't Think They'd Be Such Damned Fools," in Stillwell, ed., *Air Raid: Pearl Harbor!* p. 269.

139. Beach, *Scapegoats*, p. 100; Weintraub, *Long Day's Journey into War,* p. 230; Prange, *At Dawn We Slept*, p. 497.

140. PHA 22:35.

141. Prange, *At Dawn We Slept*, p. 497. See also note 150, below.

142. Weintraub, *Long Day's Journey into War,* p. 270 (golfer anecdote); Army Times, *Pearl Harbor and Hawaii* (New York: Walker, 1971), p. 48 (lifeguard anecdote).

143. Army Times, *Pearl Harbor and Hawaii*, p. 100.

144. Ibid., p. 49.

145. PHA 32:444; Prange, *At Dawn We Slept*, p. 517; Gannon, *Pearl Harbor Betrayed: The True Story of a Man and a Nation under Attack* (New York: Henry Holt, 2001), p. 3.

146. His fighter aircraft were on four-hour alert, and the majority of his antiaircraft batteries were able to come into action two and a half to three hours after the attack. See the Knox investigation for a detailed discussion of response times.

147. For an explanation of the significance of the "14-part" message, see Fig. 2, endnote 207.

148. Beach, *Scapegoats*, p. 100.

149. PHA Part 23, pp. 1125, 1193; Prange, *At Dawn We Slept*, p. 497.

150. "Japanese Submarine Sunk at Pearl Harbor Is Found," *New York Times,* 30 August 2002. At least one other historian has identified this event as clear tactical warning to Kimmel and Short. "After the sighting

of the first submarines within the security zone . . . the entire command should have been alerted immediately" (Hans L. Trefousse, *Pearl Harbor: The Continuing Controversy* [Malabar, Fla.: Krieger Publishing, 1982], p. 92). For more on the Japanese submarines at Pearl Harbor, see Ken Hackler, "Myths Surrounding the Midget Subs," *World War II* (Pearl Harbor 60th Anniversary Commemorative Issue) (December 2001): 26–32.

151. Kimmel, op cit., p. 4.

152. PHA 6:2539; 14:1408.

153. PHA 6:2539–43.

154. Six mobile radar stations had been operating daily. They were, however, only training. As General Short said: "At that time we had just gotten in the machines and set up. I thought this was fine training for them. I was trying to get training and was doing it for training more than any idea that it would be real . . ." PHA 22:35.

155. E.g., Michael Gannon, "Reopen the Kimmel Case," *Naval Institute Proceedings* 120 (December 1994): 51–56.

156. Husband E. Kimmel, "Admiral Kimmel's Own Story of Pearl Harbor," *U.S. News and World Report*, 10 December 1954, p. 71.

157. Ibid. (emphasis in original).

158. NARA, Record Group 38, Strategic Plans Division Records, Box 147J: Plans, Strategic Studies, and Related Correspondence (Series IX), Part III: OP-12B War Plans and Related Correspondence, WPL-46-WPL-46-PC, Chief of Naval Operations to the Commander-in-Chief, U.S. Pacific Fleet, 10 February 1941; Gannon, *Pearl Harbor Betrayed*, pp. 162–63.

159. Gannon, *Pearl Harbor Betrayed*, p. 162.

160. For more on changes forced upon the Doolittle raiders after being spotted by Japanese picket boats, see Carroll V. Glines, *Doolittle's Tokyo Raiders* (Princeton, N.J.: Van Nostrand, 1964).

161. KC, Roll 3, "Outline of Testimony Given before Army Board," Washington, D.C., August 1944, p. 3.

162. PHA 4:2045.

163. Ibid.

164. Most were in action in four minutes. The fratricide wrought on U.S. aircraft from the *Enterprise* attempting to land at Ford Island later that day suggests what fully alerted gun crews might have done to the first wave of Japanese torpedo bombers.

165. An Army radar, scheduled to have been shut down, in fact detected the approaching Japanese aircraft 50 minutes before they struck the fleet, but the contacts were erroneously presumed friendly. Given the newness of the equipment, and its inexperienced operators, the belief that the approaching aircraft were "friendlies" was not unreasonable.

166. The few fighter aircraft able to take to the air were highly effective. See Knox investigation.

167. See Weintraub, *Long Day's Journey into War,* pp. 243–44.

168. Admiral Kimmel's predecessor, Admiral Richardson, had decided against torpedo baffles or nets, and Admiral Kimmel inherited this decision. Had Admiral Kimmel seen the possibility of a torpedo aerial attack, however, he might have requested the Navy Department to furnish him with such items, or at least the equipment to manufacture them. PHA 5:2350. Certainly, Admiral Kimmel was aware that his ships were vulnerable to such an attack. For example, CNO Stark, in a letter to Admiral Kimmel, 13 June 1941, wrote: "A minimum depth of water of 75 feet may be assumed necessary to successfully drop torpedoes from planes. About 200 yards of torpedo run is necessary before the exploding device is armed, but this may be altered . . . . Recent developments have shown that United States and British torpedoes may be dropped from planes at heights of as much as 300 feet, and in some cases make initial dives of considerably less than 75 feet, and make excellent runs. *Hence, it may be stated that it cannot be assumed that any capital ship or other valuable vessel is safe when at anchor from this type of attack if surrounded by water at a sufficient distance to permit an attack to be developed and a sufficient run to arm the torpedo*" (emphasis added). PHA 5:2266. Because Pearl Harbor's depth was between 30–40 feet, Admiral Kimmel considered the use of baffles or nets to be limited, and did not press the Navy Department to supply them.

169. The use of these sausage shaped balloons tethered to long wires was suggested by Secretary of the Army Stimson to Secretary of the Navy Knox on 7 February 1941; a copy of this letter went to General Short. He was "direct[ed] . . . to cooperate with local naval authorities" in deciding whether to use such balloons to protect the Fleet and base facilities. PHA 14:1003–4.

170. See Fig. 2 for an explanation of these messages and their relevance.

171. See, for example, JCC, pp. 181–89.

172. See, for example, Harry E. Barnes, *Perpetual War for Perpetual Peace*, Caldwell, Id: Caxton Printers, 1953; Robert A. Theobald, *The Final Secret of Pearl Harbor*, New York: Devin-Adair Co., 1954.

173. Prange, *At Dawn We Slept*, pp. 623–28. See also Martin V. Melosi, *The Shadow of Pearl Harbor: Political Controversy over the Surprise Attack* (College Station: Texas A&M University Press, 1977).

174. For a dated, but comprehensive refutation of the conspiracy theory, see Donald M. Goldstein and Katherine V. Dillon, "Revisionists Revisited," in Prange, *At Dawn We Slept*, pp. 839–52. A similar, more detailed analysis of revisionist theories is found in Hans L. Trefousse, *Pearl Harbor: The Continuing Controversy* (Malabar, Fla.: Krieger Publishing, 1982). See also Stephen E. Ambrose, "Just Dumb Luck: American Entry into World War II," in *Pearl Harbor Revisited*, ed. Robert W. Love, Jr. (New York: St. Martin's Press, 1995), pp. 94–95.

175. Beach, *Scapegoats*, p. 159.

176. Ibid., p. 158.

177. Ibid., p. 157.

178. Ibid., pp. 171–72: "It is clear today that, among those with responsibility for the Japanese attack, first must be President Roosevelt himself . . . Roosevelt had determined on war with Japan . . . he engineered our entry into World War II . . . he had received multiple warnings for days that something was about to happen [on 7 December].... The national leadership [Roosevelt, Marshall, Stark, Turner] utterly failed our commanders at Pearl Harbor, and then blamed them for their own lack of alertness."

179. John Toland, *Infamy: Pearl Harbor and Its Aftermath* (New York: Doubleday, 1982). For a refutation of Toland's claims, see David Kahn, "Did FDR Invite the Pearl Harbor Attack," *New York Review of Books*, 27 May 1982. See also David Kahn, "Did Roosevelt Know?" *New York Review of Books*, 2 November 2000.

180. Daryl S. Borgquist, "Advance Warning? The Red Cross Connection," *Naval History Magazine* (June 1999): 13. See also John McCaslin, "Dredging Pearl Harbor," *Washington Times*, 1 June 2001, p. 7.

181. Robert B. Stinnett, *Day of Deceit: The Truth about FDR and Pearl Harbor* (New York: Free Press, 1999).

182. Stephen Budiansky, *Battle of Wits: The Complete Story of Codebreaking in World War II* (New York: Free Press, 2000), pp. 8–9. Not

a single Japanese naval code message transmitted at any time during 1941 had been read by 7 December 1941; the message traffic used by Stinnett to support his claims was decoded and translated in 1945 and 1946. See also David Kahn, "Why Weren't We Warned?" *World War II* (Pearl Harbor 60th Anniversary Commemorative Issue) (December 2001): 82–97. The "main" diplomatic code could be read "rapidly and completely"; other diplomatic and consular codes could be deciphered "with a few days delay"; the "main naval [code] could be read only slightly" (ibid., p. 90).

183. Edward J. Drea, "Review: *Day of Deceit*," *Journal of Military History* 64, no. 2 (April 2000): 583.

184. For more on the conspiracy theory, see Bruce R. Bartlett, *Cover Up: The Politics of Pearl Harbor, 1941–1946* (New Rochelle, N.Y.: Arlington House, 1978): "Roosevelt's guilt consisted not in a conspiracy to set up the fleet but in pursuing a policy he knew would lead to war . . . the petty effort to lay all the blame on Kimmel and Short is totally inexcusable." Also see John E. Costello, *The Pacific War* (New York: Rawson, Wade, 1981), claiming that Roosevelt had received a "positive war warning" from Prime Minister Winston Churchill eleven days before Pearl Harbor; Churchill specifically warned Roosevelt that the Japanese would attack America at the end of the first week of December.

185. Gore Vidal, *Golden Age* (New York: Doubleday, 2000).

186. Gannon, *Pearl Harbor Betrayed: The True Story of a Man and Nation under Attack*, pp. 261–82.

187. Michael Schaller, "The Debacle in the Philippines," in Love, ed., *Pearl Harbor Revisited*, pp. 123.

188. Ibid., pp. 126, 129n.34.

189. See Section IV, infra, fn 229 and accompanying text.

190. *Mullan v. United States*, 212 United States Reports 516 (1909).

191. Felix Belair, Jr., "Truman Says Public Must Share Blame for Pearl Harbor," *New York Times*, 31 August 1945, p. 1.

192. Letter, Secretary of the Navy Forrestal to Rear Admiral Kimmel, 28 August 1945. Reprinted in PHA 19:3944; "Kimmel Defers Bid for Court-Martial," *New York Times*, 13 September 1945, p. 2.

193. The "bomb plot" message was an instruction from Tokyo to the Honolulu consulate to give precise locations of all ships moored in Pearl Harbor. The import of this request to set up a grid system for reporting the presence and position of ships in Pearl Harbor was not appreciated,

as the "bomb plot" message did not by itself prove that the Japanese intended to attack Pearl Harbor. Rather, a pre-attack reading of the message might have reinforced the suspicion of sabotage.

Advocates for Kimmel and Short frequently claim that had they known about the "bomb plot" message, the two commanders would have immediately recognized that the Fleet was in danger. But they conveniently ignore that no one thought the "bomb plot" message was particularly important at the time it was decoded and translated. As Roberta Wohlstetter concluded in *Pearl Harbor: Warning and Decision* (Stanford, Calif.: Stanford Univ. Press, 1962), naval intelligence in Washington, D.C., viewed the message as simply reflecting the "incredible zeal and efficiency" with which the Japanese collected detail. "*No one read into it a specific danger to ships anchored at Pearl Harbor.* At the time, this was a reasonable estimate, since somewhat similar reports for information were going to Japanese agents in Panama, Vancouver, Portland, San Diego, San Francisco, and other places" (emphasis supplied). Wohlstetter, p. 390. Their claims to the contrary, the import of Wohlstetter's conclusion is clear: even if they had been provided the bomb plot message, there is every reason to believe that Kimmel and Short also would have concluded that the message reflected the efficiency of Japanese intelligence gathering.

194. First translated by the Army in Washington on Oct. 9th.

195. The "winds" code was established by the Japanese to give a "special message in an emergency" and was to be broadcast in the middle of the daily Japanese-language short-wave news broadcast. The "winds" codes were: "East wind, rain" (war between Japan–US); "North wind, cloudy" (war between Japan–USSR); "West wind, clear" (war between Japan–Britain). The "winds" code was a diplomatic—not military—code. JCC, p. 470. The existence of the "winds" code did not surprise Washington; most believed war with Japan was imminent. Additionally, the "winds" code never revealed that Pearl Harbor would be attacked. Note that implementation of the "winds code" required a complementary "winds execute" message.

196. Washington received its first "winds" code traffic on Nov. 26 and 28; its last "winds" code information on Dec. 4th. JCC, p. 470.

197. Admiral Kimmel learned of the "winds" code in a Nov. 28th dispatch to him from the US Asiatic Fleet. JCC, p. 470.

198. Washington learned that the Japanese Navy unexpectedly changed its call signs on Dec. 1st. Previously, call signs were changed every six months, and had last been changed on Nov. 1st. JCC, p. 134.

199. Admiral Kimmel learned of this call sign change on Dec. 1st. JCC, p. 134.

200. No radio traffic from four Japanese carriers had been monitored for between 15–25 days. Consequently, their location was unknown. Washington learned this on Dec. 2. JCC, p. 134.

201. JCC, p. 133. Admiral Kimmel did not pass this information to General Short because he assumed the four Japanese carriers remained in "home" waters. JCC, p. 135.

202. Washington learned of Japan's orders to certain consulates and embassies to burn codes on Dec. 3. JCC, p. 130.

203. Admiral Kimmel learned of Japan's orders to certain consulates and embassies to burn codes on Dec. 3. JCC, p. 130. He did not consider it to be of "vital importance." JCC, p. 130. Consequently, he did not pass it on to General Short. JCC, p. 131. General Short, however, did receive information from his staff that the Japanese were burning their codes and papers on Dec. 6th. JCC, p. 132. The JCC concluded that "[w]hile the order to burn codes may not always mean war in a diplomatic sense, it very definitely meant war—and soon—in a military sense after the 'war warning' of November 27." JCC, p. 131.

204. Probably did not exist. Capt. L. Safford testified before the JCC that an implementing winds execute message was received in the Navy Department on the morning of Dec. 4th. This message announced war between the US and Japan. No credible evidence, however, supported Safford's claim. The JCC concluded, after "considering all the evidence relating to the winds code . . . that no genuine message . . . was received in the War or Navy Department prior to December 7, 1941." JCC, p. 486. Assuming arguendo that a genuine execute message had been intercepted, the JCC "concluded that such fact would have added nothing to what was already known concerning the critical character of our relations with the Empire of Japan." That is, a "winds execute" message would not indicate the timing or location of any Japanese attack.

205. The "Pilot" message was a message from Japan to her Ambassadors in Washington advising them that the Japanese reply to the American note of 26 November was ready and being sent to them

in 14 parts; that it was to be treated with great secrecy pending instructions as to the time of its delivery; and that time for its delivery was to be fixed in a separate message. JCC, p. 210.

206. Washington had the text of the "Pilot" message on Dec. 6th. JCC, p. 210.

207. The first 13 parts of the 14-part Japanese memorandum were received by the Navy on Dec. 6th. These 13 parts indicated that negotiations were at an end. Although President Roosevelt apparently stated that 'this means war', "it is significant that there was no indication as to when or where war might be expected." JCC, p. 217. The 14th part of the message was decoded and available for distribution between 7:30 and 8:00 AM on Dec. 7th. JCC, p. 221. The 14th part of the message also stated that negotiations were at an end. Nothing in "Part 14" indicated that Pearl Harbor would be attacked.

Little has been said about why the Japanese were timing the delivery of their 14- part message to coincide with the attack on U.S. forces at Pearl Harbor. In retrospect, it seems as if the Japanese government was trying to comply with the Law of War as it then existed. The Hague Conventions of 1907 required Japan to declare war prior to initiating hostilities. While Part 14 did not contain an express declaration of war, the language contained therein made it clear that hostilities were imminent. Japan intended for the U.S. to receive Part 14 just minutes before its aerial forces appeared in Honolulu skies.

208. The "one o'clock" [Eastern Standard Time] message specified the time for delivery of the Japanese 14-part memorandum to the United States. When Washington officials learned of the "one o'clock" message, they knew that something important would happen. General Marshall, for example, stated that he was certain "something was going to happen at 1 o'clock." JCC, p. 223. No one in Washington, however, knew what would happen, or where it would happen.

209. Mr. Edward R. Kimmel, Thurmond transcript, p. 19.

210. Prange, p. 584.

211. Kimmel, op. cit., p. 170. General Short was largely silent during these years and did not write his memoirs.

212. The sections pertinent to Admiral Kimmel and General Short are quoted in Section III, supra.

213. Stimson Diary, December 17, 1941.

214. Kimmel, p. 170.

215. James B. Reston, "Roberts Board Blames Kimmel and Short," *New York Times,* Jan 25, 1942, p. 1, col. 8.
216. Kimmel, p. 170.
217. "Inquiry on Hawaii Urged in Congress," *New York Times,* Jan 27, 1942, p. 4, col. 1.
218. Kimmel, p. 182.
219. "Inquiry on Hawaii Urged in Congress," *New York Times,* Jan 27, 1942, p. 4, col. 1. By the next day, a list of specific topics that many in Congress wanted to further investigate was published in the press, including the degree of responsibility of the Administration, and the reason messages from Washington focused on the Far East as the most likely point of attack. Arthur Krock, "Pearl Harbor Issue: Many in Congress Want Inquiry," *New York Times,* Jan 28, 1942, p. 5, col. 2.
220. "Republicans Push Inquiry on Hawaii," *New York Times,* Jan 28. p. 5, col. 1 (Representative Whittington of Mississippi told the House that Pearl Harbor "could not be permitted to rest by finding the Hawaiian area commanders derelict in their duty.").
221. Kathleen McLaughlin, "House Votes Trial for Short, Kimmel," *New York Times,* June 7, 1944, p. 11, co1. 8.
222. E.g., "Hints Vindication of Kimmel, Short," *New York Times,* Nov. 26, 1944, p. 44, col. 3; Lewis Wood, "Kimmel and Short Will Not be Tried," *New York Times,* Dec. 2, 1944, p. 1, col. 7.
223. *New York Times,* Dec. 2, 1944, p. 5, col. 6.
224. In December 1941, a brigadier general and Chief, Army War Plans Division.

Note that Gerow later served on the board that recommended advancement of general officers who had been relieved of command and reduced in grade. See note 47 and accompanying text.

225. E.g., "Army, Navy Report On Pearl Harbor; Marshall, Hull And Stark Censured," *New York Times,* Aug. 30, 1945, p. 1., col. 1. The full texts of the Army and Navy reports were reproduced in section 2 of the same issue of the *Times.*
226. JCC, Appendix C.
227. C. P. Trussell, "Angry Senators Debate on 'Records' of Pearl Harbor," *New York Times,* Nov. 3, 1945, p. 1, col. 6; "Hannegan Says Republicans are Trying to Smear the Memory of Roosevelt," *New York Times,* Nov. 18, 1945, p. 2, col. 5; W. H. Lawrence, "Pearl Harbor Inquiry Enmeshed in Politics," *New York Times,* Nov. 18, 1945, p. 5, col. 1.

228. William S. White, "Roosevelt Found Blameless for Pearl Harbor Disaster," *New York Times,* July 21, 1946, p. 1, col. 2.

229. "Short Reiterates Stand," *New York Times,* July 21, 1946, p. 12, col. 6.

230. Kimmel, op. cit.

231. See Section II, above.

232. Henry C. Clausen and Bruce Lee, *Pearl Harbor: Final Judgment* (New York: Crown Publishers, 1992), pp. 300–311.

233. U.S. Const., Article II, Section 2. The President "shall have the Power, by and with the Advice and Consent of the Senate ... [to] appoint ... Officers of the United States." Today, Senate confirmation is required before an officer appointed to a three-star or four-star position may serve in such a grade. 10 U.S.C. § 601 (a).

234. During times of national emergency, the President has expanded powers to make temporary 1 year appointments of officers in the Armed Forces. 10 USC 603.

235. Thurmond transcript, p. 19.

236. See notes 187 and 188, above.

Chapter 3. Aftermath

1. David C. Richardson, "A Critical Analysis of the Report by the Department of Defense Dated December 1, 1995, Regarding Advancement of Rear Admiral Husband E. Kimmel and Lieutenant General Walter C. Short on the Retired List," 21 July 1997, pp. 20–25 (reprinted as Appendix C, below).

2. Those co-sponsoring the resolution included Senators Biden, Helms, Thurmond, Stevens, Cochran, Inouye, Durbin, Spector, Ford, and Faircloth.

3. H.R. 3050, 106th Cong., 1st sess., "A bill to provide for the posthumous advancement of Rear Admiral (retired) Husband E. Kimmel and Major General (retired) Walter C. Short on the retired lists of their respective services."

4. Public Law 106-398.

5. Kimmel family Web site, as of 1 October 2002: http://www2.com/~tkimmel.

6. Ibid.

7. Ibid.

8. Goldstein, remarks as panelist, 3 December 2001, U.S. National Park Service Symposium, "Pearl Harbor 1941–2001: A Day to Remember, A Time Not Forgotten." The panel's subject was "Air Raid Pearl Harbor: A Historical Review of the Attack."

9. David F. Winkler and Jennifer M. Lloyd, eds., *Pearl Harbor and the Kimmel Controversy: The Views Today* (Washington, D.C.: Naval Historical Foundation, 2000), p. 27.

10. Norman Polmar, "Promotion for Fleet Commander at Pearl Harbor Ignores History," *Navy Times*, 4 December 2000, p. 54.

11. Dan van der Vat, *Pearl Harbor: The Day of Infamy: An Illustrated History* (New York: Basic Books, 2001), p. 151 (emphasis supplied).

12. NBC, *The News with Brian Williams*, segment on Pearl Harbor, 8 December 2000.

13. Gannon, *Pearl Harbor Betrayed*, p. 322n.50.

14. Gannon, remarks as panelist, 3 December 2001, National Park Service Symposium; see above, note 8.

15. Stilwell, oral statement to Borch, 3 December 2001. Stilwell expressed this view while moderating the National Park Service Symposium on Pearl Harbor.

16. NBC, *News with Brian Williams*, 8 December 2000.

17. Telephone conversation with Alice Rhee, staff member, *News with Brian Williams*, 15 December 2000.

18. Emily S. Rosenberg, *A Date Which Will Live: Pearl Harbor in American Memory* (Durham, N.C.: Duke University Press, 2003), p. 139.

19. Ollie Reed, Jr., "A Family's Battle for Honor," *Albuquerque Tribune*, 7 December 2001, p. A-1, quoted in Rosenberg, *A Date Which Will Live*, p. 139.

Conclusion

1. Prange, *At Dawn We Slept*, p. 738.

Annotated Bibliography

Primary Sources: Official Records

U.S. Congress, Joint Committee on the Investigation of the Pearl Harbor Attack. "Investigation of the Pearl Harbor Attack: Report of the Joint Committee on the Investigation of the Pearl Harbor Attack." Pursuant to S. Con. Res. 27, 79th Cong.: A concurrent resolution to investigate the attack on Pearl Harbor on December 7, 1941, and events and circumstances relating thereto. 20 July 1946. Reprint. Laguna Hills, Calif.: Aegean Park Press, 1994.

U.S. Defense Department. *The Magic Background of Pearl Harbor.* Washington, D.C.: Government Printing Office, 1977. 8 vols. containing "Magic" intercepts.

Secondary Sources: Books and Articles

Army Times, ed. *Pearl Harbor and Hawaii: A Military History.* New York: Walker, 1971. Popular history of Japanese attack on Pearl Harbor and its aftermath, with many firsthand accounts. Theme is that disaster resulted from American unpreparedness.

Bartlett, Bruce R. *Cover-Up: The Politics of Pearl Harbor, 1941–1946.* New Rochelle, N.Y.: Arlington House, 1978. Roosevelt is responsible for Pearl Harbor because he pursued a policy he knew would provoke war with Japan.

Beach, Edward L. *Scapegoats: A Defense of Kimmel and Short at Pearl Harbor.* Annapolis, Md.: Naval Institute Press, 1995. An important book frequently cited by those defending Kimmel and Short.

Berry, Henry. *"This Is No Drill": Living Memories of the Attack on Pearl Harbor.* New York: Berkley Publishing Group, 2001. Stirring firsthand accounts by those on Oahu who experienced the events of 7 December 1941.

Borch, Frederic L. "Comparing Pearl Harbor and 9/11." *Journal of Military History* (July 2003): 845–60. Examines the often heard claim that Pearl Harbor and the terrorist attacks of September 11, 2001, are similar events in terms of intelligence failure, unpreparedness, and military responsibility. Concludes that while there are some similarities, the two events are more dissimilar than they are alike.

———. "Guilty as Charged?" *MHQ: The Quarterly Journal of Military History* 13, no. 2 (Winter 2001): 54–63. Argues that Kimmel and Short failed at Pearl Harbor and are responsible, at least in part, for the disaster.

———. "Justice Was Served" (Opposing Views: Pearl Harbor Commanders' Culpability). *MHQ: The Quarterly Journal of Military History* 14, no. 2 (Winter 2002): 33–37. Continues the debate, with an opposing view from the Kimmel family.

Borgquist, Daryl S. "Advance Warning? The Red Cross Connection." *Naval History* (June 1999): 20–26. Claims that Roosevelt, knowing of an imminent attack on Pearl Harbor, requested that the Red Cross secretly send medical supplies to the West Coast.

Brownlow, Donald G. *The Accused: The Ordeal of Rear Admiral Husband Edward Kimmel, U.S.N.* New York: Vantage Press, 1968. Collected biographical materials and interviews of Kimmel.

Budiansky, Stephen. *Battle of Wits: The Complete Story of Codebreaking in World War II.* New York: Free Press, 2000. A comprehensive examination of U.S. and U.K. cryptographers in World War II. Demolishes the claims by conspiracy theorists that U.S. intelligence was reading Japanese naval codes, and consequently had advance warning of the Japanese attack on Pearl Harbor.

———. "Too Late for Pearl Harbor." Naval Institute *Proceedings* 125 (December 1999). Brief look at the extent to which U.S. Navy codebreakers were reading the main Japanese naval code in the months preceding the attack; concludes that cryptanalysts did not decipher the Japanese fleet codes in time to warn Pearl Harbor.

Clausen, Henry C., and Bruce Lee. *Pearl Harbor: Final Judgment.* New York: Crown Publishers, 1992. The author, appointed by Secretary of War Stimson to investigate the "root causes of Pearl Harbor," concludes that many individuals are to blame—including Kimmel and Short.

Cohen, Stan. *East Wind Rain: A Pictorial History of the Pearl Harbor Attack.* Missoula: Pictorial Histories, 1999.
Conroy, Hilary, and Harry Wray, eds. *Pearl Harbor Reexamined: Prologue to the Pacific War.* Honolulu: University of Hawaii Press, 1990.
Costello, John. *The Pacific War.* London: Collins, 1981.
Fichida, Mitsuo. "I Led the Attack on Pearl Harbor." Naval Institute *Proceedings* 78 (September 1952): 939–52. Firsthand account by Japanese aviator who led the aerial strike.
Fukudome, Shigeru. "Hawaii Operation." Naval Institute *Proceedings* 81 (December 1955): 1315–31. "Hawaii Operation" was the Japanese Imperial Headquarters official name for the Pearl Harbor surprise attack; Fukudome, a vice admiral, gives an insider's view as someone who helped plan the attack.
Gannon, Michael. *Pearl Harbor Betrayed: The True Story of a Man and a Nation under Attack.* New York: Henry Holt, 2001. Gannon, who believes that Kimmel and Short merit posthumous advancement, argues that Washington's inattention and derelictions were the primary reasons for unpreparedness at Pearl Harbor.
———. "Time to Reopen the Kimmel Case." Naval Institute *Proceedings* 120 (December 1994): 51–56. Argues that Kimmel was unjustly blamed for failing to conduct long-range aerial reconnaissance.
Goldstein, Donald M., and Katherine V. Dillon, eds. *The Pearl Harbor Papers: Inside the Japanese Plans.* New York: Brassey's (US), 1993.
Goldstein, Donald M., Katherine V. Dillon, and J. Michael Wenger. *The Way It Was: Pearl Habor, the Original Photographs.* New York: Brassey's (US), 1991.
Hoehling, A. A. *The Week before Pearl Harbor.* New York: W. W. Norton, 1963. Washington's "apathy" was to blame for the Pearl Harbor attack.
Jacobsen, Philip H. "Who Deceived Whom." *Naval History* (December 2003): 27–31. Shows that recently declassified naval communications intelligence records prove that Japanese radio deception masked movement of their carriers in late November and early December 1941. This explains why the Pearl Harbor attack was a surprise. It also refutes claims from Robert B. Stinnett and other revisionists that President Roosevelt "knew" in advance—from Japanese radio intercepts—that an attack on the Hawaiian Department was imminent.

Kimmel, Larry, and Margaret Regis. *The Attack on Pearl Harbor: An Illustrated History*. Seattle: Navigator Publishing, 1992. Good outline of plan to attack Pearl Harbor, including discussion of targets, weapons, high-level bombing, and midget submarine attacks.

Kimmel, Thomas H., Jr. "Unfairly Shouldering the Blame" (Opposing Views: Pearl Harbor Commanders' Culpability). *MHQ: The Quarterly Journal of Military History* 14, no. 2 (Winter 2002): 30–33. Kimmel's grandson recites the Kimmel and Short family positions on who was responsible at Pearl Harbor.

Layton, Edwin T., Roger Pineau, and John Costello. *And I Was There: Pearl Harbor and Midway: Breaking the Secrets*. New York: Morrow, 1985. Firsthand account by Kimmel's intelligence officer.

Lewin, Ronald. *The Other Ultra: Codes, Ciphers and the Defeat of Japan*. London: Hutchinson, 1982.

Lord, Walter. *Day of Infamy*. New York: Holt, 1957.

Love, Robert W., Jr., ed. *Pearl Harbor Revisited*. New York: St. Martin's Press, 1995. Published proceedings of a one-day symposium of scholars charged with considering Pearl Harbor "as a unique international event and to approach the issues it raised for historians from unconventional, oblique or eccentric angles."

Miller, Edward S. *War Plan Orange*. Annapolis, Md.: Naval Institute Press, 1991. Comprehensive history of the U.S. Navy's plans for war with Japan.

Mintz, Frank Paul. *Revisionism and the Origins of Pearl Harbor*. New York: University Press of America, 1985. Scholarly study of revisionist historiography relating to the war with Japan.

Morgenstern, George. *Pearl Harbor: The Story of the Secret War*. New York: Devin-Adair, 1947. Early conspiracy theory.

Prado, John. *Combined Fleet Decoded: The Secret History of American Intelligence and the Japanese Navy in World War II*. New York: Random House, 1995.

Prange, Gordon. *At Dawn We Slept: The Untold Story of Pearl Harbor*. New York: McGraw Hill, 1981. Masterfully researched and written. The best secondary source on Pearl Harbor.

Rosenberg, Emily S. *A Date Which Will Live: Pearl Harbor in American Memory*. Durham, N.C.: Duke University Press, 2003. In examining "the contested meanings of Pearl Harbor in American culture," Rosenberg sees the Kimmel-Short controversy as part of the larger culture and history "wars" of the 1990s. While agreeing that the Kimmel and Short families are the prime moving force behind the crusade to rehabilitate Admiral Kimmel's and General Short's reputations, Rosenberg argues that those supporting the two Pearl Harbor commanders were "part of a larger, conservative movement that, after 1992, focused its wrath on President Clinton, the popular Democrat who had a group of Clinton haters that recalled the Roosevelt haters of the 1940s" (p. 126). By 1999 and 2000, with Senate impeachment hearings under way against Bill Clinton, exonerating Kimmel and Short and blaming the executive branch and a Democratic president (Roosevelt) for failing to prevent Pearl Harbor "held a special resonance" (p. 138).

Rusbridger, James, and Eric Nave. *Betrayal at Pearl Harbor: How Churchill Lured Roosevelt into World War II.* New York: Summit Books, 1991. The British had broken JN-25, the Japanese naval code. Consequently, Churchill knew that a task force had sailed from Japan in late November 1941, and that one of its likely targets was Pearl Harbor. However, Churchill deliberately withheld this information from Roosevelt because he knew that the attack would bring America into the war. The U.S. Navy also had broken JN-25, and knew an attack on Pearl Harbor was imminent. The authors conclude that Adm. Richmond K. Turner probably withheld this intelligence from Roosevelt, and subsequently conducted an extensive housecleaning of naval records to cover up his actions. Unfortunately for Rusbridger and Nave, their claims lack evidence. In fact, no one had successfully deciphered JN-25, and neither U.S. nor British officials knew that the Japanese planned to attack Pearl Harbor on 7 December.

Sakamaki, Kazuo. *I Attacked Pearl Harbor.* New York: Association Press, 1949. Firsthand account.

Scott, Roger D. "Kimmel, Short, McVay: Case Studies in Executive Authority, Law, and the Individual Rights of Military Commanders." *Military Law Review* 156 (June 1998): 52–199. The definitive source on the legal aspects of relief from command and posthumous advancement. Scott concludes that Kimmel and Short did not suffer any legal wrong; that they are not legally entitled to posthumous promotion; and that any relief is a matter of discretion rather than legal right.

Stilwell, Paul, ed. *Air Raid: Pearl Harbor.* Annapolis, Md.: Naval Institute Press, 1981. Collection of firsthand accounts and memories about the events before, during, and after the Japanese attack on Pearl Harbor.

Stinnett, Robert B. *Day of Deceit: The Truth about FDR and Pearl Harbor.* New York: Free Press, 1999. Claims that the Japanese did not maintain radio silence while steaming from Japan to Hawaii in late November and early December 1941; that Allied radio listening stations intercepted and decoded this radio traffic; that this information was passed to President Roosevelt; and that Roosevelt consequently knew that Pearl Harbor was to be attacked. Stinnett also maintains that the United States provoked the Japanese attack. The book's claims are totally false, and Stinnett represents the worst kind of scholarship.

Theobald, Robert A. *The Final Secret of Pearl Harbor: The Washington Contribution to the Japanese Attack.* New York: Devin-Adair, 1954. Early revisionist theory, with "corroborative forewords" by Admirals Kimmel and Halsey. Claims that Roosevelt intentionally withheld intelligence from the senior commanders in Pearl Harbor; that the president knew the Japanese intended to attack U.S. forces in Hawaii; that Kimmel and Short were "splendid officers who were thrown to the wolves as scapegoats for something over which they had no control," (Halsey's foreword, p. ix).

Trefousse, Hans L. *Pearl Harbor: The Continuing Controversy.* Malabar, Fla.: Krieger Publishing, 1992. An examination of conspiracy theories about Pearl Harbor. Concludes that "the Pearl Harbor attack was an operation compounded by error on all sides . . . and appears to have succeeded because of errors in Washington and at Pearl Harbor." Also, while "later treatment of Kimmel and Short was not justified, their lack of foresight was certainly a matter for censure" (pp. 92–93).

Van der Vat, Dan. *The Pacific Campaign: The U.S.–Japanese Naval War 1941–1945.* New York: Simon & Schuster, 1991. Highly acclaimed history.

———. *Pearl Harbor: Day of Infamy: An Illustrated History.* New York: Basic Books, 2001. Photographic history of Pearl Harbor by author of several books on modern warfare. Endorses view that, as senior commanders in Pearl Harbor, Kimmel and Short were "accountable" for U.S. unpreparedness on 7 December.

Weintraub, Stanley. *Long Day's Journey into War: December 7, 1941.* New York: Truman Talley Books, 1991. Looks at this single day, hour by hour. Consequently, Pearl Harbor is examined in the context of the ongoing war in Russia, North Africa, Malaya, and Singapore.

Winkler, David F., and Jennifer M. Lloyd. *Pearl Harbor and the Kimmel Controversy: The Views Today.* Washington, D.C.: Naval Historical Foundation, 2000. Published proceedings from the symposium held 7 December 1999 at the Navy Memorial, Washington, D.C.

Wohlstetter, Roberta. *Pearl Harbor: Warning and Decision.* Stanford, Calif.: Stanford University Press, 1962. A comprehensive look at Pearl Harbor as an intelligence failure. Argues that the United States failed to anticipate the Japanese attack because too much "noise" masked those signals pointing to an attack.

Wrixon, Fred B. "American Cryptanalysts Successfully Cracked the Japanese Diplomatic Code Known as 'Purple.'" *World War II* (November 1997): 22–28. Good summary of U.S. success in deciphering Japanese embassy radio message traffic between 1935 and 1939. Includes much technical information on cipher machines used to produce "Magic," the name given to decoded "Purple" diplomatic messages.

Index

advance warning, assumption of, 68
aerial reconnaissance. *See* long-range aerial reconnaissance
air attack on Pearl Harbor. *See* attack on Pearl Harbor
aircraft: long-range reconnaissance, 65, 68–69; massed to prevent sabotage, 58
air patrols, 68–71
Akagi (carrier), 47
alerts against enemy attack: Alert Number I, defense against sabotage, 56. *See also* war warnings
ammunition, difficulty in obtaining, 59
anti-torpedo netting, Kimmel's decision not to use, 73
Arizona (battleship), 45
Army Board for Correction of Military Records, 11–12, 100
Army Pearl Harbor Board. *See* investigations
Aspin, Les, 7
At Dawn We Slept (Prange), 19, 103
Atlantic Campaign (Van der Vat), 104
attack on Pearl Harbor: advance planning, 39, 46–47, 53–54, 73; American losses, 45–46; antiaircraft protection, 52–53, 74; anti-torpedo protection, 73; Army's defenses, 52–53, 73–74; "Battleship Row," 60, 74; disbelief in possibility of, 60–64; effective use of air power, knowledge of, 53; Hickam Air Base, 27; Japanese losses, 46; pre-attack RADAR sighting, 62–63, 73; pre-attack submarine reconnaissance, 56; pre-attack *Ward* sinking of submarine, 66–67, 110–11; radio silence, 56; route across Pacific, 72; surprise, 50–51; torpedoes, 73
attack on World Trade Center and Pentagon (9/11), 101, 105–6
AXIS alliance, 49–50, 76

B-17 (long-range bomber), 62, 69
B-25 (long-range bomber), 71
Baird, Henry W., 36
Ball, William L., III, 4–5
balloons, barrage, 74
Barnes, Julian F., 36
Battle of Britain, 63
Battle of the Atlantic, 76
"Battle of the Bands," 58
"Battleship Row," 60, 73
Beach, Edward L., 7, 19, 27, 76–77

209

Bellinger, Patrick N. L., Jr., 53. *See also* Martin Bellinger Report
Bentley, Helen D., 6
Betrayal at Pearl Harbor, 70
Bicknell, George, 93
Biden, Joseph R., 6–7
Bloch, Claude C., 64, 66, 70
"bomb plot" message. *See* messages
Borch, Frederic L., 17, 105
Borgquist, Daryl S., 78
Bratton, Rufus S., 94
Brewer, Carlos, 36
British Broadcasting Corporation, 10
Brooks, Edward M., 9
Brown, Lloyd D., 36
Bush, George H. W., 6
Bush, George W., 101, 105

California (battleship), 60
call signs, changed by Japanese navy, 56
carriers, Japanese: *Akagi,* 47; attack route across Pacific, 72; failure to locate, 54; radio silence, 56–57, 77–78
carriers, U.S., 56
carrier warfare, 53–54
Casey, William J., 76–77
casualties: Japanese, 46; U.S., 45–46
Catalina aircraft, 68–69
Central Intelligence Agency (CIA), 76–77
Cheney, Richard, 4, 101–2
China, Japanese forces in, 49
Christian Science Monitor, 60
Clark, Mark W., 37
Clark Air Field, Philippines, 81
Clausen, Henry C., investigation by, 28, 92–95
Clinton, William J., 8
codes: burning of as indication of war, 57, 84, 93; decoding, 78; Japanese JN-25 code, 205; MAGIC, 68, 78, 80, 86–87, 94; purple code, 57, 93–94
command, relief from, 30–33
congressional investigation. *See* investigations
"conspiracy" theories of Pearl Harbor, 74–79
Costello, John, 13
court-martial, of Kimmel and Short, 41, 83, 85
cryptology. *See* codes
Cummins, Joseph M., 36

Dalton, John, 24
Date Which Will Live: Pearl Harbor in American Memory, A (Rosenberg), 105–6
Dawley, Ernest J., 36–37
Day of Deceit: The Truth About FDR and Pearl Harbor (Stinnett), 78
declaration of war by Germany, 76
Defense, Department of, investigation. *See* Dorn Report
Defense Authorization Act (2001), 101
"dereliction of duty" charge, 34, 40–42, 86
Deutch, John, 12–14, 24
"Diamond Head" (Hawaii), 54
Doolittle, James, 71
Dorn, Edwin P., 12, 16–22, 25. *See also* Dorn Report
Dorn Report, 101–5; Approach and Methodology, 16–22; Part I, "Introduction," 23–29; Part II, "The Personnel Actions," 29–38; Part III, "The Pearl Harbor Investigations," 38–83; Part IV, "The Court of Public Opinion,"

INDEX

83–90; Part V, "Options for Further Action," 90–98
Dusenbury, Carlisle C., 92–93

economic freeze against Japan, 76
Elliott, George, 62–63
embargoes on U.S. exports to Japan, 76
"errors of judgment" finding, 44, 91, 97

Fairfull, Thomas M., 20
Fielder, Kendall J., 92–93
first attack wave on Pearl Harbor, 52, 54, 60, 64–65
Forrestal, James V., 42
fourteen-part message of 6–7 December 1941, 65, 74, 84, 93–94
Fourteenth Naval District, 70, 94–95
French Indo-China, 49–50
Fuchida, Mitsuo, 54

Gannon, Michael, 70–71, 80, 104–5
Gates, Thomas S., Jr., 4
Germany, 34, 50, 76
Gerow, Leonard T., 36, 88, 95
Golden Age, 79
Goldstein, Donald, 103
Goodwin, Doris K., 104–5
Great Britain, 53

Halsey, William F., 56
Hanify, Edward F., 13, 33
Harsch, Joseph C., 60–61
Hawaiian Department: air defense of Pearl Harbor, 51–53, 55–56; mission of, 48; protection of Pacific Fleet, 48; Short assumed command of, 30; war warnings, 48, 55–56, 84

Hickam Field, 27
Honigman, Steven S., 1, 13–14, 24
Honolulu Advertiser, 20, 27, 54
Honolulu Star-Bulletin, 20, 27
Hoover, Herbert D., 9
Horky, Otto, 64–65

Indo-China. *See* French Indo-China
Infamy: Pearl Harbor and Its Aftermath, 77–78
intelligence: "bomb plot" message, 74; change in Japanese radio call signals, 84; in Hawaii, 54, 93–94; inability to locate Japanese carriers, 54, 84; in Washington, 50–51, 93–95. *See also* messages
investigations: Army Pearl Harbor Board, 10, 28, 41–42, 82–83, 100; Clarke investigation, 28; Clausen investigation, 28, 92–95; Hart investigation, 28; Hewitt inquiry, 28; Joint Congressional Committee, 19, 28, 37, 43–45, 72, 82, 100; Knox investigation, 28, 38–40, 85; Navy Court of Inquiry, 28, 33, 41–42, 82–83, 87–88, 100; Roberts Commission, 28, 34, 40–41, 85–88

Joint Congressional Committee on the Investigation of the Pearl Harbor Attack. *See* investigations
Journal of Military History, 78–79
Judge Advocate General, Army, 9–11, 27, 42

Kelso, Frank B., II, 7
Kimmel, Edward R., 4–5, 21, 102–3, 105

Kimmel, Husband E.: *Admiral Kimmel's Story*, 3, 19, 27; aware of possible surprise attack, 50–51, 54; blamed Navy for withholding information, 68; character and personality of, 26, 47; commander in chief of U.S. Fleet, 30; cooperation with Short, 40–41, 44, 48; court-martial of, 41–42, 82–83, 85, 87; decision not to use anti-torpedo netting, 73–74; decision to keep fleet in Pearl Harbor, 55; "dereliction of duty" charge, 41–42, 85; destruction of Japanese codes and, 57; "Diamond Head" statement, 54; errors of judgment, 37, 57–67, 80, 91; evaluation of "war warning" messages, 55–56; failure to implement long-range aerial reconnaissance, 65, 69–70; golf with Short, 62; mistakes and errors, 37, 56–57, 80, 91; and Navy Court of Inquiry, 28, 33, 82; on needs of Pacific Fleet, 52; possibility of posthumous restoration of highest rank, 9, 24, 98; reaction to Army-Navy investigations, 87–88; reaction to Joint Congressional Investigation report, 89–90; relationship with Short, 57; relieved of command, 30, 33; retirement of, 34; and Roberts Commission findings, 33, 40–41; Stark's failure to pass on coded messages, 68; and war warning messages, 48, 51, 53, 55–56, 65, 84
Kimmel, Manning M., IV, 8, 12, 21
Kimmel, Thomas K., 4–5, 12, 21
King, Ernest J., 18, 42
Knox, Frank, 28, 30, 38–40, 85
Kramer, Alwin D., 95
Kuborn, John R., 20

Layton, Edwin T., 54, 93
Lockard, James, 62–63
long-range aerial reconnaissance: failure to implement, 68–72; historical commentary on, 70; Kimmel's statements on, 69–71; Navy's responsibility to implement, 48
Love, Robert W., Jr., 103
Lucas, James T., 11–12

MacArthur, Douglas, failures in the Philippines, 81, 97
MAGIC, 86–88, 94; congressional investigation and, 86–88, 94; decoding, 68; not given to Kimmel and Short, 68, 99
Marley, James P., 36
Marshall, George C.: on defense of Hawaii, 48; first concern to protect the fleet, 48; knowledge of possible Japanese attack, 51; messages to Short, 48, 52–53; and war warnings, 55–56
Martin, Frederick L., 53
Martin-Bellinger Report, 53
Martinez, Daniel A., 20
Matthews, John R., 12
Mayfield, Irvin H., 94
McCain, John, 6
McMahon, William C., 36
messages: "bomb plot," 74, 84; "fourteen-part," 65, 74, 84, 93–94; "one o'clock," 74, 84; "pilot," 74, 84; "war warning," 74, 84; "winds," 74, 84; "winds execute," 74, 84

Mitchell, Billy, 53
Muir, James I., 36
Murphy, Frank, 81

Naito, Takeshi, 53–54
National Park Service, U.S., 20
National Personnel Records Center, 25, 27
naval aerial warfare, torpedo bombing, 51, 53
naval intelligence. *See* intelligence; messages
Naval Records, Board for Correction of, 4
Nave, Eric, 77
Navy Court of Inquiry, 4, 28, 33, 82
Navy Department, warnings sent to Kimmel, 48, 55–56, 65, 84
Netherlands, Dutch naval attaché, 27, 86–87
Netherlands East Indies, 77
nets: antisubmarine, 73–74; anti-torpedo, Kimmel's decision not to use, 73–74
News with Brian Williams, The, 105
New York Times, 27, 86
Nomura, Kichisaburo, 40

Oahu: defense of, plans for joint action in event of attack, 40, 51; Sunday activity on, 39, 58–60, 62–65, 73. *See also* attack on Pearl Harbor
Officer Personnel Act (1947), 36
oil embargo by U.S., 49–50
Oklahoma (battleship), 43, 59
Outerbridge, William W., 66–67

Pacific Fleet: aviation, 68–70; battleships, 69; carriers, 69; disposition in Pearl Harbor on 6 December 1941, 58–60; protection by Army, 48; ships in port every Saturday and Sunday, 39, 58–60, 73; Short's responsibility to defend, 48; and war warnings, 48, 55–56, 65, 84
patrols: antisubmarine, 56, 65–67; Kimmel's views on, 69–72; long-range aerial reconnaissance, 48, 68–72; searches not implemented by Kimmel, 68–72
Pearl Harbor: aircraft disarmed and massed to prevent sabotage, 73; American disbelief in likelihood of Japanese attack, 57, 60–62; antisubmarine netting, 67; antitorpedo netting, 73–74; "Battleship Row," 60, 73; "bomb plot" message, 84; casualties at, 45–46; disposition of ships and aircraft, 39; effect on U.S. public opinion, 84–85; Japanese air attack on, 39, 45–47, 53–54, 73; protection of, 48, 50–53; responsibility for losses, 38–47, 91–98; submarine sunk off entrance to, 66–67, 110–11; and war warnings, 48, 55–56, 65, 84
Pearl Harbor Betrayed (Gannon), 104
Pearl Harbor: Final Judgment (Clausen), 92
Pearl Harbor investigations. *See* investigations
Pearl Harbor Revisited (Love), 103
Pearl Harbor Survivors, Association of, 10
Pearl Harbor: Warning and Decision (Wohlstetter), 74
Perry, William J., 1–2, 7
Philippine Islands, 68, 81
Pierce, Archie, 59

Poindexter, John M., 35–36
Polmar, Norman, 103
Prange, Gordon W., 19, 103
press: pro-Roosevelt sentiments, 88; reaction to congressional investigation, 87; reaction to Kimmel and Short, 86–88; Short speech, 88

radar operations: in the Battle of Britain, 63; at Opana Point on 7 December, 62–63
radio call signs, Japanese changes in, 56
radio silence, by Japanese carriers, 56
Ramsey, Logan C., 65
Ranson, Paul L., 36
Reagan, Ronald, 36
reconnaissance aircraft. *See* long-range aerial reconnaissance
Red Cross, U.S., 78
relief from command. *See* command, relief from
Republican Party, 75
revisionist school of history, 74–79
Richardson, David C., 99–100; analysis of Department of Defense report, 123–74
Richardson, James O., 33
Roberts, Owen J., 40. *See also* Roberts Commission
Roberts Commission: findings of, 40–41; report submitted to Roosevelt, 41
Rochefort, Joseph J., 95
Roosevelt, Franklin D.: charge of withholding information, 3; conspiracy theory, 74–79; exonerated, 88; freezing of Japanese assets, 49–50; sanctions against Japan, 49–50

Rosenberg, Emily S., 105–6
Roth, William V., 100, 105
Rugg, Charles B., 87–88
Rusbridger, James, 77
Russo-Japanese War, 50

sabotage: aircraft massed as protection against, 73; alert against, 56; fear of local Japanese, 73; precautions against, 60; Short's refusal to issue ammunition, 60
Sacrifice at Pearl Harbor, 10
Safford, Laurence F., 94
Scapegoats (Beach), 19
Schofield Barracks, 27
Scott, Roger, 17
September 11, 2001, attack. *See* attack on World Trade Center and Pentagon (9/11)
Short, Walter C.: aircraft available to, 68–69; on air defense, 54, 58; alerts, 56; command of Hawaiian Department, 30; congressional investigation, 88; court-martial of, 42, 87; death of, 10; denied information by Washington, 100; "dereliction of duty" charge, 41–44; errors of judgment, 37, 44–46, 58, 60, 62–63, 91–92; failure to cooperate with Navy, 40–41, 43–45; failure to perform his mission, 44; failure to protect fleet, 44; failure to understand air power, 57–58, 62–63; fear of invasion by Japanese, 58; golf with Kimmel, 62; knowledge of possible surprise attack, 50–51, 54; military career of, 30–31; orders aircraft disarmed and massed, 58; plan to train Air Corps men for

ground combat, 58; posthumous restoration of highest rank, 24; preoccupation with training, 31, 58; reaction to congressional report, 88; relieved of command, 30, 33; retirement of, 34; testimony of, 88; training and experience of, 31; and war warning messages, 48, 51, 53, 55–56, 65, 84
Short, Walter D., 10–11
Silvester, Lindsay M., 36
Simpson, Alan K., 6
Sino-Japanese conflict, 49–50
Spence, Floyd, 101, 104
Spy Book: Encyclopedia of Intelligence, 103
Standley, William H., 33
Stark, Harold R., 10, 86
Stillwell, Paul, 105
Stimson, Henry L., 92
Stinnett, Robert B., 78–79
submarines, attack on Pearl Harbor, 56, 66–67, 110–11
surprise attack: advantages, 47, 53, 58–59, 73; Kimmel aware of the possibility of, 50–53, 54; Martin-Bellinger Report on, 50, 53; possibility of, 50–51, 53
survivors, 74

Taft, William H., IV, 5
Taranto, British naval air attack on Italian fleet at, 53–54
Thurmond, Strom, 1–2, 6, 12–15, 22, 24, 99, 102, 104, 107–8, 122
Timenes, Nicolas, 17
Toland, John, 77
torpedoes: anti-torpedo measures, 73–74; Japanese, 73; nets, 73–74
Trost, Carlisle A. H., 4, 38

Truman, Harry S., 83, 88
Turner, Kelly, 71–72, 94
Tyler, Kermit A., 62

U.S. Army: mission in Hawaii, 48; responsible for defense of Pearl Harbor, 44, 48
U.S. Fleet: Kimmel appointed commander in chief, 30; psychological unpreparedness for Pearl Harbor, 57–58; resources available, 68–69
U.S. House of Representatives, 85; H.R. 13, 7; H.R. 534, 6–7
U.S. Senate, Joint Resolution 19, 100–101

Van der Vat, Dan, 103
Vidal, Gore, 79

Wagner, David H., 64
Ward (destroyer), 66–67, 110–11
war games: involving Japan, 48, 53; involving Pearl Harbor, 53
war plans, involving Japan, 55
war warnings, 48, 55–56, 65, 74, 84
weather and sea conditions, 72
West, Togo D., Jr., 12
White, John P., 15, 22, 25, 122
"winds execute" message, 74, 84
"winds" message, 74, 84
World War II: Battle of the Atlantic, 76; Battle of Britain, 63

Yamamoto, Isoroku, 47

Zero aircraft, 59, 66

About the Authors

Col. Fred Borch, USA, is a career Army lawyer. His areas of expertise are criminal law and international law, and his last assignment was as chief prosecutor, Office of Military Commissions, Department of Defense. In that position, he supervised the prosecution efforts involving terrorists detained in Guantánamo Bay, Cuba. He currently serves as the special assistant to the commander of the Army's legal center and school in Charlottesville, Virginia. He holds a J.D. from the University of North Carolina at Chapel Hill, an LL.M. in military law from the Judge Advocate General's School, Charlottesville, Virginia, and an M.A. in national security studies from the Naval War College, Newport, Rhode Island.

Colonel Borch is the author of several books and articles, including *Judge Advocates in Combat: Army Lawyers in Military Operations from Vietnam to Haiti*.

Daniel Martinez is a career National Park Service employee and the chief historian at the USS *Arizona* Memorial, Honolulu, Hawaii. He holds a B.A. in history from California State University at Dominguez Hills. Before joining the Park Service, he taught high school history and journalism in Torrance, California.

Mr. Martinez has written and edited several books and articles about Pearl Harbor. A popular media consultant and commentator, he has appeared on the *Today Show* and *Good Morning America* and has reviewed scripts for, narrated, or acted as an adviser on television documentaries ranging from Pearl Harbor and the Battle of Midway to the Battle of Little Big Horn and the West Loch disaster. Since 2002 Mr. Martinez has been the host and historian for the Discovery Channel series *Unsolved History*, which uses forensic science to examine historical mysteries.

The Naval Institute Press is the book-publishing arm of the U.S. Naval Institute, a private, nonprofit, membership society for sea service professionals and others who share an interest in naval and maritime affairs. Established in 1873 at the U.S. Naval Academy in Annapolis, Maryland, where its offices remain today, the Naval Institute has members worldwide.

Members of the Naval Institute support the education programs of the society and receive the influential monthly magazine *Proceedings* and discounts on fine nautical prints and on ship and aircraft photos. They also have access to the transcripts of the Institute's Oral History Program and get discounted admission to any of the Institute-sponsored seminars offered around the country.

The Naval Institute also publishes *Naval History* magazine. This colorful bimonthly is filled with entertaining and thought-provoking articles, first-person reminiscences, and dramatic art and photography. Members receive a discount on *Naval History* subscriptions.

The Naval Institute's book-publishing program, begun in 1898 with basic guides to naval practices, has broadened its scope to include books of more general interest. Now the Naval Institute Press publishes about one hundred titles each year, ranging from how-to books on boating and navigation to battle histories, biographies, ship and aircraft guides, and novels. Institute members receive significant discounts on the Press's more than eight hundred books in print.

Full-time students are eligible for special half-price membership rates. Life memberships are also available.

For a free catalog describing Naval Institute Press books currently available, and for further information about subscribing to *Naval History* magazine or about joining the U.S. Naval Institute, please write to:

Membership Department
U.S. Naval Institute
291 Wood Road
Annapolis, MD 21402-5034
Telephone: (800) 233-8764
Fax: (410) 269-7940
Web address: www.navalinstitute.org